DUE DATE

			Printed in USA

THE ECONOMIST

The Economist

Henry Thoreau and Enterprise

LEONARD N. NEUFELDT

ew York   Oxford
xford University Press
89

Oxford University Press

Oxford New York Toronto
Delhi Bombay Calcutta Madras Karachi
Petaling Jaya Singapore Hong Kong Tokyo
Nairobi Dar es Salaam Cape Town
Melbourne Auckland

and associated companies in
Berlin Ibadan

Copyright © 1989 by Oxford University Press, Inc.

Published by Oxford University Press, Inc.,
200 Madison Avenue, New York, New York 10016

Library of Congress Cataloging-in-Publication Data
Neufeldt, Leonard.
The economist : Henry Thoreau and enterprise /
Leonard N. Neufeldt.
p. cm. Includes bibliographies and index.
ISBN 0-19-505789-9
1. Thoreau, Henry David, 1817–1862—Knowledge—Economics.
2. Economics in literature. 3. Economics—
United States-History—19th century. I. Title.
PS3057.E25N48 1989
818'.309—dc 19   88-21000   CIP

1 2 3 4 5 6 7 8 9

Printed in the United States of America
on acid-free paper

For Sandra, Tamera,
and Jonathan

Preface

This book is a study of Thoreau's participation in the economic discourse of his time and place. The following complex question prompted my research: What difference did it make that New England and America underwent an unprecedented transformation in economic thinking and behavior in Thoreau's lifetime, that this cultural change was evident at the level of language, and that Thoreau was keenly aware of the transformation? Although this study might be of interest to economic historians and to the economists who still acknowledge a historical dimension to the field of economics, my title has been selected not to get their attention but to signify the major concern of the book in as concise a way as possible. Those of my literary colleagues who hold to straight-and-narrow formalist and aesthetic definitions of literary scholarship (with few exceptions, this includes Thoreau scholars of the last three decades) may not regard *The Economist* as a literary study. If that is their judgment, I hope they will not dismiss this book. I share their conviction that the study of literature is a way of knowing, yet I cannot believe that literary documents represent a unique way of knowing or that the language of literary works and literary criticism is autonomous in its essence, self-referential in its relations, or self-regulating in its claims, including its claims to signification and authority.

Nor can I, in good conscience, regard literary works as epiphenomena of economic culture, history, or any transcendent universals.

Rather than approaching Thoreau's language as self-referential, as a linguistic trace of universals, or as an echo or mirror image of his culture, I accept what I regard as an obligation to "historicize" his language, thus rejecting the working principle of formalists and a surprising number of deconstructionists that there is no ground but Thoreau's language and that for the practical purposes of the critic Thoreau's language contains all language and culture. At the same time, I refuse to march to the beat of those who insist that there is no "reality" but history and that Thoreau's language is fully "contained" by history or by any putative "scientific" or other laws of history.[1] Those of my colleagues in the field of history who dismiss intellectual history as a form of archaic elitism and who assume that a statistical study of trades in a particular village is, by definition, sounder scholarship than the examination of the so-called ideas of a region or a culture will notice that I estimate the integrity of intellectual history to be about the same as that of economic, social, and political history. Fashions in historiography aside, the multiplicity of practices in the enterprise of historical scholarship is tied to institutional conventions and, consequently, to conventional purposes and valuations. I am willing to accept the proposition that each of these practices can be useful, but my acceptance is linked to the question: Useful to what end? As for the current disrepute of intellectual history, my extended stays in foreign cultures have reinforced my conviction that shared beliefs and habitual modes of thinking are not insignificant factors in the definition and understanding of a culture and of the dynamics of power.

In characterizing this book as interdisciplinary scholarship by a literary scholar interested in conducting cultural criticism, and in acknowledging that my assumptions and methods probably cannot be accommodated in traditional formalist and aesthetic criticism, I am joining many of my colleagues in a polyglot poststructuralist diaspora of philosophical speculation and practical critical experimentation. A source of energy and joy, the speculation and experimentation are also a serious—and I would add moral—undertaking. Let me explain "moral" by focusing on the project of writing *The Economist*. Once I had reached the point of no return in my commitment to this project, I was no longer free to sidestep the question of what kind of book I might write and could not write, given my assumptions about the nature of the artist's and critic's work in general and the nature of my work with Thoreau in particular. What I have accepted is a number of assumptions I have not been able to deny and, consequently, a number of obligations that these assumptions have placed on me.

My study of Thoreau rests on the following premises: (1) neither Thoreau nor his critics have conducted their work outside of, and therefore independently of, literary and cultural conventions; (2) no impermeable distinctions can be drawn between literary and cultural conventions; (3) no fundamental differences can be demonstrated (so as to be enforced) between the language of Thoreau's literary works and the language of his culture; (4) the "language" of Thoreau's culture is, in fact, a nest of "languages"; and (5) the language of Thoreau's literary art "contains" his culture.

To contain culture means, among other things, to contain its most important process, language. In a sense, the discourse of Thoreau's culture can be called stable: it constitutes, registers, and passes on the inscriptions of experience and understanding. In recognizing that language contains the inscriptions of experience and in acting upon that recognition, Thoreau and the Thoreau scholar contain language. Frequently, however, those inscriptions are not uniform, and often they are consistent neither with themselves nor with each other. In another sense, then, the language of Thoreau's culture is highly unstable: under the pressures of cultural developments and changes, and of collective and individual appropriations of language, the language of a culture is easily diffused and multiplied. As cultural agent or process, language is "quickly mobilized," as Lewis Mumford observed, "to function on particular occasions for particular uses."[2] In particular, changes in economic discourse in Thoreau's culture are "contained" in thoroughly familiar yet enigmatic terminology, lexical clusters, and groups of statements, as well as in the frequency of all of these, in their relation to their context, and in the conditions of their emergence, appropriation, and reappropriation. The stability/instability of the language of Thoreau's culture and the impossibility for him, as a writer, to assume with any freedom and certainty a position external to his culture were acknowledged by Thoreau, as we shall see. If he occasionally quarreled with the implications of these conditions for himself as a writer, the quarrel registers what the speaker of *Walden* describes as "a desire to speak somewhere *without* bounds" (*Walden*, p. 324).

To contain one's culture also means to select, distribute, arrange, and shape—to invent as one reports and to create even as one registers. In this sense, "contain" signifies Thoreau's recognitions, validations, valuations, and re-presentations. To say that his language contains his culture or some aspect of its life is to acknowledge that his appropriation of his culture was an act of containment. Such an acknowledgment is also appropriate in considering the action of those citizens of Concord who, in their attempt to determine the meaning of Thoreau, relocated his grave in the late 1860s to the crest of the highest ridge in Sleepy Hollow Cemetery, where he lies buried with distinguished literary figures. The acknowledgment of containment, however, is a de facto admission of the scholar's situation as he tries to make sense of Thoreau's language.

The two parts of this book conduct a twofold conjugation of the verb "contain." Part I situates Thoreau in significant economic conditions of his time and place, and examines how these conditions contained him even as he sought to contain them. Throughout this section the focus is on cultural conditions, his awareness of them, and his responses to them as a literary artist who identified his writing as his vocation. Thus, to be contained by history or culture does not mean to be contained by a narrowly defined *kairos*, on the one hand, or to be swept forward by some abstract, limitless march of history, on the other. Nor does it mean that Thoreau's attempts to contain conditions that contained him were inconsequential. Part I locates Thoreau inside the boundary markers of his culture and its discourse, and focuses on attitudes and practices in the presence of which—indeed, in the confinement of which—he developed his practice.

While in no way dismissing or ignoring any of this containment of Thoreau by his culture, Part II acknowledges that ever since Thoreau has become a subject of stature to literary historians and critics, his stature has had something to do with his legacy of contesting confinement and with the related history of a scholarship emphasizing his permanent suggestiveness. It is chiefly Thoreau's language of "*extra vagance*," to cite the term he uses to describe the achievement of the *Walden* account, that has made him interesting to modern readers. Using *Walden* as an example, Part II attempts to offer an answer to the question of why and how Thoreau—who was very much contained by his culture and its conventions—also contested the limitations of those conventions and used his condition to transform some of them. *Walden* has been selected as central to my examination for several reasons: it is Thoreau's best-known work; among Thoreau's writings it most consciously and clearly connects "enterprise," "economy," "vocation," and "*extra vagance*"; it announces and demonstrates that "*extra vagance*" is linked to confinement and cannot be understood apart from confinement; through parody it appropriates and transforms conventions that confine both a species of literature and the behavior of his culture; and the compositional history of *Walden* as I represent it in Part I is a useful preparation for an examination of the containment and "*extra vagance*" of the language of *Walden*.

Although contained by his culture, Thoreau used the terms of that containment to cultivate a vocation and writing in which he could demonstrate the possibility of co-opting conventions of the culture that confined him. Co-optation along with transformation of this kind in the name of one's vocation and out of moral integrity or "principle" was Thoreau's most practical definition of and claim to the much bandied-about term *transcendentalist*. *Walden* neither transcends (exists above and independent of) the conditions in which it was situated nor can it be reduced to those conditions. Part II, then, is a supplement to past efforts to account for Thoreau's perennial importance to readers, an importance that extends beyond his richness as archeological exhibit. In demonstrating that *Walden* is contained by literary conventions that were inseparable from the economic culture of Thoreau's age, but that *Walden* surveys the conditions of his containment in order to identify passages beyond the containment of those conditions, I do not hesitate to use his own carefully chosen metaphors to describe his achievment. The "*extra vagance*" of *Walden* is directly linked to how and how thoroughly the work is "yarded." Thoreau is situated in a field of powerful conventions; he is also presented as a writer who accepts as his greatest challenge the work of creating the condition for "more liberal laws" to be established or for current conventions to "be expanded, and interpreted . . . in a more liberal sense" (*Walden*, pp. 323–24).

Because of the dearth of scholarly material in American literature to which I could turn for assistance in an undertaking for which I was not trained, I am grateful for the bountiful encouragements, information, advice, and criticisms I have received in the course of writing this book. For their advice and encouragement during my labors, I wish to thank Thomas Blanding, Lawrence Buell, William Epstein, James Gilbert, Robert Gross, George Hendrick, Hans-Joachim Lang, Virgil Lokke, Joel Myerson, Janice Radway, Hugo Reichard, David Robinson, Malini Johar Schueller, Nancy Simmons, G. Richard Thompson, Leland Warren, Gordon Wood, and Harold Woodman. Special thanks go to Lawrence Buell, Joel Myerson, David Robinson, and Richard Thompson, who patiently perused parts of the book in an unreadable first draft; to Vincent Leitch, Joel Myerson, and Elizabeth Boyd Thompson, who read the intermediate version of the entire manuscript; and to Merton Sealts, who read the final draft. The suggestions of these readers have been enormously helpful. I also owe a debt to John Broderick, who years ago conscripted me to assist in the project of editing the manuscript Thoreau Journal for *The Writings of Henry D. Thoreau*, and to William Howarth, who invited me to organize my schedules and budget so as to work from time to time at the Textual Center of this Princeton University Press edition of Thoreau's writings. My association with the seemingly endless Thoreau editorial project has been a constant source of education and re-education, a rich tutelage full of surprises.

Marcia Moss of the Concord Free Public Library, Herbert Cahoon of the Pierpont Morgan Library, Lola Szladitz of the Berg Collection in the New York Public Library, Rodney Dennis of the Houghton Library, the research staff of the Henry E. Huntington Library, and the staff of the Textual Center of *The Writings of Henry D. Thoreau* at the University of California–Santa Barbara have all been generous with their cooperation and assistance. I am grateful to the editors of *American Quarterly* for publishing an earlier version of my first chapter. I am also pleased to acknowledge the substantial assistance of Purdue University and its Center for Humanistic Studies. It was as a fellow of the center in 1983 that I began the research that resulted in this book and as a faculty member on sabbatical leave that I completed the writing.

This book is dedicated to many, including Mera, who for many years has been my closest companion; to Virgil Lokke, who has spent much time debating literary theory with me; to Joel Myerson, whose interest in the genetic history of literary works and zeal for revision are entirely compatible; to David Robinson, who encouraged me to devote more than a paragraph to the subject of *Walden* and the young man's guide to success; and to Victor Raskin, whose expertise in semantics and whose research in the apparently unrelated subjects of the semantics of lying and artificial intelligence helped me to keep my work and our friendship in perspective. By their willingness to exchange drafts of poems with me when the work on Thoreau needed to be set aside, Jared Carter, Allen Mandelbaum, and Neil Myers also helped with perspectives. In a special way, however, this study is intended for three enterprising young people who have enriched my life beyond any expectations with their energy, love, delight in knowledge, and zest for debate. Mera and I are privileged to call them our children.

West Lafayette, Ind.   L. N. N.
June 1988

Notes

1. I find Michel Foucault's characterization of his duty and intention both instructive and perhaps a little exaggerated in its implied claims for his achievements: to discover precisely where strands of discourse and behavior "become reflective techniques with definite goals, the point at which a particular discourse emerged from these techniques and came to be seen as true, the point at which they are linked with the obligation of searching for the truth and telling the truth." Michel Foucault, *The Foucault Reader*, ed. Paul Rabinow (New York: Pantheon, 1984), p. 7.

2. Lewis Mumford, *The Myth of the Machine* (New York: Harcourt, Brace & World, 1967), p. 97.

Contents

Key to Abbreviations

CSmH HM 924   Manuscript *Walden*. Thoreau's autograph worksheets of *Walden* in the Henry E. Huntington Library, San Marino, California.

NNPM MA 1302   Manuscript Thoreau Journal. Thirty-nine notebooks of autograph Journal in the Pierpont Morgan Library, New York.

1906 J   Thoreau's *Journal*, vol. VII–XX of *The Writings of Henry David Thoreau*, ed. Bradford Torrey and Francis Allen (Boston: Houghton Mifflin, 1906). Also numbered separately as vols. 1–14, which is the numbering used here.

PE J   Thoreau, *Journal*, ed. John Broderick et al., in *The Writings of Henry D. Thoreau* (Princeton University Press, 1981–).

Reform Papers   Thoreau, *Reform Papers*, ed. Wendell Glick, in *The Writings of Henry D. Thoreau* (Princeton University Press, 1973).

Walden   Thoreau, *Walden*, ed. J. Lyndon Shanley, in *The Writings of Henry D. Thoreau* (Princeton University Press, 1971).

Fordyce   James Fordyce, *Addresses to Young Men*, 2 vols. (Boston: Manning & Loring, 1795).

Franklin   Benjamin Franklin [with Dr. Stuber], *The Life of Dr. Benjamin Franklin* (Salem, Mass.: Cushing & Carlton, 1796).

Hawes   Joel Hawes, *Lectures Addressed to the Young Men of Hartford and New-Haven* (Hartford, Conn.: Oliver D. Cooke, 1828).

West   Mrs. [Jane] West, *Lectures Addressed to a Young Man, on His First Entrance into Life and Adapted to the Peculiar Circumstances of the Present Times*, 3 vols. (London: Longman and Rees, 1801).

THE ECONOMIST

Introduction

The views that Henry Thoreau expressed on enterprise and economy during his mature years in the late 1840s and 1850s were not sanctioned by Concord opinion. Nor did his views sanction prevailing economic beliefs and behavior in his hometown and in his culture at large. Just what the subscribers to the Concord Lyceum (the intellectual elite of the town) believed is difficult to ascertain from the Lyceum records, since the Lyceum administration usually sought to offer some speakers and addresses that would test the intellectual tolerance and generosity of spirit of the subscribers. We do know that in February 1847 Thoreau delivered either two consecutive lectures or the same lecture twice to a large but unconsenting Concord Lyceum audience based on material he eventually used for the "Economy" section of *Walden*. We also know that his first lecture version of "Life without Principle," presented at the Town House Lyceum in February 1855, was not well received.[1] Five days later he was still irritated by the reaction of his audience to his address, which he referred to by the titles of "What Shall it Profit" and "What Shall it Profit a Man." "If you wish to know how I think," he wrote in his *Journal*, "you must endeavor to put yourself in my place. If you wish me to speak as if I were you, that is another affair" (1906 J 7:197).

Outside the Lyceum, the view that probably counted most with the majority of Concordians was the one from the porch of the rebuilt Middlesex Hotel, usually occupied by the local politicians

3

and patriarchs. The Middlesex had risen like a small miracle after the completion of the Fitchburg Railroad, surpassing its old glory, which the fire that destroyed the first Middlesex Hotel had turned into a memory of the good old days. The new version of the Middlesex had also come to represent a potential incompatibility in Concord's socioeconomic attitudes—the desire for continuity with the older order and a preoccupation with new definitions of progress and success. Defenders of the Concord of the old Middlesex Hotel, of the rummy wisdom of the fathers, but also of the need for Concord to recover her commercial importance in the region through new enterprise, these local politicians and patriarchs had learned without the help of the McGuffey *Reader* to identify piety, progress, and usefulness when any of these presented themselves in modern habit.

Several of Townsend Scudder's paragraphs in his book on Concord join the usual cluster of head-shaking, tooth-picking hotel porch sitters in the 1850s.

What was going to happen to Concord? Loafers spitting tobacco juice in the dusty square where the booths and tents of Court Week used to stand growled there was no place even to enjoy a drink. Husky, tow-headed, ruddy-faced George Prescott there, the widow's son, on his way to the coal and lumber yard he ran (folks said he did a pretty good business) was in part to blame—with his teetotalling notions and his Young Men's Total Abstinence Society. There was that good-for-nothing failure, Bronson Alcott, on his way up Main Street towards Mrs. Thoreau's, to hobnob, likely, with Henry, his equal. The idlers curiously watched another crank, Ephraim Bull, once a prosperous goldbeater, trudge across the green toward his land along the sidehill on Lexington Road. Trying to play tricks on nature, was he? Thought he could make grapes better than God intended? . . . (Charlie Bartlett, though, they say, is getting good money for his strawberries, which no one ever before thought to grow here.)

If you lolled long enough in the shade of the big oak by the Town House, you'd be likely to see most of the people passing. Tall, long-shanked young Ed Wheeler striding by—why didn't he go pioneering; head West for gold like other men? (Some folks were remarking he was doing pretty well with that part of his father's farm he'd taken over—raising asparagus and other truck along with the usual Wheeler cattle.) Rockwood Hoar, coming from the train (the Governor had just named him Judge of the Court of Common Pleas). . . . There goes John

Shepard Keyes, the big man's son (doing quite a legal practice, ain't he?). . . . There was Mr. Emerson, with a smile and nod for the swarm of boys playing ball on the square. Heading down Main Street toward the station, a bundle under his arm—some book, most likely, he'd written, to be printed in Boston.

Well, times had changed. Men weren't what they used to be.[2]

A brief yet remarkably revealing document on the change in the times anecdotally registered by Scudder and of some of the forces behind the change is contained in Thoreau's Journal entry for 27 January 1852. On that day Thoreau climbed the hill just south of the house inhabited at this time by Joseph Hosmer, Sr., an aged farmer who had moved off his ancestral farm a half mile to the north. Thoreau's position afforded him a panoramic view of the Assabet River basin, including the family farm now worked by Joseph Hosmer, Jr., and the ancestral house now occupied by him and his family. Joseph Hosmer, Jr., had recently tried life in the city; he and his wife had returned to Concord and to farming "in despair" according to Thoreau (see his Journal for 27 January 1852). To Thoreau the Hosmer estate represented ancestral farms and traditional farming away from the village center. The old family farm also represented traditional values, attitudes, and regimen associated with such farms and farmers. The narrator of *Walden* notes that in the Concord vicinity one no longer finds many "men on their farms" (*Walden*, p. 267). Indeed, Joseph Hosmer, Sr., died in the year in which *Walden* appeared, and three years thereafter Joseph Hosmer, Jr., "sold the old ancestral farm," to quote his brother Horace, "which had been in the family possession, (passing from father to son) for 220 years."[3] On 27 January 1852, however, Joseph Hosmer, Jr., was still on his farm (back on his farm, to put it more accurately) as Thoreau looked north and west over cultivated and deserted farms that formed his landscape and that registered the march of time and fundamental changes in the region. The coherence and poignancy of Thoreau's version of Hosmer, other young men like him, and a changing Concord are much more the functions of Thoreau's nay-saying than sympathetic identification with his boyhood friend and a town that elsewhere in his *Journal* he described as "the most estimable place in all the world" (1906 J 9:160).

Thoreau's Journal entry concerning his hilltop view and the reflections it prompted is lengthy. "Mill Road S of Ministerial Swamp 3 P.m." is a subheading-like introjection at the beginning of a paragraph that registers a shift from the immediately preceding paragraphs. In the interior oration that follows, Thoreau impressionistically reports looking "over the plains westward toward Acton" and seeing

> the farm houses nearly half a mile apart—few & solitary—in these great fields between these stretching woods—out of the world—where the children have to go far to school—the still stagnant—hearteating—life-everlasting gone-to-seed country—so far from the post Office where the weekly paper comes— Wherein the new-married wife cannot live for loneliness— And the young man has to depend upon his horse—— See young J Hosmer's House whither he returns with his wife in despair—after living in the City. I standing in Tarbells' road which he alone cannot break out. (NNPM MA 1302:15)[4]

This scene and the conditions it typifies become the immediate backdrop for Thoreau's comments on Joseph Hosmer, Jr., and other young men like him. The source of Hosmer's despair is unclear: perhaps the stagnant rural environment has been eating his heart, perhaps he recognizes the new economic facts of life for farmers, perhaps he has been confused by his temporary stay in the city, perhaps he has set heart and mind on a business profession in the city. Whatever the cause, Thoreau reports one aspect of Hosmer's despair: Hosmer is desperate to "break out," but is convinced that, unlike others, he cannot. Although the "he alone" is somewhat ambiguous, Thoreau probably is not suggesting that Hosmer's wife, Martha Bacon Hosmer, is the problem. After all, she, too, has returned to the farm "in despair." The characterization of Hosmer's entrapment, a description that appears to have been influenced by discussions with Hosmer or with others who knew of his "despair," gains some of its edge from its image of the road, which is open for Thoreau but closed for Hosmer. In Hosmer's case, the road is much too far from "the P.O. & the Lyceum" and does not lead him to the railroad "Depot" with its ticket agent. Instead, the reference to Tarbell's Road is followed immediately by two winter images: the farmer sealed off from the town by the snow drifts and all "springs ceiled [*sic*] up & no digressions."[5]

Whereas "the old man thinks he may . . . rust it out not having long to live," the "young man" is "restless—& resolves to go to California, because the Depot is a mile off.—" Among the penciled revisions Thoreau made to this passage at a later date is a sentence interlined above and below "to go to California, because the Depot is a mile off" (the interlineation is not marked for position and may have been intended as an alternate version): "He hears the rattle of the cars at a distance & thinks the world is going by & leaving him." The tonal shift in these statements—to an unmistakable dubiousness and ironic dissociation from Hosmer and other young men resolved to "break out" of rural Concord—makes one wonder if something has been missed. Have ironic pointers in the text been overlooked? Or has Thoreau concealed his ironic sense until this moment? This is, in fact, his second ironic note on Hosmer's aspirations and dilemma. The first note to register an ironic attitude to Hosmer's situation is Thoreau's characterization of Hosmer's despair as an exaggerated and confused view: "I standing in Tarbell's road which *he alone* cannot break out" (emphasis added). Others have broken out, but Hosmer supposedly sees himself as a tragic exception. Yet the irony directed against the one who is convinced that he cannot break out almost immediately governs images of breaking out—dreams of California and the railroad as the golden arches of one's prospects, and, hitched to those dreams, actual passage west. On the other hand, Thoreau's bleak depiction of the "stagnant—hearteating" life in the old farm clearings has not been reversed or, for that matter, called into question.

Young men like Hosmer, we are told, are "restless" and resolve "to go to California." A few days later Thoreau wrote in the same Journal notebook, "I know of no more startling development of the morality of trade and all the modes of getting a living that [*sic*] the rush to California affords. . . . Going to California. It is only 3000 miles nearer to Hell. . . . Satan showed mankind the kingdom of California and they entered into a compact with him at once—." This much longer diatribe against America's new mother lode of dreams of enterprise, a passage which Thoreau reworked for his lecture versions and published text of "Life without Principle," concludes with a self-reflective note on its tone and moral position: "There are some things which God may afford to smile at—man can-not" (NNPM MA 1302:15). To see the railroad and a ticket to

the city or to California as the economic and moral alternative to
the condition of Hosmer on his ancestral farm is not a smiling
matter.

Nor is the desolation of a number of old farms something to
smile at. That desolation adds urgency to the theme of breaking out
of a cycle of hopelessness. In a memorable wasteland passage
reminiscent of the twelfth chapter of Ecclesiastes, Thoreau offers a
catalogue of images of decay, lifelessness, loss, and futility, thus
evoking the sense that a once praiseworthy way of life is passing,
indeed is past, and that the worthy practitioners have passed with it:

> Where rabbits & partridges multiply & muskrats are more numerous than
> ever.— And none of the farmer's sons are willing to be farmers— And the
> apple trees are decayed—& the cellar holes are more numerous than the
> houses— And the old maids—wish to sell out & move into the village—&
> have waited 20 years in vain for this purpose—& never finished but one
> room in the house— Lands of which the Indian was long since dispos-
> sessed—and now the farms are run out—& what were forests are grain
> fields—& what were grain-fields—pastures— Dwellings which only those
> Arnolds those Coureurs de bois the baker & the butcher visit—to which at
> least the latter penetrates for the annual calf—& as he returns the cow lows
> after— Whither the villager never penetrates . . . and if he does not who
> does? Where the owls give a regular serenade.

In a later revision Thoreau added a less poetic penultimate sentence
in pencil: "where some men's breaths smell of rum—having
smuggled in a jug-full to alleviate their misery & solitude." No one
penetrates the run-down farm region, but the misery and solitude of
the small residual population penetrate Thoreau's descriptive language, encumber it, and resonate in the owls' night calls.

Old traditional farms may once have been praiseworthy, but as
this Journal entry makes clear, Thoreau withholds his praise. As
indicated by this entry and another one that he made four months
earlier upon beholding another traditional farm in the region, both
the thought of living on such a farm and the thought of remaining
on it provoke revulsion and dismay in him. In the earlier Journal
report the traditional farmer living in retirement on his farm has no
prospects:

> There is somewhat exceedingly pathetic to think of in such a life as he
> must have lived—with no more to redeem it—such a life as an average

Carlisle man may be supposed to live drawn out to 80 years. . . . Here was the cider mill & there the orchard & there the hog-pasture—& so men lived & ate & drank and passed away.— like vermin. Their long life was mere duration. As respectable is the life of the woodchucks which perpetuate their race in the orchard still. . . . We only know that they ate & drank and built barns & died and were buried, and still perchance their toomb-stones cumber the ground. But if I could know that there was ever entertained over their cellar hole some divine thought which came as a messenger of the gods—that he who resided here acted once in his life from a noble impulse— . . . if only a single verse of poetry or of poetic prose had ever been written or spoken or conceived here beyond a doubt—I should not think it in vain that man had lived here.— (NNPM MA 1302:13)[6]

In Thoreau's reflections on Hosmer's despair, his note on chang-ing land use in Concord, from grain cultivation to what he sees as the paradoxically more modern yet more primitive dairy farming, adds a crucial element to the evocation of a wasteland scene—the principle of irrevocable change. This cycle of change and disposses-sion impressionistically imaged by Thoreau offers no alternative to farmers like Hosmer but to "break out." In an era now referred to in the preterit, they practiced their "enterprise" on the traditional farm; now they must revitalize their hope and conduct their Yankee "enterprise" in a new context. The end of the former and the uncertain prospects of the latter, however, directly challenge a Yankee and national myth as well as the speaker's own moral version of that belief. The settled assurance of possession and repossession implied in the supposition that the enterprise of each new generation of Americans will overcome desolation and misery and through its achievements will continue to guarantee progress— this assurance is unsettled by what Thoreau describes as the hope-lessness of Hosmer and of the alternatives entertained by young men like him. Indeed, that myth is as unsettled as the traditional farms and the condition of the farmers. "I cannot realize," the speaker concludes, "that this is that hopeful young America which is famous throughout the world—for its activity & enterprise—& this is the most thickly settled & Yankee part of it." The semantic register of "realize" makes this unsentimental coda a richly sugges-tive and fitting conclusion to a complex passage about the troubled young farmers of Concord. The speaker cannot "realize" the present condition as his reality, nor can he recover past versions of an enterprising America for the despairing young men, thereby reestablishing the "activity & enterprise" befitting a "hopeful young America." Nor do the national myth and actual conditions agree. Consequently, the concluding observations in Thoreau's description of dispossession and desolation counter any predilection the reader might have to equate loss with lament and thus to regard this Journal entry as an ode to dejection. But the coda also reports another kind of resistance: Thoreau's honorific language about "activity & enterprise" rejects popular new forms of such enterprise— business life in the city and flight to the other end of America.

Hosmer's alternatives—persevering on the farm, entering a business career in the city, or catching a train to the West—are thus rejected. But where does that leave Thoreau? In the concluding paragraph, Thoreau draws the various concerns in his Journal entry (the old cultural ways, economic transformation, modernity, individual failure and collective exhaustion, and the nature of one's citizenship in the modern culture) into the commodious schema of what we might call historical process. This process, which Thoreau presents as an unavoidable principle of growth, change, dissolution, and reconstitution, is patron and guarantor of enterprise:

> In new countries men are scattered broad cast— They do not wait for roads to place their houses on . . . & each man is a prince in his principality & depends on himself— Perchance when the virgin soil is exhausted a reaction takes place & men concentrate in villages again— become social & commercial—& leave the steady & moderate few to work the country's mines.

A paean to persisting American enterprise, one might say. Settlers are building the roads of their direction and destiny after laying foundations for their dwelling, they are cultivating self-reliance as much as land, they refuse to be trapped in the past or victimized by exhaustion, they keep stride with change and play an important role in that change, they learn through their undertakings what must be undertaken. There is no detectable censure in the observation that cultural change is bringing about an America that is "social & commercial."

Yet the very principle that serves as guarantor of enterprise seeks to stand free of traditional and current American definitions of "activity & enterprise." The act of rising above particulars to the vantage provided by the principle of incessant cultural change does not resolve irreconcilable elements or reconcile the various alternatives noted; rather, it marks a departure—in behalf of another enterprise. The leave-taking recalls Thoreau's "Reform and the Reformers," an unfinished product of the 1840s. "Reform and the Reformers" searches for a trustworthy footing outside the strong current of belief in a special destiny secured by popular definitions of cultural progress. The most promising footing is identified when the speaker pleads the case for "some pure product of man's hands, some pure labor, some life got in this old trade of getting a living— some work done which shall not be a mending, a cobbling, a reforming. . . . One generation abandons the enterprises of another. Many an institution which was thought to be an essential part of the order of society, has, in the true order of events, been left like a stranded vessel on the sand." The constant in this historical and cultural flux is "the free labor of man, even the creative and beautiful arts" (*Reform Papers*, pp. 188–89). In the Journal entry the leave-taking is described as a being left alone to follow a vocation distinct from any noted thus far: "the steady & moderate few" are left "to work the country's mines." Rather than plowing the soil or returning it to pasture, a steady few burrow beneath it; rather than moving to the city, some remain where they are in order to perform a labor ignored by those who leave to improve their lot; rather than staking out gold claims in California, some (a "few," with whom the speaker identifies) work richer mines. To quote a passage that Thoreau wrote at Walden Pond in his first version of *Walden*: "My instinct tells me that my head is an organ for burrowing, as some creatures use their snout and fore-paws, and with it I would mine and burrow my way through these hills. I think that the richest vein is somewhere hereabouts" (*Walden*, p. 98). A similar mining image provides the gravitational force for several successive paragraphs of "Life without Principle," the first draft of which Thoreau composed two years after his Journal entry on Hosmer's despair. With the vision of money-frantic western miners before him, the speaker asks himself "why *I* might not sink a shaft down to the gold within me, and work that mine" (*Reform Papers*, p. 164). In both passages the mining image refers principally to self-culture and a literary vocation, concepts that, in Thoreau's case, were inseparable, reciprocally constitutive, and central to his rationale for his life. Thus to "work the country's mines" is both a personal rejection of apparently attractive new alternatives for young Concordians and a recommitment to his own private business, a business demonstrated by the literary tour de force on Hosmer, Concord, and the question of enterprise.

That commitment is pointedly confirmed in Thoreau's notations immediately following the passage on Hosmer and Concord's farmers. The apparent dissociation from what has just been presented is an integral part of the message of the passage:

> In going across lots I walk in the woods where the snow is not so deep— part having been caught on the trees & dissipated in the air—and a part melted by the warmth of the wood & the reflection.
>
> The poison sumac with its stems hanging down on every side is a very agreeable object now seen against the snow
>
> I do not know but thoughts written down thus in a journal might be printed in the same form with greater advantage—than if the related ones were brought together into separate essays.

Thoreau's account is of the rambler who notes scenes, particulars, and events, who writes them down as he walks through the woods and farm clearings and then reworks his notes and transcribes them in his Journal notebook, whose literary instincts tell him that his Journal is assuming a literary life of its own and may be a worthy enterprise in its own right. Yet, while acknowledging that his Journal is a fitting literary expression of his life and imagination, Thoreau also decided to revise and transcribe the Journal passage on the desolation of Concord farms and the despair of the children of enterprising farmers in order to use it with related passages in a lecture/essay appropriately titled "Life without Principle" and in its earlier lecture versions, "What Shall it Profit" and "Life Misspent." Keeping a Journal was a profitable enterprise, and composing lectures and essays was time and energy well spent. Moreover, although the Journal passage on Hosmer and Concord's young farmers may have profited Thoreau's worksheets for "What Shall it Profit,"[7] as "Life without Principle" developed, Thoreau decided against incorporating this Journal passage and mined a similar passage instead. Such mining and separating both tested and reinforced the strength required in the business of self-culture as literary vocation.

Thoreau's observations, closing with a self-conscious reflection on the value of his Journal and his commitments as a writer, conclude his Journal entry for 27 January 1852. They also circle back to the beginning of the entry, supplementing the beginning, and, together with the beginning, providing a personal frame of reference in a strikingly impersonal voice. The entry for 27 January begins:

> The peculiarity of a work of genius is the absence of the speaker from his speech— He is but the medium. . . . I read its page but it is as free from any man that [*sic*] can be—remembered as an impassable desert.
>
> I think that the one word which will explain the Shakspeare miracle— is unconsciousness. . . . There probably has been no more conscious age than the present.
>
> Mill Road S of Ministerial Swamp 3 P.m.

And so we begin with Thoreau's discussion of the heart-eating life of rural Concord and of Joseph Hosmer, Jr., a geographical scene and cultural problem awaiting the artist/historian's response. That response, according to Thoreau, is marked by genius to the extent that the writer's culture richly resonates in his or her response, even though the response is personally shaped. If the writer's consciousness is a cultural consciousness, the "speaker" will function as medium and the "speech," inhabited by the age rather than the demands of a private and separate ego, will be much more memorable than the speaker. Since there "probably has been no more conscious age than the present," such an economy of awareness and writing, Thoreau concedes, is severely tested by the very age it attempts to articulate.

Hosmer was not one of the few friends privy to Thoreau's Journal notebooks. Thus he could not have learned of Thoreau's entry for 27 January 1852 or known that in the rapidly expanding Journal Thoreau commented increasingly on Concord, the surrounding region, friends, and acquaintances. Nor would he have known that the entry which so memorably notes his "despair" highlights a prominent theme in the Journal of the early 1850s and a number of Thoreau's non-Journal compositions of this decade—the effects of individual and collective dedication in America to a powerful new version of enterprise. (No doubt Hosmer's knowledge of the Journal notebooks was limited to the passages that Ellery Channing had selected, and in numerous cases freely edited, for use in his *Thoreau: The Poet-Naturalist*, 1873.) What Hosmer knew in 1852, among other things, was that he would rather not be farming and that he would rather reside in the city than in Concord.

Boyhood friend to both Henry Thoreau and his brother, John, and frequent visitor to their home in those years, Hosmer much later recalled another visit, in 1845, when, at Thoreau's invitation, he spent a Sunday with him at the cabin at Walden Pond, a visit Hosmer remembered with obvious pleasure some thirty-five years after the fact. Hosmer's reminiscence of this visit is included in a memoir of Thoreau that he wrote in Chicago, where he had lived since 1857, where he had been remarkably successful by most standards, and where two of his sons had recently become millionaires.

Why an old-stock New Englander like Hosmer would sell the family farm and move with his family to the relatively small immigrant city of Chicago is no doubt explained in part by statistics directly pertinent to Hosmer's situation. In the years 1850–1880 the number of rural Americans decreased in ratio from 82 percent to 61 percent of the population; the number of people living on farms (farm laborers included) decreased in ratio from somewhat over 50 percent to slightly over 40 percent of the population; the number of farms in Massachusetts increased only marginally in a period of strong population gains in the state (especially in the cities);[8] the number of farms in Middlesex County (in which Concord is located) decreased; the average size of farms in New England and the nation decreased, while productivity increased. Moreover, farms in the vicinity of Concord shifted to more intensive cultivation, more farmhands (especially immigrant labor), new crops, significantly more dairy farming, and new markets, all of which made the traditional farm a precarious business and the exodus of considerable numbers of people from farming the pattern. In the same thirty-year span Chicago's population soared from 29,963 to 503,185, the population of Cook County increased fourteen-fold (whereas the national population doubled), and the business of Chicago, as of much of the victorious North, became business enterprise.[9] In trying New England city life, in taking rail passage a few years later to Chicago to start a business life there, and in assisting his sons to become entrepreneurial giants in Chicago, Hosmer can be consid-

ered a more typical representative of economic and social developments than was Thoreau, whom Hosmer described in his memoir as
"product" and "heritage" of Concord.[10]

Two years and nine months older than Thoreau, Hosmer outlived
him by more than twenty-four years. In the 1870s and 80s he witnessed the extraordinary economic and social successes of his sons,
especially the two oldest, and he appears to have played no small role
in his sons' economic success.[11] The oldest son married a socialite in
Chicago; he and the second son, both of them new millionaires,
joined some of Chicago's most prestigious social clubs; and both were
subsequently listed for years in *The Elite of Chicago*, the *Chicago
Blue Book*, and the *Chicago Social Register*. In the late seventies and
early eighties Hosmer held a political patronage position in the
Federal Revenue Department that required little work on his part.
He suffered from a damaged liver but, in his brother's words, had
"sound teeth" and "looked younger than many men of 50."[12]

With a somnolent job and much free time on his hands, Hosmer
looked for interesting and useful diversions. One of these diversions
was to frequent the Chicago Public Library, where, in the course of
his reading, he worked through the published volumes of Thoreau,
for him an apparently pleasant activity that played a role in the
memoir of Thoreau that Hosmer wrote for the *Concord Freeman* in
1880. This memoir notes the importance of following a "profession
or business," which Hosmer defines as a "useful" occupation. In
Hosmer's view, he had found a useful place, and he would leave
signs of having done so. Thoreau, on the other hand, "followed no
profession or business," and "went in and out among us his life
long, waiting, and hoping to find a place where he could be useful
and happy." Yet Thoreau's failure to find a useful place did not
discredit him in Hosmer's eyes or hold back Hosmer from identifying with, and co-opting, his erstwhile friend. Hosmer dismissed as
ridiculous the "romantic and unreal idea" that readers had of
Thoreau, and his memoir offered as the real Thoreau a realist who
subscribes to a version of realism Hosmer admired. Thoreau "was a
matter-of-fact man." "No guessing or theory would answer for
him"; he "was one of the most practical of men, but without
imagination or fancy and, what was not real was unworthy of his
thought." Indeed, if "ever a man stood on the multiplication table,
he, Thoreau, did."[13]

The version of Concord that Thoreau epitomizes in Hosmer's memoir is a Concord that does not threaten Hosmer's values in 1880. Quite taken with the spirit of enterprise before the Civil War and very much the citizen of a post–Civil War, capitalistic America, the memoirist has canceled the weight of his Concord past while nurturing self-confirming mnemonic ties to it. As for Thoreau, his Journal provides ample evidence that the Concord in which he "travelled a good deal" was a place of unsettling changes. In fact, often the place and state of change are indistinguishable. Not even nature was spared these changes according to *Walden*, to his essays on the Maine woods, Canada, and Cape Cod, to his growing notes on autumnal tints in the proximity of Concord, and to his unfinished and somewhat inchoate fruits and seeds project. Stability was to be found elsewhere, in his unorthodox vocation. As he admitted in his Journal, this was one of the lessons he drew from his consuming preoccupation with the fate and meaning of John Brown.

Thoreau's resistance to America's prevailing forms of modernity, his refusal to find consolation in retreating to the past,[14] his attachment to and persistent quarrel with Concord, and his linking of self-confirming bonds to a literary activity that negotiated between his American culture and self-culture and between stability and change through a kind of "history" writing are all clearly evident in his Journal passage on Hosmer and Concord.

From his observation post south of Hosmer's farm, Thoreau surveyed his culture at a significant moment in its development. We cannot imagine him surveying his generation from a hurly-burly Chicago. Nor can we imagine that Hosmer would have been able to change Thoreau's perspective or Thoreau Hosmer's. Notwithstanding its double negative and elliptical final three words, Hosmer's personal note at the end of his memoir of Thoreau, a note of affectionate combativeness, is an appropriate conclusion for a comparison of the two men in their times: "We never agreed as boys or men in hardly anything, but always friendly."[15]

Concord presented Thoreau with a local version of the spirit of the age. Thus he saw fit to reflect on individuals like Hosmer in addressing the ambiguities of America's socioeconomic transformation, which, in the history of the emergence of modern America, has been characterized as "The Great Transformation."[16] It is not at all surprising that Thoreau titled his first chapter of *Walden* "Economy," or that the persona presented therein assumes the role of economist. Nor is it surprising that the personae of Thoreau's works are presented as men of enterprise whose most crucial enterprise is that of contesting the age on the meaning and function of "economy."

Notes

1. On the February 1847 lectures, see Walter Harding, *The Days of Henry Thoreau* (New York: Alfred A. Knopf, 1965), pp. 187–88. On the relation of this material to *Walden*, see chapter 2, section II, of the present study.

2. Townsend Scudder, *Concord: American Town* (Boston: Little, Brown, 1947), pp. 198–99.

3. George Hendrick, ed., *Remembrances of Concord and the Thoreaus* (Urbana: University of Illinois Press, 1977), pp. 91–92. This volume contains both Horace Hosmer's letters to Dr. Samuel Jones and the memoir of Thoreau by Joseph Hosmer, Jr.

4. All quotations of Thoreau's Journal notebooks MA 1302:13, 15 are with the permission of The Pierpont Morgan Library, New York. Thoreau's numbering of the latter of the two notebooks is 9. In the Torrey and Allen edition of the *Journal*, see 1906 J 3:237–39. The two other discussions of this essaylike Journal passage are as unlike each other as they are unlike mine. See Ronald Wesley Hoag, "A 'Life without Principle' Manuscript Fragment: What to Make of a Diminished Thing?," *Essays in Literature* 12 (Spring 1985): 139–43, and Mary Elkins Moller, *Thoreau in the Human Community* (Amherst: University of Massachusetts Press, 1980), pp. 145–50. Moller bases her explication on Torrey and Allen's unreliable edition of the *Journal*. The problematical inferences she draws from the physical appearance of the autograph Journal reveal an unfamiliarity with Thoreau's manuscripts, and her close reading of the words of the text reveals considerable unfamiliarity with geography, community, and the socioeconomic changes of Concord that provide the context for Thoreau's observations. Hoag is more familiar with that context.

5. For a strikingly different treatment of the subject of entrapment by snowstorms, see Emerson's poem "The Snow-Storm" and the prose version out of which Emerson fashioned the poem, in *Journals and Miscellaneous Notebooks of Ralph Waldo Emerson*, ed. William Gilman et al., 16 vols. (Cambridge: Harvard University Press, 1960–82), 6:246. In these texts Emerson uses the imprisonment in the blizzard-swept farmhouse as the occasion for "new thought" that transforms prisoner, farmhouse enclosure, and the winter scene. In Thoreau's early essays, images of entrapment compete with the motif of uninhibited privacy and freedom of the saunterer; in *Walden*, however, the narrator does not allow himself to be shut in by the winter. During the season

of snowdrifts and ice, the saunterer is less dependent on roads and familiar paths as passports to his destinations, and so can follow his own directions.

6. Thoreau's numbering of this Journal notebook is 7. Even the old family farmer Thoreau most admired, his friend Edmund Hosmer (not closely related to Joseph Hosmer, Jr.), prompted a Journal report of considerable exasperation. This "long-headed farmer, . . . one of the few of his vocation who are 'men on their farms . . .'" (*Walden*, p. 267), who "admits that he has property enough for his use without accumulating more, & talks of leaving off hard work, letting his farm, and spending the rest of his days more easily and better, cannot yet think of any method of employing himself but in work with his hands—only he would have less of it. Much as he is inclined to speculation in conversation, giving up any work to it for the time, and wise as he is in many respects, he talks of working for a neighbor for a day now and then, and taking his dollar. 'For,' says he 'I would not like to spend my time sitting on the Mill-dam.' That is one exchange. As if that were the only alternative." The passage quoted here is the transcription of a Journal passage that Thoreau made in the fall of 1854 for use in his lecture "What Shall it Profit." Houghton Library, Harvard University (MH): bMS Am 278.5, folder 6D; quoted by permission of the Houghton Library. Compare 1906 J 4:194–95.

7. Hoag's conjectures about Thoreau's intentions to use the Journal passage in lecture drafts and his eventual decision against incorporating it into "Life without Principle" strike me as judicious and accurate ("A 'Life without Principle' Manuscript Fragment," pp. 141–43), especially when considered in the light of the evidence painstakingly and brilliantly assembled by Bradley P. Dean in "The Sound of a Flail: Reconstructions of Thoreau's Early 'Life without Principle' Lectures" (Master's thesis, Eastern Washington University, 1984).

8. Most of the population expansion in Massachusetts in the forties and fifties is accounted for by city growth. The population of Boston, for instance, increased close to 50 percent per decade. A number of back country, higher counties, in contrast, experienced little or no increase and some lost population in these years.

9. Statistics reported here are drawn from the following sources: the United States census reports for 1850, 1860, 1870, and 1880; *Historical Statistics of the United States: Colonial Times to 1970*, 2 vols. (Washington, D.C.: Bureau of the Census, 1975); and Donald Joseph Brogue, *The Population of the United States* (New York: Macmillan, 1985).

10. Hendrick, *Remembrances*, p. 136.

11. For an account of Hosmer's Chicago years, see Leonard Neufeldt, "'We Never Agreed . . . In Hardly Anything': Henry Thoreau and Joseph Hosmer," *Thoreau Quarterly*, forthcoming.

12. Hendrick, *Remembrances*, p. 31.

13. Ibid., pp. 135, 136, 144, 145.

14. Michael Gilmore, in an important and provocative study, argues that

Thoreau was inspired by the agrarian ideals of the past (which Gilmore identifies with European civic humanism of the seventeenth and eighteenth centuries), that *Walden* gives symbolic form to those ideals, and that in so doing
Walden "fails as a rejoinder to the nineteenth century." Leaving aside Gilmore's
arbitrary and dated view of real as opposed to exchange value and of the
historical/cultural significance of symbolic discourse, as well as the unanswered
and unanswerable question of what constitutes a successful literary rejoinder to
the nineteenth century, I suggest that the view of Thoreau as a culturally
homeless, alienated writer who sought refuge in irrevocably past orders doesn't
wash with the evidence. See his *American Romanticism and the Marketplace*
(Chicago: University of Chicago Press, 1985), pp. 5, 35, 36.

　15. Hendrick, *Remembrances*, p. 146.

　16. Karl Polyani, *The Great Transformation: The Political and Economic
Origins of Our Time* (1944; reprint, Boston: Beacon Press, 1957).

PART I

Enterprise, Economy, and Vocation

1

An Enterprise of Self-Culture in a Culture of Enterprise

Were we to consider the prevalence of the subject of enterprise in Henry Thoreau's writings apart from his cultural environment, we might conclude that in his literary performances a hard Yankee business head and literary inventiveness found each other and decided to live together in a self-constructed and self-regulated house of art. Such a view would privilege a formalist reading of Thoreau's language while admitting biographical data to the extent that these could be translated into aesthetic considerations. Thoreau scholars will recognize that, allowing for qualifications that acknowledge individual differences, I have just characterized the bulk of Thoreau scholarship in the 1960s and 70s. A close analysis of Thoreau's texts, however, leads us into the heart of his culture, to distinctive habits of language and behavior, and to questions about cultural discourse. I am convinced that our understanding of Thoreau's writings is impoverished or enriched by the extent to which we probe his culture, recognize the new economic vernacular with its range of semantic shifts and differentiations, and acknowledge the implications of the linguistic changes for the culture in which he had to locate himself. The culture and economic discourse of Thoreau's time are the subjects of sections I and II, respectively, of this chapter.

Without question, however, Thoreau's works should be read with reference not only to his times but also to his personal agenda: they constitute an ongoing personal narrative about an autobiographical problem that overshadowed all other concerns in his life and that throws considerable light on the inter-textuality of culture and literary works in his case—the question of his literary vocation in an age of enterprise. That subject is addressed in sections III and IV of this chapter. Section III focuses on the record of Thoreau's problem of language in his years-long attempt to develop an alternative to the economic vernacular and values of his culture; section IV notes connections between Thoreau's excursions into the economic discourse and behavior of his times and the shape of his career.

Why is the problem of vocation the major ligature between culture and literary text in Thoreau's case? First, he identified vocation with self-culture or what the narrator of *Walden* calls the "art of life." Second, in defining self-culture for himself, he equated it with a literary career, albeit an unusual one that, in the language of *Walden*, reregistered *business* as a moral/vocational term, *commerce* as the profitability of resistance to mass culture, and *profit* as "virtue" and "*extra vagance.*" In other words, the art of life and the life of art were from early on two sides of the same fact, and both were identified with means as with ends and with cause as with effect. One of Thoreau's reasons for conducting his two-year "experiment" at Walden Pond was to drive his vocational ideals into a corner in order to determine whether his art of life could be secured by terms tolerable to his society yet compatible with his aspirations as a writer. But the move to Walden was not without precedent. Already in February 1841, less than a year after he published his first literary work (a poem), he reported that he was thinking of purchasing or renting a site in retirement in which the art of life and the life of art could meet under one roof. Both Emerson and Fuller seemed to have understood his desire to find a writer's studio and succeed in his career. In this context Emerson's role in persuading Thoreau to compose "Natural History of Massachusetts" for *The Dial* (1842) takes on special significance in that the essay Thoreau produced is, among other things, the manifesto of a would-be writer.

The third point to be made—for the last two sections of this chapter the most important one—is that the spirit of enterprise exerted powerful pressures on Thoreau's idea of vocation as well as on his practice of a literary career. What he understood as the enterprise of vocation was increasingly at odds with the vocation of enterprise. To be sure, most of his lexicon on self-culture, vocation, and enterprise belongs to the discourse of his culture. Yet he also quarreled with the contemporary language and assumptions of enterprise, and he was more unrelenting in his criticism of new and narrow conceptions of enterprise than he was of slavery, territorial expansion, political institutions and processes, reformers, and exploitation of the wilderness. His response to enterprise as defined and practiced by his contemporary culture is an important element in the intellectual, social, and economic history of his America.

I

The more one examines the lexical and semantic forms of thought, attitude, and behavior of American culture in the years spanning Thoreau's youth, early adulthood, and literary career, the more massively the evidence mounts that Thoreau's age represented a new departure. For good reasons it has been described as the beginning of industrial capitalism in America. A more appropriate characterization might be the age of enterprise. The term *enterprise* houses suggestions of a range of altering and altered assumptions, values, beliefs, agendas, and language. It also registers both the ambiguities of the new age and the ambivalences with which many literary artists viewed it.

Although Thoreau's age has been studied extensively and specifically in socioeconomic terms, these studies, instructive as they are, have focused on economic history, social history, economic activities and transformations, the social impact of economic changes, and the ideological dimensions of the age of enterprise. To date, no study of the economic *lexicon* and *discourse* of the times has been conducted; the spirit of the age of enterprise has not as yet been examined at the level of language and linguistic shifts. This chapter assumes that studies in socioeconomic thought and behavior and examinations of lexicon and meaning can richly inform one another and that the latter kind of examination is particularly useful in illuminating Thoreau's literary language on enterprise. Both changes in economic lexicon and in the meaning of key terms, moreover, offer insights into his vocational agenda.

As preamble to the subject of linguistic changes, let me offer a brief summary statement on the new behavioral tendencies of the age of enterprise. As historians have noted, the new economic activities and behavior represented an unprecedented transformation in American economic and social life. Communally and state controlled manufacturing, external trade and commerce, and internal trade (all of these centered in island communities that competed with one another) were either crowded out or drawn into the dynamic center of a new economic age by an astonishing growth not only in what we today refer to as private enterprise but also in new forms of private enterprise, including individual and group investment and speculation in numerous fields of new economic development.[1]

According to economic historian George Taylor, the chief signs of the new era were the rapid development of regional and national transportation networks; unprecedented technological advances; increased division of labor; greater specialization and interrelatedness of commercial, financial, and industrial activities; phenomenal land development; the development of corporations and rapid increase of money investors and investments; a society that regarded the economic developments as instruments for meeting regional and local needs; and laissez-faire principles applied to corporations, companies, and entrepreneurs in order to promote economic success and prevent the disastrous failures in many state enterprise initiatives in earlier decades.[2] Bray Hammond has succinctly described the spirit and practice of the age: "People were led as they had not been before by visions of money-making. Liberty became transformed into *laisser faire*. A violent, aggressive, economic individualism became established."[3] Rush Welter's view is both less pejorative and less vivid: "[A]n expansive economic orientation well in evidence by the 1840s . . . involved a national predisposition to increase individual wealth by any acceptable means even if it also meant sacrificing some of the scruples of the past. The paths by which Americans arrived at enterprise, and the measures they took to be acceptable, were key facts in the intellectual history of the epoch."[4]

Many clergymen in New England and New York, as well as the pillars of their congregations and the congregations themselves, were caught up in the restive dynamism of the age. On the whole, the middle- and upper-middle-class religious communities adjusted to the rapid economic transformation as well as any other sector. "We of the East," Horace Hosmer of Acton and friend of the

Thoreau family wrote with his customary bluntness, "have a commercial look even at heavenly things."[5] The list of eastern liberal ministers and transcendentalists with impressive business acumen is long, and includes notables like Theodore Parker, Ralph Waldo Emerson, Cyrus Bartol, Henry Bellows, James Freeman Clarke, and Convers Francis. One recalls Bartol's moral benedictions on his newly gotten wealth through real estate transactions and Emerson's inspection of the Fitchburg Railroad depot that was being constructed in Concord in the spring of 1844 (at least some of his interest is to be explained by his investment in the new company, an investment that in short order had already gone up 10 percent).[6] Publishing records of the 1830s to the 50s also disclose that shrewd investments by clergymen by writing popular and profitable books were hardly limited to Unitarian and transcendentalist ministers. Ann Douglas has offered historical and social explanations for what the book trade records reveal: an unprecedented number of ministers of liberal and conservative theological persuasion who lived economically and vocationally by the immediate aid of their books and who cooperated closely with editors and publishers whose role and influence were defined largely by transactions between demand and supply, consumer and producer.[7]

In the area of literary production, then, ministers joined other writers, including full-time professional authors, in producing formulaic sentimental romances promoted for their virtuous influence, vaguely edifying and clearly sentimental religious books and tracts, exotic travel literature, profiles of the newly and venerable rich, etiquette books for young women, treatises on domestic economy, and guides to success for the young man. There was an unprecedented commercial look to the various forms of human enterprise, including the literary profession. The major theme of the times was progress, the concept of progress was parsed by cultural definitions of success, and the economic component of these definitions increased markedly.

II

As noted earlier, neither historians nor literary critics have investigated at the level of language the cultural shift just summarized.[8] The last two sections of this chapter suggest that Thoreau was keenly aware of the vigorous and powerfully influential language of enterprise and of the extent to which it contested language and values that he regarded as crucial to self-culture and to the fortunes of the American culture. Whether he was more right than wrong or more wrong than right in his assessments, whether he was modernist or antimodernist in his stance on American culture, or progressive or conservative in his economic assumptions, is not the issue here. What is at issue is the lexical and semantic changes discernible in the language of enterprise, the confirmation of the meaning of these linguistic shifts by cultural behavior, and both Thoreau's vocational agenda and his linguistic forms within the context suggested by the dynamic new forces registered in cultural language and frenetic economic activity. Concord, as Robert Gross has documented, vigorously participated in the era and its spirit.[9] By staying at home, Thoreau could travel a good deal in the history of economic discourse and the economic vernacular of his age.

In a few decades both the language and the sometimes uneasy consensus that had served a mercantile/agrarian society from the beginning of nationhood to the administration of John Quincy Adams underwent rapid transformation. Perhaps the clearest indicators of this transformation are the speeches made by a succession of presidents to their government and nation. Consider, for example, the speeches that bracketed each administration—the "Inaugural Address" and the "Fourth Annual Message" (in Andrew Jackson's case his inaugural speech and "Farewell Address"). On the whole, the inaugural speeches are couched in a ritualistic, formulaic, and somewhat archaic language whereas the final address, and for that matter every annual address, is much more steeped in the current political/economic terminology. As one might expect, the economic terminology manifests the kind of economic preoccupations totally or largely absent from the inaugural speeches. Moreover, a chronological review of the final annual addresses of the presidents from John Quincy Adams to Millard Fillmore reveals not only an increasing degree of specificity in the economic review and proposals but also an increasing domination of the speech by economic considerations. (In the speeches of Franklin Pierce and James Buchanan, as one might expect, the immediate and explosive issues of slavery, sectional conflict, and the federal union overshadow all other issues.)

A more telling change in the speeches from Adams to Fillmore is the shift in moral assumptions and tone on the subject of America's new economic vigor. Adams registered traditional republican values in his warnings against wealth, pursuit of luxuries, and the equation of prosperity with spiritual fulfillment.[10] Andrew Jackson, however, celebrated the national march to prosperity and spoke honorifically of "our free institutions" which offer every citizen the opportunity to attain "prosperity and happiness without seeking to profit themselves at the expense of others" (*Presidents*, 4:1513, 1517). Indeed, the individual should look forward to sharing in the blessings of a national prosperity. Yet Old Hickory also intoned in his strange farewell address that the "planter, the farmer, the mechanic, and the laborer all know that their success depends upon their own industry and economy, and that they must not expect to become suddenly rich by the fruits of their toil" (*Presidents*, 4:1524). In this speech—dark with references to the evil coercion of "monied corporations," "monopoly," "exclusive privilege," speculation, paper money, and paper stocks—the overseer of the early halcyon days of enterprise appealed to the producing groups of the old order to recover the rights they had allowed to slip away. As in the case of several presidential farewells in our century, Jackson's address is marked by expressions of private reflection, regret, censure (including self-censure), nostalgia, and warnings against potentially evil new geniuses countenanced and perhaps even encouraged by the current administration. One is inclined to conclude that the nation was as nostalgically ready for the Jacksonian moralisms of his farewell address as for the vigorous enterprise of the Jacksonian era. Martin Van Buren, whose administration had been bitten in the heels by the 1837 economic panic, repeated Jackson's chastisements for "capitalists" (Van Buren's term), speculators, and monopolists, and warned against a return to the past—a reference, it appears, to the Jacksonian boom. On the other hand, he regarded the nation's top priority as a program of economic stabilization and strong advance (*Presidents*, 5:1823–33).

One of the features distinguishing James Polk's addresses from those of his predecessors is his enthusiastic endorsement of all forms of enterprise, the direct connection in his thinking between a vigorous expansion of agricultural, industrial, commercial, and business production and manifest destiny (*Presidents*, 6:2496–

2500), and the absence of any doubt or ambivalence in his soporifi-
cally long-winded speeches over the country's program of economic
expansion. Fillmore is an even more enthusiastic apologist for
enterprise than Polk. The entire nation is "full of enterprise." Indeed, luxuries, wealth, and "exuberance of enterprise" are referred
to favorably. The "progress of the people" reveals itself economically, and the responsibility of the government is to "keep pace with
the progress of the people" and participate in their "spirit of enterprise" by fostering and protecting industry and lending powerful
governmental assistance toward the further promotion of "our
internal commerce" (*Presidents*, 6:2717).

Semantically, the economic transformation can be traced in
gradual alterations of key ideological terms such as *commerce*,
business, *profit*, *industry*, and *corporation*, and in changes in their
conjunction with other terms or, one might say, in their valency.
John Quincy Adams used a conventional triangulation of terms to
describe the nation's economic life—the "agricultural, commercial,
and manufacturing" interests (*Presidents*, 3:979). *Commerce* de-
noted international trade to Adams, Jackson, Van Buren, and
Polk, but was extended to internal exchange of goods and services
in the speeches of Fillmore. Thus a term that originally meant
"dealings" gradually came to be associated with commercial port
cities in the East and, by Thoreau's time, with international and
domestic exchange of goods and services (especially domestic) for
profit. *Profit*, both a moral and economic term in the speeches of
Adams, Jackson, and Van Buren, came to signify simply financial
profit. *Industry*, in the early nineteenth century a synonym for
diligence, self-discipline, concentrated effort, and perseverance,
gradually replaced the traditional *manufactures*, thereby, like
profit, shedding much of its moral meaning. As for *business* and
corporation, not until the speeches of Jackson did they emerge as
key economic signifiers with close affinities to our modern use of
the terms. *Business* had dual meanings for Jackson: "ordinary
pursuits of business" signified traditional, individual, and collective
undertakings for profit (entrepreneurship, farming, mechanic arts,
merchants' activities, and so on) whereas the insidious new business
of "corporations," "monopoly," "exclusive privilege," and "speculation" subverted the "independent spirit," "love of liberty," "intelligence," and "moral character" of the citizens in their "ordinary

pursuits of business" marked by "honest industry" (*Presidents,* 4:1520–21). Van Buren referred to the promoters of the new business as "capitalists" and warned of "the bitter fruits of that spirit of speculative enterprise to which our countrymen are so liable" (*Presidents,* 5:1825, 33). Polk's updated terminology for the domestic production system aside from farming was not the conventional *manufactures* but *business and industry* (*Presidents,* 6:2498). Indeed, *business* is his most frequent and multi-faceted term, referring to activities such as agriculture, manufacturing, the construction, expansion, and maintenance of transportation systems, building trades, merchant's functions, corporations, and investment capital. Neither Polk nor Fillmore registered moral or other concerns about the direction America's "business" development was taking.

Probably the richest register of lexical and semantic shifts linked to economic developments is contained in the history of the term *enterprise.* By the 1840s *enterprise* had pretty much disengaged itself from its much earlier associations with moral discipline, courage, and self-sacrifice, characteristics that might be summed up as a conflation of the Greek *oikonomia,* the Latin *virtus,* and the Late Latin *interprendere.* As the presidential addresses reveal, in Thoreau's era *enterprise* contained both negative and positive connotations. In its negative sense the term recalled seventeenth- and eighteenth-century usage, especially of the adjectival form *enterprising*: misadventurous, unduly ambitious, scheming, self-aggrandizing, usurpative, compulsive, distorted (ethically crippled and morally impotent). Some of these associations have survived to our day as secondary meanings in the French cognate and most recent ancestor of the English term, especially in the verb *entreprendre* and its past participial form *entrepris,* the adjective *entrepris/entreprise,* and the noun *entreprise.*

By Thoreau's time, however, *enterprise* had also firmly established a favorable connotation which was rapidly crowding out the negative. In its positive sense the term referred to an admirable risk taking, a venturesome spirit, the shrewdness and diligence to conceive a design and follow through with it. This was the kind of enterprise celebrated by Freeman Hunt in his influential *Hunt's Merchant's Magazine* and in his financially successful books *Worth and Wealth* (1856) and *Lives of American Merchants,* 2 vols. (1856). President Van Buren's finger-pointing at the "spirit of speculative enterprise" invokes a history of negative connotation whereas Fillmore's panegyric to the "exuberance of enterprise" and his ringing declaration that "the whole country is full of enterprise" (*Presidents*, 6:2717) invoke the favorable connotation.[11]

A second point to be made about *enterprise* is that a term whose seventeenth- and eighteenth-century history indicates multiple and general applications (see the OED) was increasingly being appropriated by economic discourse and thus was undergoing transformation into a term that in one of its primary usages was specifically associated with business and the rapid expansion and systemic change in industry, business, corporations, trade, and commerce. For instance, in Francis Bowen's *The Principles of Political Economy*, the major economic text to appear in the 1850s, *enterprise* is employed throughout in both its general (and favorable) meaning and in its specifically economic sense. On the one hand, the term stands as the opposite to "indolence, feebleness, gayety, and *insouciance*"; it is synonymously linked to "industry," "risk," and "undertaking"; it is defined as "industrious and adventurous habits"; and it is associated with "the restlessness, the feverish anxiety to get on," the "effective desire of accumulation," and the "unceasing energy and activity in the pursuit of wealth, . . . which actually generate enthusiasm of character." In his general use of the term, the Harvard-trained, politically conservative Bowen followed his economic mentors, Adam Smith, J. B. Say, and John Rae. On the other hand, Bowen also uses *enterprise* specifically as a referent to agriculture, commerce, trade, manufacturing, shop and factory production, canal or railroad building and investment, finance, and corporation stockholding.[12] Kate McKean's 1864 *Manual of Social Science*—which abbreviated, simplified, and popularized Henry C. Carey's pioneering, three-volume *Principles of Political Economy* (1840) (and which went through at least eight editions by 1888)— agrees with Bowen in the general and specific use of *enterprise*. Bowen's text also contains the earliest American usage I have been able to find of the terminology *private enterprise* in its modern sense. According to the OED, *private enterprise* was first used in 1844 in a report on activities that the British East India Company (a virtual monopoly) had left to others. Bowen distinguishes between private enterprise and government monopolies in industry, commerce, business, and finance,[13] and strongly links the former with the cultivation and manifestation of "character."

Bowen's association of "enterprise" and "character" invites another observation on the term *enterprise* as a general and specific signifier of economic desire and activity. The industrious and adventurous habits connoted by the term and its synonyms were justified in terms of the individual by the moral doctrine of self-culture and in terms of the body politic by the national expansionist doctrine of manifest destiny. Morally minded eastern Whigs, especially Unitarian moralists, tended to view favorably the expansionism of the age of enterprise, for, as Daniel Howe has noted, "only a man of secure economic position could really lead the rewarding life of self-development and refinement idealized by the Unitarians." This argument became something of a cliché in the sermons of Unitarian ministers from the time of William Ellery Channing to that of post–Civil War clergymen like Henry Bellows, James Freeman Clarke, and some of their younger colleagues. In the words of Howe: once the individual "had achieved a competence of material things," he was "expected to turn to spiritual development. Furthermore, the habits acquired in the process of material advancement— prudence, industriousness, sobriety, and the like—ought to serve as the foundation for this higher, moral development."[14]

Congressman Robert C. Winthrop of Boston understood such a doctrine of self-culture in social terms when he declared the paramount symbol of the time to be "the rapid and steady progress of the influence of commerce upon the social and political condition of man." Vigorous enterprise, Winthrop argued before his receptive Boston Mercantile Library Association audience, was renovatingly virtuous. "I would vindicate the commercial spirit from the reproaches which are too often cast upon it, and hail its triumphant progress over the world as the harbinger of freedom, civilization, and peace." His call to America was to put wars, militarism, and the enervating slave trade behind her and zealously pursue commercial enterprise. This direct descendant of Governor John Winthrop of the Bay Colony linked his enterprising view of progress to the work of God's kingdom when he addressed the religiously faithful in his audience. The enterprise he championed was inseparable not only from individual industry, invention, skill, discipline, and virtue, but also from his Christian convictions. Surely, he reminded his listeners, "I can advocate no system before men, which I may not justify to my own conscience, or which I shrink from holding in humble trust before my God." As one would expect, extracts of Winthrop's speech to the Mercantile Library Association were reprinted by Freeman Hunt.[15]

A more secular millennial rationale for enterprise was the exuberant mid-nineteenth-century version of enlightenment as articulated by Polk and Fillmore in their invocations of manifest destiny. The principal theme of Polk's annual messages on the state of the Union can be summarized by a statement made at the Texas Convention in 1845. The destiny of enterprising Americans, a Mr. Volney Howard offered, was to "force back the savage and carry civilization into the useless and unproductive wilderness."[16]

A final point to be made about *enterprise* and its allied terms is that they developed into prominent lexical signifiers in the culture at large, as evidenced in the samples of rhetoric of politicians, clergymen, and economists already discussed, in other kinds of documents such as governmental reports, newspapers, magazines, journals, and popular as well as highbrow literary texts. A "Report to the Special Commissioner of the Revenue" in the late 1860s announced and documented approvingly to the federal government a "spirit of enterprise," by which it meant vigorous economic activity, "which seems to redouble its energy with every burden placed upon it."[17] A House of Representatives Executive Document produced about the same time used *enterprise* to designate "channels of trade" and trading policies. Just over a decade later the "Resolutions of the Chicago Convention for the Promotion of Commerce," a special-interest document presented to the House of Representatives, noted the "pushing enterprise of the American merchant" and observed patronizingly that "in material enterprise [business and commerce] the South may look to the North." Indeed, American "business and commerce" are lauded as the "greatest of all enterprises." As a witness in a series of written and oral depositions to the House in the same year on the topic of depression in labor and business, journalist and labor specialist Charles C. Coffin of Boston repeatedly used the term *enterprise*, both in its general and specific applications, precisely as Francis Bowen had done in his economic writings.[18]

In two extraordinarily popular new kinds of publications, the sentimental romance precursor to the Horatio Alger economic/ moral success stories and the success manuals for young men, *enterprise* is a watchword, the age of enterprise the backdrop, and the spirit of enterprise the principle of action and source of moral victory. Since success manuals will be treated in relation to *Walden* in the second part of this book, let me note Timothy Shay Arthur here as a sterling example of the economic possibilities of exploiting the theme of enterprise for sentimental romances. Celebrated by his generation and lampooned by ours for his *Ten Nights in a Bar Room*, Arthur was actually just as successful with his business and money romances of the 1840s and 50s, in which his fascination with prosperity as the crowning glory of enterprise was properly dressed up in moral concern over the perilous seductions of evil enterprise. The nine or more editions of his *Making Haste to be Rich; or, the Temptation and Fall* brought him quick financial returns, as did his morally tongue-clicking *Nothing But Money* (which went through at least seven editions).[19] Louisa Tuthill's inspirational romances on the theme of enterprise were fewer in number, but were extraordinarily profitable. *I Will Be a Gentleman*, for example, appeared in close to forty editions and the just as mellifluously platitudinous *Onward! Right Onward!* passed through at least twenty-one editions. Her heroes, like Arthur's, are naturally enterprising. Yet they must earn their successes in an environment of corruption and dangerous evils, where enterprise is not a natural expression.

"It is natural that we should be enterprising," Thoreau noted in an enigmatic *Journal* entry in 1852 (1906 J 3:270). *Walden* features an enterprising narrator who concludes his narrative with a declaration that focuses the theme of *"extra vagance"* through economy while reminding readers of the theme's cultural connection: "I delight to come to my bearings, . . . not to live in this restless, nervous, bustling, trivial Nineteenth Century, . . . to travel the only path I can, and that on which no power can resist me" (*Walden*, pp. 329–30). Both the speaker of *Walden* and the work itself must earn their success. Unfavorable conditions are turned into favorable ones in this account of "uncommon success." The speaker of *Walden* manipulates the language of enterprise so as to acknowledge, parody, and counter the current language and behavior of America, to define his vocation with a logic of opposition, and to justify his art and life with the principle of *"extra vagance"* (standing outside the circle of extravagant enterprise). "I have always endeavored to acquire strict business habits"—this is the kind of statement in *Walden* (p. 20) that registers both linguistic and vocational agendas and suggests the inseparability of the two.

III

Thoreau's awareness of lexical and semantic shifts in the cultural vernacular and of changes in values and behavior linked to these shifts gradually led him to identify reregistration as central to his linguistic and vocational agendas. For that reason archeological probing of his culture and examinations of cultural discourse are crucial to a study of Thoreau's language. This point is brought home succinctly in a passage he drafted probably in the fall of 1854 as he began to prepare material for the first lecture version of his most concentrated discussion of enterprise, "Life without Principle." "I find commonly that that relation to Nature which had so attracted me in the farmer's life," Thoreau wrote, "exists only in my imagination." His surveying of the farmers about him also convinced him that the farmer's "boasted independence is merely a certain slight independence on the market, and not a moral independence,—that he is a *speculator*,—not in the old sense of an observer, or contemplator, but in the modern sense which is yet, for the most part, ashamed to show itself in the dictionary, and his *speculum* or mirror, is a shining dollar."[20]

To draw attention to Thoreau's awareness of historical and cultural reregistration of words is to underscore that he was philologically informed, particularly about the traditionally assumed roots of words. Although etymology fascinated him in and of itself, his interest also went beyond etymology to the social and moral significance of lexical and semantic shifts. The clearer one's sense of originary forms of the dynamic words of one's culture, the more discerning one's recognition of lexical and semantic shifts over the span of millennia, centuries and continents, generations, one's own generation, and one's own development. (One does no violence to a witty observation Thoreau supposedly made about Harvard's deficient educational program by applying his quip here: it is unsound policy to study all the branches of knowledge while ignoring all of the roots.)

As Thoreau himself notes in his reflections on the historical and cultural reregistration of terms such as *speculator*, his thinking on the subject underwent changes as his youthful imagination was gradually re-educated by a more careful attention to his culture. "Explain the phrases,—a man of business, a man of pleasure, a man of the world": here is the topic sentence of one of Thoreau's earliest surviving compositions. One should not confer on this piece an exaggerated status. It was one of those writing exercises deemed by Harvard College and E. T. Channing to be a prerequisite for the more advanced and largely interchangeable programs of manhood, true citizenship, worthy service, professional success, and, more immediately, graduation from Harvard. Thoreau walked through the assignment with the stilted clichés of a second-year student. He also used the opportunity to demonstrate some etymological expertise. A "man of business" is defined as "energetic," "persevering," "always on the lookout," "ever awake to his interest," "well calculated"; he is one who possesses "despatch . . . method and perseverance, industry and activity, united with prudence and foresight."[21] In this definition Thoreau runs his bow across old and new saws about the enterprising man, and offers a glissando of details provided by the French and English history of *enterprise* and Thoreau's cultural environment, which is placing new claims on the term.

Another writing assignment, this one included in Thoreau's commencement obligations, addresses "the commercial spirit of modern times," which Thoreau discusses in terms of behavior, attitude, and value. By averring that "the spirit we are considering is not altogether and without exception bad," he introduces a moral judgment and principle not evident in the earlier assignment. Commerce, traditionally the most touted form of economic enterprise in eastern Massachusetts, is usually bad in that it is a materialistic running for luck that has turned means into ends. Thoreau also envisions the redemption of that spirit when "men, true to their natures, cultivate the moral affections, lead manly and independent lives . . . make riches the means and not the end of existence."[22] His conclusion recalls William Ellery Channing's sermons linking enterprise and prosperity to self-culture and the moral philosophy of Thoreau's Harvard mentors, who, as Daniel Howe has described, linked frenetic materialistic enterprise to self-culture and, for that matter, to

national moral maturation by a principle of means and end.[23]
Thoreau rejoices—at least rhetorically—in the "avarice . . . din and
bustle" of the times because they are the preliminary means to a
higher end that he defines as "a more intellectual and spiritual life."
Thus, although America's "ruling principle" is "counting [financial]
gains," "we [he assumes the consent of his Harvard readers] glory in
those very excesses which are a source of anxiety to the wise and
good, as an evidence that man will not always be the slave of
matter."[24] Clearly Thoreau had been much more influenced by his
Harvard training than he was willing to admit in later years when
his views changed.

Specifying the extent to which Thoreau's manipulations of language in later writings register altered meanings and convictions is
problematical. For instance, in "Life without Principle" he borrows
a pronouncement from his 1852 Journal: "I think that there is
nothing, not even crime, more opposed to poetry, to philosophy,
ay, to life itself, than this incessant business." Yet the essay also
describes New Englanders as "warped and narrowed by an
exclusive devotion to trade and commerce and manufactures and
agriculture and the like" (*Reform Papers*, pp. 156, 175; emphasis
mine). What at first appears to be an elaboration of the sentiment in
the first statement exists in a contestatory relation to it by apparently implying an updated version of the principle Thoreau has
espoused in his commencement assignment. The adjective *exclusive*
strongly suggests that devotion to enterprise is not in and of itself
evil or always to be disparaged. Another statement in the essay
invites the same inference: "The ways by which you may get money
almost without exception lead downward" (*Reform Papers*, p. 158,
emphasis mine).

If the reader must reconcile the incompatibilities between these
two kinds of statements ("Life without Principle," with its play of
oppositions, does not attempt to make them compatible), one can,
for instance, privilege the second kind of statement and paraphrase
it as a call to direct "enterprise" toward moral ends. One could also
privilege the former pronouncement and regard the essay as an
unrelenting jeremiad against America's spirit and practice of enterprise. Or one might attend to Thoreau's manipulations of the terms
life and *living*, for both of which the term *enterprise* is at times a
richly suggestive synonym. Enterprise with principle is itself a

generative principle in the essay, but *enterprise* is a term of multiple intentions and sometimes good ends. So are related terms in the essay such as "labor," "value," "profit," "invest," "business," "commerce," "success," "wealth," and "culture." Thus one should not treat too narrowly the speaker's interest in "the comparative demand which men make on life" and the comparative demand which he and his countrymen make on the language of enterprise. As he notes toward the end of the essay, the "same ear is fitted to receive" more than one communication. The renovating virtue proposed in this wary essay on enterprise is "wariness" (*Reform Papers*, pp. 161, 172, 173).

That wariness is keenly evident in a *Journal* passage that acknowledges the importance of enterprise even while resisting it with a negative example. "It is natural that we should be enterprising," Thoreau declares, "for we are descended from the enterprising, who sought to better their fortunes in the New World." The immediate preamble to this observation suspends the apparent endorsement of enterprise in ambiguity and draws on both the positive and negative potential of the term:

> The race that settles and clears the land has got to deal with every tree in the forest in succession. It must be resolute and industrious, and even the stumps must be got out,—or are. It is a thorough process, this war with the wilderness,—breaking nature, taming the soil, feeding it on oats. The civilized man regards the pine tree as his enemy. He will fell it and let in the light, grub it up and raise wheat or rye there. (1906 J 3:269-70)

What begins as an apparently affirmative discussion of land-clearing suddenly shifts into an acerbic comment on civilized man's war against trees, the kind of turn one finds in "Chesuncook" and "The Allegash and East Branch," especially in their treatment of the effects of a voracious logging enterprise. The Journal passage implicates a number of key terms in the potential ironies produced by its shift: "descended," "better," "fortunes," and "new world." Thoreau's use of the predicate adjective *natural* in conjunction with *enterprising* after describing the enterprise as one of "breaking nature" is perhaps the most complicated reregistration of any term in the passage. In *Walden*, for instance, cave man interests, house building, Greek literary classics, nature, the sound of church bells, the lowing of the cow, Alek Therien, the stones in the beanfield, the

Walden shore, rabbits and partridges, virtue, business, and commerce are all described as "natural." Some of these are identified with lack of moral and intellectual development, others figure prominently in Thoreau's fable of self-culture, and still others are neutral. What is "natural" is often not enterprising, and too often enterprise does not represent sound economy. Indeed, the speaker of "Life without Principle" declares, "I wish to suggest that a man may be very industrious, and yet not spend his time well." "Even if we grant that the American has freed himself from a political tyrant, he is still the slave of an economical and moral tyrant" (*Reform Papers*, pp. 160, 174).

It is easier to see a progression in Thoreau's appropriation and manipulation of economic vernacular than it is to mark precise semantic boundaries for his terminology or an essential position at this or any stage in his career. And, although the chronological history of Thoreau's use of economic vernacular is related to the progression of his career, a precise correspondence cannot be marked. Nonetheless, the shape of his career is as relevant as his culture of enterprise in examining his excursions into the economic discourse and behavior of the times.

IV

On the whole, the American culture of enterprise in which Thoreau endeavored to find his place and language, especially in the late forties and the fifties, helped to focus his vocation and concentrate his energies. His dedication to his personal enterprise of vocation offers no legitimate basis for mythologizing him as a misplaced, tragic, or pathetic literary figure or as an aesthetic escape artist. To say of Thoreau, as Emerson did, that "with his energy and practical ability he seemed born for great enterprise" is to provide an index of what *enterprise* meant to this extraordinarily successful patron, who in his eulogy at Thoreau's funeral repeated the disappointment in Thoreau's lack of enterprise that he had been noting for more than a decade.[25] It is more difficult to explain and assess with any precision the nature of Thoreau's complicated relation to his culture than it is to explain why contemporaries rejected his version of enterprise, ridiculed his personal economy, and questioned his literary production, and why a culture thoroughly absorbed by its powerful new version of enterprise would ignore his writings for decades to come.

Thoreau's actions as a young writer are ambiguous predictors of his future in that they point to both commonly held and unusual values and to a conventional as well as unconventional career. If anything, the Thoreau of Harvard College seemed quite given to cultural commonplaces, particularly in his views of American economic practices and his own career goals. Certainly his decision, shortly after graduation, to start a writer's journal could point either way. By 1839–40 he was attempting publishable essays. In 1840 he published his first poem and tried, unsuccessfully, to place a lengthy, idiosyncratic essay with Margaret Fuller, keeper of the door at *The Dial*, and to understand her reasons for rejecting it. He did not rewrite the essay along the lines suggested by her telling criticisms. In 1841 he published additional poems, and his acquaintances began to think of him a promising and enigmatic new poet. At this time he also reported his desire to purchase or rent living quarters, preferably a farm, that would offer solitude outside of Concord. This desire did not conform to conventional expectations for Harvard graduates or, for that matter, for literary writers in Concord. (If Concord had not known what to expect of its literary sons, they now had an answer in the example of Emerson, a professional man of letters and civic hero whom the 1850 Census identified as one of Concord's well-to-do citizens.) At Emerson's encouragement, however, Thoreau made a more conventional move in 1843, settling on Staten Island in the hope of restarting his literary career—in New York. By 1844, however, he was putting the New York disappointments behind him and filling an oversized notebook in Concord with preliminary drafts of material for *A Week on the Concord and Merrimack Rivers*, a work that he may have planned as early as 1841.[26]

Thoreau's move to Walden Pond and his extraordinary productivity there as a writer reveal signs of an unorthodox private enterprise taking shape on his own terms: four Journal notebooks, two lyceum lectures on why he was living alone at the pond, the highly unusual and virtually unmarketable travel book *A Week*, and a highly idyllic evocation of an unconventional experiment at the pond (his first draft of *Walden*). He also wrote "Thomas Carlyle," "Ktaadn," two somewhat diffuse and unfinished compositions on reform (the basis for the Princeton edition of "Reform and the Reformers"), and began, like the entrepreneurial Indian of *Walden*, to search out angels who might minister to his business of *A Week*.

There is also an unmistakable shift in these years in Thoreau's treatment of America's economic transformation, a shift much more evident in his Journal and preliminary draft of "Ktaadn" than in his first-draft versions of *A Week* and *Walden*. In the initial and intermediate versions of "Ktaadn," for instance, the early pages give almost as much prominence to restless and indefatigable business activity as to the motif of excursion into the wilderness. In the early pages these two themes contend for influence on the essay. "New Bangor," Thoreau writes near the outset of the narrative, is "still in its swaddling clothes—built of the lumber saved from exportation" (PE J 2:281). Concerning the lumber mill in Stillwater, he has more to say about the frenetic activity of mills such as this one and their far-flung network of commerce than about the destruction of virgin forest in the Maine wilderness:

> Here the river is particularly restless and uneasy and the falls furnish the power which carries the mills night and day by which the sorely driven logs are at last driven through the narrowest gut of all and most finely slitted. . . .
>
> The log which has shot so many falls only with injury to its sap wood—and bears the scars of its adventures—may think here to lie quietly embraced by its boom with its companion's as in a fold—but not so. for here comes the closest rub of all—one inch—two 3 inches at a time. . . . The best of eastern stuff—to Boston or New Haven—or New York. (PE J 2:281-82)

His report on taking the makeshift ferry near Indian Island focuses on the peddler who suddenly appeared on the bank and hailed the ferry, which had already shoved off, because he was "earnest to carry his wares still further into the woods" (PE J 2:283). And Thoreau subsequently interlined this addition: "I was greatly astonished by this apparition for I expected momentarily to reach the end of the civilized world—and could not imagine why one should be carting a load of tinware of this sort. I despaired of ever reaching the wilderness with him in company."[27] Next to a back-country inn, Thoreau, who calls himself a "pencil maker," observed a business engaged in making pencils, "which are made in a singularly bungling way by grooving the side of a round piece of cedar putting in the lead and filling up the cavity with a strip of the same wood."[28] While these observations disclose an increased awareness of economic activities in New England, the apprehensiveness one detects in Thoreau's notations has less to do with increased economic activity in the nation or his region and with a national economic transformation per se than with obtrusive, mindless, and destructive economic behavior. Moreover, all but one of the passages quoted in this paragraph were deleted by Thoreau when he prepared "Ktaadn" for publication, and in the one passage that was saved only a few words survived.

On the basis of the available evidence, one should be cautious about drawing inferences from the passages on various economic activities in the first draft of "Ktaadn." It seems clear from these notations that at this time in his career (later 1840s) Thoreau did not subscribe to a single, clear-cut point of view on enterprise. He probably never did, even in the 1850s, when business, speculation, and the scramble for money and profits in his culture became one of the major topics in his writing, and his attitude toward American economic enterprise became notably more negative. The attitudes disclosed in the passages quoted in the preceding paragraph range from affirmation to ambivalence to uneasiness to exasperation to protest. And in one of the most negative passages, the report on the pencil maker, Thoreau does not criticize the business undertaking as such (a business thoroughly familiar to him) but only the shoddy workmanship. Nor can one legitimately infer from the deletions that Thoreau made as he reworked "Ktaadn" for publication that he was inclined at this stage of his life to suppress materials pertaining to enterprise and to check his moral impulses in behalf of a doctrine of aestheticism or of private refuge in purely aesthetic performance. Although some material on enterprise was deleted, not all of it was. The deleted material appears in the early pages of the preliminary version, and the effect of the deletions is to stress the motif of excursion and to strengthen the governance of the theme of excursion into "unhandselled" nature. Precisely the opposite, an increasing emphasis on America's powerful fascination with its new enterprise, is discernible in Thoreau's work after "Ktaadn," especially in the compositional history of *Walden* and in "Life without Principle."

Much more preoccupied by the mid- to late 1840s than previously with America's expansive enterprise, Thoreau is both attracted to and repelled by it. More often, however, his responses disclose ambivalence. One might cite a revealing passage in his *Journal* for December 1846, which is fairly representative of his Journal notations on enterprise while he lived at the pond. The topic of this entry is the Fitchburg Railroad train that regularly passes by along the causeway on the western shore of the pond. The ambivalent and richly complex response to this preeminent avatar of America's economic transformation anticipates the range of response in *Walden* to this new engine of land development and commerce; indeed, Thoreau incorporated the passage, with slight revisions, into his first version of *Walden*:

> When I meet the engine with its train of cars moving off with planetary motion or say rather like a comet—for the beholder knows not if with that velocity and that direction it will ever revisit this system—its steam-cloud like a banner streaming behind like such a fleecy cloud as I have seen in a summer's day—high in the heavens unfolding its wreathed masses to the light—as if this travelling and aspiring man would ere long take the sunset sky for his train in livery when he travelled— When I have heard the iron horse make the hills echo with his snort like thunder, shaking the earth—with his feet and breathing fire and smoke— It seems to me that the earth has got a race now that deserves to inhabit it. If all were as it seems, and men made the elements their servants for noble ends. If the cloud that hangs over the engine were the perspiration of heroes or as innocent and beneficent an omen as that which hovers over the parched fields of the farmer.
>
> If the elements did not have to lament their time wasted in accompanying men on their errands.
>
> If this enterprise were as noble as it seems. The stabler was up early this winter morning by the light of the stars to fodder and harness his steed—fire was awakened too to get him off— If the enterprise were as innocent as it is early— For all the day he flies over the country stopping only that his master may rest— If the enterprise were as disinterested as it is unwearied.— And I am awakened by its tramp and defiant snort at midnight while in some far glen it fronts the elements encased in ice and snow and will only reach its stall to start once more
>
> If the enterprise were as important as it is protracted. (PE J 2:358–59)

This enterprise seems to be a heroic venture and an "innocent and beneficent" omen. Yet it may not be what it seems to be; the expansive descriptions and cosmic imagery of the opening sentences may be little more than literary flourish. Indeed, the most compelling feature of the passage is the series of seven similar subjunctive constructions, each introduced by "if." The wistfulness registered by the wish expressed in each of these constructions is directly tied to several kinds of irresolution. The wish expressed by the first such statement—"If all were as it seems"—makes the ironic circular point that might be paraphrased as follows: "it seems that much is not what it has seemed to be." That play on "seem" adds poignancy to the six subjunctives that follow, all of which exist uneasily somewhere between two conventional species of subjunctive, the conditional with the specifiable results linked to the terms of the condition and the condition contrary to fact. Thus questions as to whether the new American enterprise epitomized by the railroad boom is "noble," "innocent," "disinterested," or "important" are suspended in dubiousness and coupled to the wish that one did not have to doubt the avatars of economic transformation.

In the fall of 1847 Thoreau vacated his cabin at Walden and resettled in Concord, where, for a brief period, both Emerson's and his parents' house served as his residences. The Concord to which he returned was a community undergoing major changes in its social and economic life, most notably in its housing, its urban and rural land use, and its population.[29] Thoreau's surveying records, Journal, the "Economy" and "Former Inhabitants" chapters of *Walden*, and his lectures, under several titles, on "Life without Principle" disclose that many Concord citizens of the later 1840s and 1850s changed residences (built a new house, as the Thoreau family had done in 1844 with the help of mortgage money from Augustus Tuttle, or moved into a larger or better located house, as the Thoreau family did in 1849). Many also bought and sold real estate (as Thoreau himself did in the case of his cabin at Walden Pond[30]), and surveyed cultivated land for the purpose of subdividing it into building lots (usually hiring Thoreau to conduct the surveys). One concludes from these activities that a number of Concord residents, notably farmers, changed occupations, an inference supported by Concord and Middlesex County survey records, census reports, maps, and contemporary accounts of Concord. Moreover, in these decades Concordians, who had never been free from the temptation to move away, removed increasingly to other towns and regions, particularly to cities, even as old-stock New Englanders and an unprecedented number of immigrants (most of them Irish) moved into Concord or to its borders.

Thoreau doubted that things were likely to go better elsewhere than in Concord. It is probably no coincidence, however, that his first major literary effort after resettling in Concord and while seeking to place *A Week* with a publisher was to draft "Resistance to Civil Government," in which he conferred the highest moral and aesthetic authority on the principle of resistance. In this argumentative essay about potentially fatal interruptions by uncivil government, "the whole history of 'My Prisons'" concludes with a conflation of the speaker's home town and "the State" and a simultaneous withdrawal from both to lead "a huckleberry party" in a field almost exactly as far from the town center as Thoreau's cabin at Walden Pond had been (*Reform Papers*, pp. 83–84). By the end of 1848, a few months before Elizabeth Peabody published "Resistance to Civil Government," Thoreau began to accept work as a surveyor, not to pay for the cost of publishing *A Week*, as is sometimes supposed, but probably to establish his writing career on his own economic terms. The richly suggestive parable of the Indian's unsuccessful business enterprise that Thoreau added in 1852 to the opening pages of *Walden* appears, in its autobiographical turn, to comment on Thoreau's post-Walden career decisions, including his calculated program of surveying for hire on a part-time basis: "I too had woven a kind of basket of a delicate texture, but I had not made it worth any one's while to buy them . . . and instead of studying how to make it worth men's while to buy my baskets, I studied rather how to avoid the necessity of selling them. The life which men praise and regard as successful is but one kind" (*Walden*, p. 19).

In May 1849, two weeks after the publication of "Resistance to Civil Government," *A Week* came out. Within a few months Thoreau appears to have known that his first long work would be a financial failure, but he revealed no distress or change of plans. By this time he had turned to revising *Walden* in those hours not encumbered by surveying or claimed by his walks. *A Week* had appeared with an advertisement of a forthcoming book (*Walden*), but Thoreau's protracted revisionary efforts sent *Walden* through multiple versions and the work would not appear for another five years.

By 1851–52 Thoreau identified another literary enterprise as his major one—his Journal—"whose editor," the narrator of *Walden* quips, "has never yet seen fit to print the bulk of my contributions. . . . However, in this case my pains were their own reward" (*Walden*, p. 18). As he noted in his Journal five days before he wrote his memorable entry on Hosmer and the young men of Concord, observations and thoughts "accidentally thrown together" would create their own order, a "frame," a "whole new field in which it was possible to labor & to think." This "new field" has to some extent replaced both his life at Walden and his Walden account. Shortly before announcing a new field for his labors and thoughts, Thoreau mused, "But why I changed—? Why I left the woods? I do not think that I can tell. I have often wished myself back" (NNPM MA 1302:15).[31] Perhaps the Journal would be his most important labor, he conjectured. It would probably never be published, although on the day that he wrote his Journal entry on Hosmer's despair he imagined his Journal appearing in print in the form in which he was composing it. It was a unique form, he recognized, and although it did not promise profits, it was a most profitable enterprise.

Yet at the very time that he assigned to the Journal a new importance and regular (almost daily) entries, many of the entries running to six, seven, and more pages, he also mined the Journal for materials for *Walden*, which over the course of almost seven years of revision virtually doubled in length. Mining his Journal and composing entirely new passages for *Walden* also turned out to be a profitable enterprise. Moreover, the revisions of *Walden*, including the incorporation of new material from the Journal of the post-Walden years, transformed the work by making enterprise one of its principal themes and extending the theme to the entire account. The genetic history of *Walden* also marks the beginning of Thoreau's mature career in the sense that he managed to translate his vocation of enterprise into literary form in a sustained fashion and make his enterprise of vocation the economy of the work.

Notes

1. Both the subject and the scholarship are richly diverse. Rush Welter has provided the fullest intellectual history of the era in *The Mind of America 1820–1860* (New York: Columbia University Press, 1975). The most thorough

studies of Jacksonian ideology and policies and their national and local impli-
cations are Marvin Meyer, *The Jacksonian Persuasion: Politics and Belief*
(Stanford: Stanford University Press, 1957), and Harry Watson, *Jacksonian
Politics and Community Conflict* (Baton Rouge: Louisiana State University
Press, 1981). In parts II and III of *Business in American Life* (New York:
McGraw-Hill, 1972), Thomas C. Cochran offers the best examination of how
business ideology became basic to American thought and action in these years.
John Cawelti, *Apostles of the Self-Made Man* (Chicago: University of Chicago
Press, 1965), chapters 2–3; Richard Weiss, *The American Myth of Success from
Horatio Alger to Norman Vincent Peale* (New York: Basic Books, 1969),
chapter 1; and Irvin G. Wyllie, *The Self-Made Man in America* (New Bruns-
wick: Rutgers University Press, 1954) study the success myth of the self-made
man that captured the individual and collective imagination.

The following scholars have offered the most informative surveys and anal-
yses on various sectors of the economy: (agriculture) Clarence H. Danhof,
Change in Agriculture: The Northern United States, 1820–1870 (Cambridge,
Mass.: Harvard University Press, 1969), and Paul W. Gates, *The Farmer's Age:
Agriculture, 1815–1860* (New York: Holt, Rinehart and Winston, 1960); (industrialization) Marvin Fisher, *Workshops in the Wilderness: The European Response to American Industrialization, 1830–1860* (New York: Oxford University Press, 1967), and Edward C. Kirkland, *Industry Comes of Age: Business,
Labor, and Public Policy, 1860–1897* (Chicago: Quadrangle Books, 1961),
chapters 1–2; (transportation) George R. Taylor, *The Transportation Revolution, 1815–1860* (New York: Holt, Rinehart and Winston, 1951); (canal-build-
ing boom in New York State) Nathan Miller, *The Enterprise of a Free People*
(Ithaca: Cornell University Press, 1962); (railroads) Alfred D. Chandler, *The
Railroads: The Nation's First Big Business* (New York: Harcourt, Brace and
World, 1965), parts I and II; (technology) John Kasson, *Civilizing the Machine: Technology and Republican Values in America, 1776–1900* (New York:
Grossman Publishers, 1976), chapters 2–4; (changes in American work force)
Stanley Lebergott, *Manpower in Economic Growth: The American Record
Since 1800* (New York: McGraw-Hill, 1964), parts I and II; (banking and
finance) Bray Hammond, *Banks and Politics in America from the Revolution
to the Civil War* (Princeton: Princeton University Press, 1957), pp. 286–499,
605–30; (patterns of income and wealth) Edward Pessen, *Riches, Class and
Power Before the Civil War* (Lexington, Mass.: D. C. Heath, 1973).

On publishing and the book trade, a subject largely economic in nature,
the most important studies are: Lawrence Buell, *New England Literary Culture
from Revolution Through Renaissance* (New York: Cambridge University
Press, 1986), chapter 3; William Charvat, *The Profession of Authorship in
America, 1800–1870* (Columbus: Ohio State University Press, 1968);
Charles A. Madison, *Book Publishing in America* (New York: McGraw-Hill,
1966), part I; and Ronald J. Zboray, "Antebellum Reading and the Ironies of
Technological Innovation," *American Quarterly* 40 (March 1988): 65–82, and

idem, "The Transportation Revolution and Antebellum Book Distribution Reconsidered," *American Quarterly* 38 (Spring 1986): 53–71.

Regional socioeconomic studies have also appeared. The most notable are: (the South) William R. Taylor, *Cavalier and Yankee: The Old South and American National Character* (New York: George Braziller, 1961); (southern communities) Watson, *Jacksonian Politics and Community Conflict*; (New England, especially Massachusetts) Oscar and Mary Handlin, *Commonwealth*, rev. ed. (Cambridge, Mass.: Harvard University Press, 1969), chapters 7–10; (Thoreau's town of Concord) Robert A. Gross, "Culture and Cultivation: Agriculture and Society in Thoreau's Concord," *Journal of American History* 69 (June 1982): 42–61, George Hendrick, ed., *Remembrances of Concord and the Thoreaus* (Urbana: University of Illinois Press, 1977), and Townsend Scudder, *Concord: American Town* (Boston: Little, Brown, 1947).

Daniel Walker Howe has commented on the economic beliefs of the moral philosophers at Harvard and among Unitarian clergymen trained by them. See *The Unitarian Conscience: Harvard Moral Philosophy, 1805–1861* (Cambridge, Mass.: Harvard University Press, 1970), chapters 8–10. Ann Douglas has explored the changing role and behavior of congregational clergymen in Massachusetts in the age of enterprise; see *The Feminization of American Culture* (New York: Alfred A. Knopf, 1977), especially chapters 1–4. Finally, Michael T. Gilmore, Robert Gross, William G. Heath, Jr., and Leo Stoller have examined the impact of the new economic culture on particular New England transcendentalists. See Gilmore, *American Romanticism and the Marketplace* (Chicago: University of Chicago Press, 1985), especially chapters 1–2; Gross, "'The Most Estimable Place in All the World': A Debate on Progress in Nineteenth-Century Concord," *Studies in the American Renaissance 1978*, ed. Joel Myerson (Boston: G. K. Hall, 1978), pp. 1–15; idem, "Transcendentalism and Urbanism: Concord, Boston, and the Wider World," *Journal of American Studies* 18 (December 1984): 361–63; Heath, "Cyrus Bartol's Transcendental Capitalism," *Studies in the American Renaissance 1979*, ed. Joel Myerson (Boston: G. K. Hall, 1979), pp. 399–408; and Stoller, *After Walden: Thoreau's Changing Views on Economic Man* (Stanford: Stanford University Press, 1957).

2. Taylor, *Transportation Revolution*, has been summarized by Meyer, *Jacksonian Persuasion*, pp. 88–89. My list abbreviates and slightly modifies Meyer's summary.

3. Hammond, *Banks and Politics*, p. 327.

4. Welter, *The Mind of America*, p. 129.

5. Hendrick, *Remembrances*, p. 5.

6. On Bartol, see Heath, "Cyrus Bartol's Transcendental Capitalism," pp. 399–408; on Emerson's investment in the Fitchburg Railroad, see Scudder, *Concord*, p. 190. On the impact of the spirit of enterprise on the clergy, Daniel Howe's assertion that the basic values of Unitarian moralists and the ministers they trained did not essentially change needs to be qualified. See Howe, *The Unitarian Conscience*, p. 205.

7. Douglas, *Feminization*, chapters 3–4.

8. The only study I am aware of that acknowledges changes in the cultural discourse closely tied to the economic transformation is Rush Welter's "Enterprise," in *The Mind of America*. There, he briefly examines the etymology and nineteenth-century American usage of the word *enterprise* (pp. 156–58).

9. Gross, "Culture and Cultivation" and "'The Most Estimable Place in All the World.'"

10. For Adams, see "Inaugural Address" and "Fourth Annual Message," *A Compilation of the Messages and Papers of the Presidents* (New York: Bureau of National Literature, 1897), 2:860–65 and 3:973–87, respectively. For Jackson, see especially his "First Inaugural Address" (3:999–1001) and "Farewell Address" (4:1511–27). Other speeches included in this survey are Martin Van Buren, "Inaugural Address (4:1530–37) and "Fourth Annual Message" (5:1819–37); James Polk, "Inaugural Address (5:2223–32); and "Fourth Annual Message" (6:2479–2521); Zachary Taylor, "Inaugural Address" (6:2542–44); Millard Fillmore, "Third Annual Message" (6:2699–3718); Franklin Pierce, "Inaugural Address" (6:2730–36) and "Fourth Annual Message" (7:2930–50). Hereafter cited in text as *Presidents*.

11. Frederika Bremer captures key aspects of the term *enterprise* in its positive connotation in the vernacular. Her description of the "enterprising" young American citizen of the 1850s is "a young man (no matter if he be old) who makes his own way in the world in full reliance on his own power, stops at nothing, shrinks from nothing, finds nothing impossible, tries everything, has faith in everything. . . . If he is unsuccessful, he says, 'Try again!' 'Go ahead!' and he begins over again, undertaking something else, and never stopping until he succeeds." *America of the Fifties*, ed. Adolph A. Benson (New York: American-Scandinavian Foundation, 1924), pp. 92–93.

12. Francis Bowen, *The Principles of Political Economy* (Boston: Little, Brown, 1856), p. 107; chapters VIII–X; pp. 93, 122, 123. On specifically economic uses of *enterprise*, see especially chapters VII–X. For typical examples see: agriculture, pp. 88, 91, 108; commerce, p. 108; trade, p. 88; manufacturing, pp. 88, 91, 126; shops and factories, p. 129; railroads and canals, p. 101; finance, p. 108; and corporation stockholding, p. 130.

13. Ibid., p. 116. The history of American dictionaries confirms the exceedingly conservative character of dictionary writing until the 1960s. Not until the past few decades, when lexicographers and linguists changed from prescriptive to descriptive principles of lexicography, was the specifically economic usage of *enterprise*, *private enterprise*, and related terms acknowledged. Thesauruses, in contrast, have acknowledged the economic meanings since early in this century. As for economic lexicons, *Palgrave's Dictionary of Political Economy* (London: Macmillan, 1894) uses the term *enterprise* in its general sense, but Horton's *Dictionary of Modern Economics* (Washington, D.C.: Public Affairs Press, 1948), a lexicon designed to describe well-entrenched American economic vernacular largely ignored by Palgrave, defines *enterprise* as a "business venture under-

taken for profit. . . . More specifically, it may be conceived of as the activities involved in initiating and operating a business venture" (pp. 114–15).

14. Howe, *The Unitarian Conscience*, pp. 227, 231–32.

15. Robert C. Winthrop, *An Address Delivered Before the Boston Mercantile Library Association . . . Oct. 15, 1845* (Boston: T. R. Marvin, 1845). Much of the address was reprinted under the title "Influence of Commerce in the Affairs of the World" in *Hunt's Merchant's Magazine* 14 (February 1846): 122–28; quoted passages on pp. 123 and 127.

16. *Debates of the Texas Convention*, William F. Weeks, reporter (Austin, Tex.: n.p., 1845), p. 645; quoted in Welter, *The Mind of America*, p. 133.

17. Quoted in Kirkland, *Industry Comes of Age*, p. 3.

18. House of Representatives Executive Document No. 78, 39th Cong. (1867), *U.S. Government Documents*, Serial 1293, pp. 27–28; House of Representatives Miscellaneous Document No. 14, 45th Cong. (1879), *U.S. Government Documents*, Serial 1861, pp. 5–6; House of Representatives Miscellaneous Document No. 29, 45th Cong. (1879), *U.S. Government Documents*, Serial 1863, pp. 515–42.

19. Several other sample titles from Arthur's storehouse of formulaic romances and tales about money, morals, and success are: *Keeping up Appearances*; *Retiring from Business*; *Riches Have Wings*; *Rising in the World*; *True Riches, and Other Tales*; and *The Way to Prosper, and Other Tales*. All of these appeared in numerous printings of multiple editions.

20. Houghton Library, Harvard University (MH): b MS Am 278.5, folder 6B, and folder 6E. The last nine words appear at the top of a worksheet that represents Thoreau's continuing composition but that has been filed in a folder different from the one in which the preceding manuscript leaf is filed.

21. Henry Thoreau, *Early Essays and Miscellanies*, ed. Joseph J. Moldenhauer and Edwin Moser, *The Writings of Henry D. Thoreau* (Princeton: Princeton University Press, 1975), p. 13.

22. Ibid., pp. 115, 117.

23. Howe, *The Unitarian Conscience*, pp. 226–35.

24. Thoreau, *Early Essays*, pp. 117–18.

25. Ralph Waldo Emerson, *Lectures and Biographical Sketches*, vol. 10 of *The Complete Works of Ralph Waldo Emerson*, ed. Edward W. Emerson (Boston and New York: Houghton Mifflin, 1903), p. 480.

26. See *The Correspondence of Henry David Thoreau*, ed. Carl Bode and Walter Harding (New York: New York University Press, 1958), p. 57.

27. New York Public Library (NYPL), Thoreau [Berg] Journal, p. 103. Unfortunately the Princeton Edition of the Berg Journal reports neither this revision nor most other revisions by Thoreau. The Berg Journal notebook is quoted with the permission of the Henry W. and Albert A. Berg Collection of the New York Public Library, Astor, Lenox and Tilden Foundations.

28. Thoreau [Berg] Journal, p. 116. The version quoted includes alterations by Thoreau to the passage as presented in PE J 2:289.

29. See especially Gross, "Culture and Cultivation"; idem, "'The Most Estimable Place in All the World.'"

30. After purchasing the cabin from Thoreau, Emerson, in turn, sold it to Hugh Whelan, an Irish immigrant. Thus the cabin which Thoreau had purchased as lumber from an Irish immigrant laborer was eventually resold to an Irish immigrant laborer.

31. Compare 1906 J 3:217.

2

The Economist of Walden

By Thoreau's time the Protestant debate over vocation had been settled among enlightened New Englanders.[1] Both the concept of vocation and its religious rationale had been pushed to the margins of personal and cultural relevance, but his age witnessed the publication of many sermons and treatises on particular occupations (the popular new term *professions* for what was once called *offices* signals the change). These sermons and treatises often presumed to speak on vocation whereas their interest in most cases was morally acceptable and above all economically successful occupations.

To follow the history of the idea of vocation in America, I suggest, is to trace a line from the quarrel between John Cotton and Anne Hutchinson in which both parties claimed authority and justified their behavior by invoking precisely the same argument of having been called by God to perform God's special work.[2] The line of development can be traced through the writings of figures like Cotton Mather to Benjamin Franklin and Thomas Jefferson with their ideal of the *homo oeconomicus*. Early nineteenth-century Unitarianism, as David Robinson has carefully documented, fostered the concept of *homo oeconomicus* as a religious doctrine or, we might say, as a moral/aesthetic religion of self-culture in which "the moral life was transformed from a sign, or an adjunct, of the religious life, into a religion in itself."[3]

An important reminder to be extrapolated from Daniel Howe's and Robinson's examinations of Unitarianism in Thoreau's time is that Thoreau invented neither his language nor his general understanding of self-culture. Thus to note the equation in *Walden* and "Life without Principle" between vocation and self-culture and to see this equation confirmed by biographical evidence is to underscore the obvious about Thoreau and his circle. Not even Thoreau's characterization of self-culture as an enterprise in *Walden* is unique, a point that a review of Unitarian sermonizing in his time and region will drive home with monotonous repetition. What is unique is his equation of self-culture with his highly unusual literary vocation and the version of enterprise inherent in it. While hardly denying that self-culture or the "art of life" is a principal theme in *Walden*, I suggest that greater significance should be attached to the fact that the narrator's agenda of self-cultivation and his artistic labors become interchangeable in his vocational "experiment" and that the two became interchangeable in Thoreau's enterprise of vocation.

I

This fusion of self-culture, literary career, and enterprise serves as matrix and theme for two memorable parables that Thoreau added to his growing *Walden* account. Approximately two years before he prepared a printer's copy of *Walden* and more than a year before he wheelbarrowed home the over 700 unsold and virtually all unbound volumes of *A Week* that publisher James Munroe had been storing on his inventory shelves for four years since he had printed 1,000 copies, Thoreau added to the early pages of *Walden* a parable of an Indian basket weaver and his failed enterprise. This anecdote and another added shortly thereafter, the exotic parable of the artist of Kouroo, provide a frame of sorts for the economist's account in the published version of *Walden*. Both parables are concerned with vocation and enterprise—more precisely, with the enterprise of vocation. It is hardly surprising that they have prompted scholars over the years to make biographical applications.

The most immediate lesson of the richly suggestive parable of the Indian's unsuccessful venture into business enterprise is offered by the narrator: "I too had woven a kind of basket of a delicate texture, but I had not made it worth any one's while to buy them . . . and instead of studying how to make it worth men's while to buy my baskets, I studied rather how to avoid the necessity of selling them. The life which men praise and regard as successful is but one kind. Why should we exaggerate any one kind at the expense of the others?" (*Walden*, p. 19). This reflection raises three significant issues: career, economic success, and vocation. Unfortunately, what the entrepreneurial Indian was capable of producing did not match what his successful neighbors needed or wanted. Whether the Indian's baskets were "of a delicate texture" isn't clear, but the narrator has "woven a basket of a delicate texture"—possibly Thoreau's literary productions to 1852 when he added this parable to *Walden*, possibly *A Week*, which, even Thoreau admitted, had turned into a business fiasco. Like the Indian, the narrator has failed to market his products. With a shrewd entrepreneurial expertise and patronizingly pedagogical tone, he explains the Indian's fundamental business mistakes by identifying several alternative actions that the Indian failed to recognize and pursue: to "make it worth the other's while to buy them, or at least make him think that it was so, or to make something else."

The narrator's explanations are not without irony, the irony directed at the community, the Indian, and himself. All three alternatives are addressed in the autobiographical reflection, "I had not made it worth any one's while to buy them." These alternatives are then rejected: "I studied rather how to avoid the necessity of selling them." Throughout, the narrator employs a language of production, promotion, and economic returns while undermining the popular assumptions and values behind the language. Even in his deliberate decision to free himself from the anxious demands and expectations of financial success in his line of work, he speaks with the aplomb and calculated idiom of a shrewd entrepreneur who has evaluated his market, his circumstances, and his career interests. He will not jeopardize his best interests; he will merely reject popular interpretations of enterprise and reward. As abrupt as the parable's "well-known lawyer" is toward the Indian (one suspects that the less than reverent reference is to Judge Samuel Hoar and his equally distinguished sons Ebenezer Rockwood Hoar and George Frisbee Hoar), and with an understatement characteristic of his discussion of vocation here and elsewhere in *Walden*, the narrator concludes that the "life which men praise and regard as successful is but one kind." Central to the parable and its function in "Economy" is this reversal of status by which the authority of presence and worth passes from those whom the business-minded Indian admired and hoped to emulate to the narrator and his unusual enterprise.

Like the moralist who must emphasize the principle of what he has just declared through an extended example, the narrator asks rhetorically, "Why should we exaggerate any one kind [of living] at the expense of the others?" The logic of the parable and the question allows for several intentions in the question and, by extension, in the telling of the *Walden* story. *Walden*, in fact, confirms three intentions: in an age that defines career success in narrow materialistic terms to argue the legitimacy of many alternatives (many kinds of lives); in an age characterized by money-making careerism and the unprecedented popularity of career manuals to add "one kind" more (the narrator's vocation) to the reader's inventory; and in a work that plays serious games to turn an apparent injunction against exaggerating his kind of life into an injunction to exaggerate. This "exaggeration" is justified at length in the final chapter of *Walden*; indeed, the speaker declares in the paragraph in which he distinguishes his *"extra vagance"* from the "extravagance" of his age, "I am convinced that I cannot exaggerate enough" (*Walden*, p. 324).

An examination of the preamble to the parable of the Indian will reveal that the rhetorical question concluding the parable is also directed at the four paragraphs immediately preceding the parable, paragraphs in which the speaker offers an obviously satirical career manual; he introduces himself as a "reporter to a journal, of no very wide circulation," a "self-appointed inspector of snow storms," a "surveyor of forest paths," a "custodian of the wild stock of the town" that has escaped its owners and yards, and a nurseryman to red huckleberries, sand cherries, nettle trees, and other varieties of customarily ignored or depreciated flora in the vicinity of Concord. In the minds of his "Townsmen" the entire range of employment belongs not only to the unconventional but also, as the speaker concedes, to the unacceptable (*Walden*, p. 18). Thus the question of why one would want to "exaggerate any one kind" of career or living "at the expense of the others" is concerned, above all, with the theme of vocation as a private enterprise of self-culture. In addressing this theme, the speaker presents himself as an anomaly but not an anachronism. The parable of the Indian, the "Economy" chapter that serves as its immediate context, and *Walden*, its more commodious context, represent an important contribution by Thoreau to a historically weakening and culturally battered idea of vocation, an ideal he sought to reauthorize in his version and which was threatened not so much by overt hostility as by neglect in a society reassured by the dynamism of its frenetic enterprise.

About the time when Thoreau added to his *Walden* account the anecdote of the Indian entrepreneur, he began to draft a sketch of an "artist in the city of Kouroo who was disposed to strive after perfection." In his next version of *Walden* (the fifth), this passage was somewhat reworded and expanded. By the sixth version, the parable was completed and its place secured in the account by now divided into titled chapters largely as we know them. Its immediate context was a newly drafted conclusion. This new chapter prominently featured the anecdote of an artist who with "singleness of purpose and resolution, and his elevated piety" worked tirelessly, or at least perseveringly, to complete his ornate staff while the culture to which he belonged by citizenship "passed away" along with his friends, who had grown "old in their works and died." The result of his protracted work was "a world with full and fair proportions," in contrast, one assumes, to the deficient secular world that was passing away (*Walden*, pp. 326–27).

Ignored by the critical commentaries on the artist of Kouroo passage is its immediate preamble with its apothegm about a man marching to a different drummer, a maxim variously packaged and trivialized in recent decades. The brief paragraph in which this well-known aphorism appears warns the "you" and "we" of *Walden* against "desperate haste to succeed" and against seeking success in "desperate enterprises." Hard on the heels of this foot-tapping reminder of a culture enthralled by and addicted to its new economic prospects is the richly suggestive image of the man out of step with his companions, an allusion that recalls Thoreau's relation to his culture, his calculated vocational decisions, his private business, his view of art, and his protracted labor on *Walden*: "If a man does not keep pace with his companions, perhaps it is because he hears a different drummer. . . . If the condition of things which we were made for is not yet, what were any reality which we can substitute? We will not be shipwrecked on a vain reality" (*Walden*, p. 326).

The "condition of things which we were made for" is presumably the reality of the *Walden* speaker. In other words, this parable concerning an unusual enterprise of vocation stands out as the supreme exaggeration of one kind of life at the expense of others. The parable reveals not the slightest hint of concern in the artist about selling his work or avoiding the necessity of selling it. His indefatigable labors allow for no alternatives, although they themselves are presented as an alternative to customary assumptions and practice. His "singleness of purpose and resolution" tolerates no vanity or desperation in the undertaking. Whether his friends "who grew old in their works and died" tolerated and even conducted desperate enterprises or made compromises with the times is not clear, but the parable suggests the likelihood that that has been the case. For his part, the artist has participated in the march of things, but at a different pace, and perhaps to different music.

Like the Indian basket weaver, the Kouroo artist uses common material from his environment, in his case wood from the forest. Although not practicing rejection per se or escapism, he rejects sample upon sample of wood, like a violin maker, until he finds material suitable for his purpose—transformation of a large stick into a splendid staff. Before he has completed his work the culture in which he was born and reared has passed away, and he records its passing only to return to his uncompromising labor, a rigorous economy and economical regimen that yield "a new system," a "world with full and fair proportions." The artist's commitments and achievement are reminiscent of a Journal entry Thoreau made in the year when he began to sketch his parable of the artist of Kouroo:

> The forcible writer does not go far for his themes—his ideas are not far-fetched—he derives inspiration from his chagrins & his satisfactions— His theme being ever an instant one his own gravity assists him—gives impetus to what he says— He minds his business. He does not speculate while others drudge for him.
> I am often reminded that if I had bestowed on me the wealth of Croesus, my aims must still be the same & my means essentially the same. (NNPM MA 1302:15)

The artist's unwillingness to settle for a work imperfect for its "compromise with Time" ("though I should do nothing else in my life") is admittedly ambiguous. Will his project of a perfect work become more than a passing enterprise? Will it become his life, disallowing any other occupation or preoccupation? Is his work so comprehensive, absorbing, and consuming that, having become his life as well as its own, it permits no other kind of life, even after its completion? Does it resist, perhaps cancel, what the speaker has referred to in the same chapter as "several more lives to live"? (*Walden*, p. 323). Or is he standing outside of his enterprise and allowing us to overhear a debate with other observers who expect, possibly demand, that he do something else in his life and with his life? In a sense, he answers these questions, yet, in so doing, shifts the focus. "But why do I stay to mention these things?" He has stayed with the parable and, in doing so, has stayed both "Conclusion" and *Walden* by it, thus carrying out his advice to the reader to "lay the foundation of a true expression" (*Walden*, pp. 327, 324). The means as well as end of "true expression," he points out, are exaggeration. The parable of the artist of Kouroo, then, is the answer to the tongue-in-cheek question that concludes the parable on the Indian basket weaver: "The life which men praise and regard as successful is but one kind. Why should we exaggerate any one kind at the expense of the others?"

To be sure, singleness of purpose, elevated piety, desire for perfection, and a self-conducted adjudication that pronounces the results to be "wonderful" are not uncompromised by presumption and vanity. Yet the vocabulary and context of the parable, while not entirely dismissing the reader's suspicions of the solitary artist, underscore the pertinence of the passage to Thoreau's life in his culture. Consider, for example, the problematical term *perfection*, which, Thoreau knew, has its semantic roots in the Greek *telos*, a polysemous term whose meanings include power, efficacy, authority, the undoing of things done, a breaking out of things as they are done, a higher degree of attainment or maturity, the fullest possible realization, a consummation issuing in fulfillment, and the end of a word, sentence, chapter, or book. As for principal meanings of *perfection* in the eighteenth and nineteenth centuries, these include the state of having been accomplished, completed, or carried out, the characteristic of excellence, faultlessness, or sufficiency, the quality of being unmixed, and, in printing, the completion of a sheet or signatures by printing the other side.

The pertinence of these meanings to the narrator's unusual vocation and alternative enterprise should be obvious to the reader of *Walden*, who by the end of "Economy" has been made aware of the connections-by-analogy among building a house and managing a farm, overseeing an estate, building a career, exploring other sides of vocation, building monuments, building a more sufficient life, constructing works of art, and bringing *Walden* to maturity. "I intend to build me a house which will surpass any on the maine street in grandeur and luxury as soon as it pleases me as much and will cost me no more than my present one," Thoreau wrote in his first draft of *Walden*,[4] presenting his private enterprise in the context of Concord's enterprise and appropriating the vernacular and values of his town for his personal agenda—to realize another enterprise and exaggerate that enterprise at the expense of more popular ones. Some two or three years after drafting the passage on the kind of house he intended to build, Thoreau moved into the house his parents had just purchased on highly desirable Main Street. He retained his passage in *Walden*, correcting the spelling of the street and adding "in Concord" (see *Walden*, p. 49). As sole occupant of the spacious garret of the house on Main Street, he sought, through six successive versions, to bring *Walden* to completion. In the process of these revisions, he increased the prominence of the theme of enterprise.

II

An inventory of *Walden* will substantiate its concern with enterprise. A word frequency check of the published version of the text alone is revealing: *enterprise*, in most cases with reference to business enterprise, risk, or undertaking, occurs nineteen times, the same number as *trade* or *traders*. The term *business* in reference to business enterprise or designs occurs more frequently than *enterprise*. *Economy* as noun and adjective occurs ten times; *railroad*, a principal avatar of economic expansion, occurs forty times. Related word usages are: *commerce* five times (also the number for *banks* and for *factories*); *profit* in a financial sense three times; *expense(s)* fourteen times; *success* as related to enterprise more frequently than *expense(s)*; *interest* as a financial term more frequently than *economy*; *venture* and *undertaking* (as connected to *enterprise*) ten times; and *industry* in the sense of diligence eight times. One might also note that in the first chapter of *Walden* alone, *money* appears eleven times.[5]

By comparison, the first version of *Walden* is noticeably less inhabited by the vocabulary and theme of enterprise. A comparison of the two texts in their entirety except for the "Economy" material produces the following numbers in a word frequency check of key terms: in the first version *enterprise* and *profit* occur half as often; *railroad, trade, trader,* and *money* less than half as often; and *business* and *expenses* less than one-third as often. Furthermore, *market,* a word that in chapters other than "Economy" in the published text occurs ten times, is absent from the corresponding material in the first draft. Two factors account for the disparity in the frequency of these terms, and other related terms, in the initial and final versions: missing leaves in the surviving worksheets of the first version (the lesser factor) and the expansion and changing conception of *Walden* as it passed through another six versions (the greater factor).

More revealing than these word frequency figures is the compositional history of *Walden,* a history that provides a context of significance for the numbers. The evidence of the *Walden* worksheets suggests that the "Economy" chapter was originally drafted as a separate lecture/essay designed, in part, as a personal statement for Lyceum purposes on his vocational enterprise of self-culture at Walden and perhaps as a comic-serious parody of success manuals for young men. At some time during his second year at Walden, perhaps simultaneously with the writing of the Lyceum lecture, Thoreau also began a larger work on his life in the woods. This account, with its own sequence of page numbers, begins, naturally enough, with the narrative which grew into "Where I Lived, and What I Lived For." The word *naturally* in the preceding sentence implies, among other things, that what was to become "Economy" is much less integrated into the rest of the account in the first version than it is in the final version. The bulk of lecture material that was to become "Economy" (probably to leaf 30 verso in this sequence and perhaps other pages as well) appears to have served Thoreau as the text for his lecture at the Concord Lyceum on 10 February 1847 and again a week later (perhaps a lecture in two installments).[6] Before he turned to revising and expanding his

Walden account, he decided to use the "Economy" manuscript as the opening section, although in his second version he debates in the "Economy" pages whether to use the terminology "this lecture" and "audience" and alters "I require of a writer" by adding the words "or lecturer."

Apart from these separately numbered lecture pages on economy, the first version of *Walden* is characterized by buoyancy, serenity, freely ranging imagination, a vacation spirit free, in the main, from contemporary Concord and New England cultural pressures, excursiveness into a timeless world created, in large part, by pastoral motifs and Edenic allusions, generous hospitality within that timeless world, and the quiet joy of an indefinitely outlined and intensely private self-culture.[7]

In the successive versions of *Walden* one of the emerging patterns is the gradual extension of the theme of economy and profitable business to materials other than the "Economy" pages but also the expansion of the "Economy" material (only some of these additions, particularly the latter, survived to the final version). The *Walden* worksheets disclose that in his second version Thoreau was preoccupied principally with the "Economy" pages; in this version the redrafted text of these pages is larger than the newly drafted material for the rest of the work. Thoreau's revisions sharpen his distinction between right and wrong economies, successful and unsuccessful business, and necessary and unnecessary labor, investments, and expenditures. The account of preparing timber and boards and then constructing the cabin is filled out, serving now as an example of profitable economy. The influence of these changes to the "Economy" pages on what follows them is unmistakable. For example, the following paragraph was added in this version to the discussion eventually forming chapter two, "Where I Lived, and What I Lived For":

> Let us settle ourselves, and work and wedge our feet downward through the mud and slush of opinion and prejudice and tradition, and delusion, and appearance, that alluvion that covers the globe—through London and Paris, through New York and Boston and Concord, through Church and State,—through poetry and philosophy and religion—till we come to a hard bottom and rocks in place, which we can call reality, and say this is, and no mistake;—and then begin, having a *point d'appui*,

below freshet and frost and fire, a place where you might found a wall or a state, or set a lamp post safely, or perhaps a guage [*sic*]—not a Nilometer, but a Realometer.[8]

Where the gauge is to be gotten or how it is to be identified is unclear, but its purpose is clear enough: this passage, consisting of a single, long, syntactically extended, probing sentence, distinguishes between being mired and finding a secure ground in one's undertaking. The hortatory voice, the imperative-like demand, and the probing sentence concluding with its "Realometer" leave no doubt about the agenda. The narrator's enterprise and *Walden*'s economy must avoid being mired. Unlike institutions and practices of the age, narrator and narrative must probe through the mire to a reliable footing.

In the third version, the one featuring the fewest changes of any of the versions, the effect of Thoreau's revisions is to link the "Economy" pages more tightly to the rest of *Walden* by means of further alterations of the "Economy" pages and, especially, by additions to the rest of his account. New reflections on Alek Therien, the gregarious French-Canadian woodchopper, post maker, and fence builder illustrate the latter. The new material on Therien serves as a suggestive comment on the maturation of *Walden* beyond its initial elysian setting and childlike joy. In Therien, Thoreau now adds, "the animal man chiefly was developed. . . . But the intellectual and spiritual man in him were slumbering like an infant." Thoreau also reports or invents the woodcutter's untroubled, self-justifying thoughts on the matter: "He suggested that there might be men of genius in the lowest grades of life, however permanently humble & illiterate, who take a view of their own always & are not indebted to their neighbors—who are as bottomless as even Walden pond was thought to be, though *they* may be dark & muddy."[9] This sentiment may have been Therien's, the images undoubtedly are Thoreau's. His affectionate yet ironic treatment of Therien establishes an expectation and norm that suggest, by extension, a parody of the narrator of the first version in the interest of maturing him and a self-criticism that underscores maturation as one of the necessaries of *Walden*. Therien is not lacking in imagination, and he seems instinctively to understand that although his labor is valuable to landowners and developers in the region, his work is a private and personally satisfying undertaking. Something less than satisfaction characterizes the narrator's new reflections on this unquestioning, untroubled, "dark & muddy" man.

Similar critiques of narrator and narrative are evident in the additions to the fourth through sixth versions, in which the lexicon of enterprise and theme of profitable economy are significantly expanded in the text that follows "Economy." A notable example of such a critique is the addition in the fifth version to the account of cultivating the beanfield. In the first version the speaker, reflecting on his not unpleasant agricultural drudgery, notes that in the future he will prepare for a more rewarding harvest by planting seeds such "as sincerity—truth—simplicity—faith—innocence."[10] In the fifth version, however, he interjects an evaluation of the undertaking that survived virtually unchanged to the final version: "Alas! I said this to myself; but now another summer is gone, and another, and another, and I am obliged to say to you, Reader, that the seeds which I planted, if indeed they *were* the seeds of those virtues, were wormeaten or had lost their vitality, and so did not come up" (*Walden*, p. 164). What he has gleaned from "this further experience" is not entered in the ledger as a loss; rather, the entire unorthodox enterprise of the narrator is troubled by the possibility of failure. Regardless of whether his aims are entirely honorable and sincere, he may succeed no more than the fathers and his fellow Concord farmers have. In short, the narrator of the fifth version is not convinced that he has outenterprised others in his undertaking.

The possibility of a ruined enterprise is a disquieting note considering the new observations in the fourth and fifth versions of the miserable undertakings of others. In the fourth version Thoreau added his famous paragraph beginning with "The mass of men lead lives of quiet desperation" (in this version, "The great mass of mankind"). The passage culminates in a lengthy sarcastic portrait of a "poor wretch," a "helpless" man who apparently came "from New York and was seeking work." The man is unaware of where he is, has been, or will be. "And so he would go on if his constitution held out to the Gulf of St. Lawrence, where he would probably jump in." In this same version the teamster is much less satisfactory than Therien, the old and experienced have no useful experience to impart, the farmer's work and worries "outweigh the value of his farm," and architecture and the belles lettres in America are a testimony to the citizens' "despair or indifference to life." Thoreau also added a passage that he later heavily crossed out: "I do not hesitate to repeat what was asserted by another in a moment of illumination that 'mankind is a damned fool.'" These additions are not devoid of humor, but they are humorless in comparison to Thoreau's final text. "There is no play" in the mass of men, Thoreau adds to the conclusion of the paragraph on lives of quiet despera- tion, "for this comes after work."

One should not forget that in this fourth version Thoreau also composed the parable of the Indian basket weaver and his failed enterprise and began to sketch the parable of the artist of Kouroo who made no compromises with his culture and so surprised him- self by outenterprising and outliving his contemporaries through his successful artistic achievement. As he builds his fireplace and chimney and prepares for his indoor labors of winter, the narrator of the fifth version is anxious that his hearth be more than a "compact utilitarian heap" before which "the present may sit down and go to sleep." "He shall put *some* things behind him; he shall pass an invisible boundary, new more universal & liberal laws shall silently establish themselves around & within him . . . or the old laws be expanded and interpreted in his favor in a larger & more liberal sense," Thoreau also added in this fifth version.[11]

By the sixth version, when Thoreau made the expanded parable of the artist of Kouroo centerpiece of a new concluding chapter, and more emphatically by the seventh version, the theme of "*extra vagance*" by means of economy (higher means to higher ends) emerged as a principal motif, supported by the parables on voca- tion and enterprise that now help to frame the work. What the economist/narrator learned from his undertaking at Walden and in *Walden* is that with the proper economy one "will meet with a success unexpected in common hours." Without this success, which is characterized as an establishing of new and more liberal laws and an appropriation and transformation of old laws, he could not "brag as lustily as chanticleer in the morning . . . if only to wake my neighbors up" (*Walden*, pp. 323, 84).

The protracted labor on *Walden* secured its success, made "success unexpected in common hours" its theme, and increasingly identified enterprising young men eager for success as its internalized readers. As such, *Walden* presented itself as a success manual, a guidebook for devotees of success in a culture of enterprise. But the protracted compositional process is also a historical reminder of the relation of *Walden* to powerful cultural forces. Present in that reminder is the implication that both the cultural conventions addressed by the speaker of *Walden* and the speaking of *Walden* refuse to behave as transcendental objects, even when formally examined. If Hawthorne was correct in his assessment that the only current American materials available to a vocation-minded artist like Thoreau were "a common-place prosperity, in broad and simple daylight,"[12] two paramount questions for the critics arise. How did Thoreau appropriate his materials? And what is suggested by the history of that appropriation? Early in *Walden*, in a paragraph Thoreau added in the fourth version, we are given a strong hint of what *Walden* will offer in the way of answers to these two questions: "The greater part of what my neighbors call good I believe in my soul to be bad, and if I repent of any thing, it is very likely to be my good behavior." Yet the power of dominant cultural values and behavior is not underestimated. A rhetorical question with a witty reference to America's new "demonology," the doctrine of economic success and the craze of moneymaking, forms part of the speaker's declaration about two powerful and different attractions: "What demon possessed me that I behaved so well? . . . I hear an irresistible voice which invites me away from all that" (*Walden*, pp. 10–11). The successive versions of *Walden* are a record of increasing response to and identification with the "irresistible voice." In the final version of *Walden* that "irresistible voice" and the economist clear in his vocational commitments have become one, and they stand as one behind the pronouncement in "Economy" that "men have become the tools of their tools" and that the "best works of art are the expression of man's struggle to free himself from this condition" (*Walden*, p. 37). The speaker's claim near the end of *Walden* of success "unexpected in common hours" includes inside its boundaries the forces of the culture, the final form of *Walden*, and the demanding enterprise of achieving such a form.

Notes

1. The most informative recent scholarship on the concept and practice of vocation in New England Unitarian circles in Thoreau's day is Daniel Howe, *The Unitarian Conscience: Harvard Moral Philosophy, 1805–1861* (Cambridge, Mass.: Harvard University Press, 1970), pp. 100–120, and David Robinson, *Apostle of Culture: Emerson as Preacher and Lecturer* (Philadelphia: University of Pennsylvania Press, 1982, especially pp. 7–29.

2. *Vocation*, from *vocatio, vocationis*, originally referred to the irresistibility of a divine summons. As understood by conservative Catholic scholars of the Renaissance and the majority of the leading Protestant reformers, this summons to exercise a special function, perform a special work, or take up a particular life's calling was contrary to man's inclination and will. Both in Protestantism and in conservative Catholicism the term gradually accommodated both this sense of an arbitrary divine call and the humanist's concept of the way of life (*genus vitae*) in which individual choice, based on the weighing of alternatives, is central. The latter view was held by liberal Catholics like Erasmus and many of the Arminian sects. The idea of a man called by a sovereign God to perform God's designated work is a concept not easily reconciled with a religious version of the *homo oeconomicus*, a concept usually associated with the humanist's understanding of *vocatio*, but the ambitions of a Cotton Mather in New England constrained him to attempt to reconcile the two. In colonial America the Puritans emphasized the former view, the liberal Anglicans, the Quakers, and some of the Anabaptists the latter. A much less frequent use of the term in early American religious writing equates vocation with the state of grace in God's economy. In this view the term is directly linked to a processive state of salvation and the harmony with God realized in such a state. Colonial texts directly or indirectly addressing vocation, calling, and appointed task (in the order of their completion and dated accordingly) include: John Cotton, *The Way of Life*, 1641; William Bradford, *Of Plymouth Plantation*, 1648; Cotton Mather, *The Way to Prosperity*, 1690; idem, *A Christian at His Calling*, 1701; idem, *Agricola*, 1727; Samuel Sewell, *Diary*, 1728; John Woolman, *Journal*, 1772; Benjamin Franklin, "The Way to Wealth," 1758; idem, *Autobiography*, 1790; Jean de Crèvecoeur, *Letters from an American Farmer*, 1782; and Thomas Jefferson, *Notes on the State of Virginia*, 1785. Instructive nonconformist British texts on the topic include: William Perkins, *A Treatise of the Vocations, or Callings of Men* (first printed separately in 1605); George Swinnock, *The Christian-Mans Calling*, 1665; John Flavel, *Husbandry Spiritualized*, 1669; idem, *Navigation Spiritualized*, 1677; Richard Steele, *The Husbandmans Calling*, 1668; idem, *The Trades-mans Calling*, 1684. For an excellent discussion of *vocatio* as understood and used by the intelligentsia in early modern Europe, see Richard M. Douglas, "Talent and Vocation in Humanist and Protestant Thought," in *Action and Conviction in Early Modern Europe*, ed. Theodore K. Rabb and Jerrold E. Seigel (Princeton:

Princeton University Press, 1969), pp. 261–98. I am indebted to Professor Douglas for some of my distinctions between the traditional conservative and enlightened humanist views of vocation.

3. Robinson, *Apostle of Culture*, p. 10.

4. J. Lyndon Shanley, *The Making of "Walden"* (Chicago: University of Chicago Press, 1957), p. 127.

5. For word frequencies in *Walden* the reader should consult Marlene A. Ogden and Clifton Keller, *Walden: A Concordance* (New York: Garland, 1984), and J. Stephen Sherwin and Richard C. Reynolds, *A Word Index to "Walden"* (Charlottesville: University of Virginia Press, 1960). This index has been reprinted, with a brief supplement of corrections, in *Emerson Society Quarterly*, no. 57 (Reference Book II 1969): 1–91.

6. See CSmH HM 924. Although Thoreau used the same paper for the Concord lecture material and the rest of the first draft of *Walden*, he also used the same paper at several other times to draft clearly later material. The kind of paper used by Thoreau, therefore, is not evidence of a single compositional process. The independent sequence for the leaves that were to become "Economy" runs 1 to 51. Leaves 31 recto to 35 verso appear to be redrafts of preliminary worksheets. At least twelve leaves, including most of the concluding pages in this sequence, were subsequently added, probably when Thoreau began to work toward a functional linguistic and thematic transition from the lecture manuscript to his growing Walden account. There is considerable evidence that these latter pages were written later. For one thing, 35 verso is only partially filled and appears to have been the conclusion of this material at one stage. The next page is an afterthought, a more extensive and poetic conclusion to substitute for the conclusion already drafted. The handwriting and ink of page 36 verso strongly suggest another stage of drafting. Moreover, about a fourth of the way down this page Thoreau wrote largely and boldly, "End of Economy," which he followed with a heavy period in the shape of a "v," an indication that he brought his pen nib down hard, as in a gesture of finality. At some later date, however, he added two notes to himself as directives on possible additions for the conclusion of this section. These notes are separated from the rest of the text on the page and from each other. Neither is followed by punctuation.

Whether Thoreau added this lecture material (on what was to become "Economy") after he had completed his first draft of *Walden* or a substantial part of it cannot be ascertained.

7. Citing Thoreau's description in the first version of *Walden* of the mist-shaped Pond as an example of his evocation of an idyllic, timeless state, Thomas Woodson offers an instructive observation: in this passage "the emphasis is again on the gradual rhythm of natural unfolding. . . . Thoreau's grammar is loose in reference; the flowing parataxis of '. . . and . . . or . . .' takes control. . . . But most important is the sense of auroral revelation as mythical and timeless, absorbing the primitive past into the present moment"

(Woodson, "The Two Beginnings of *Walden*: A Distinction of Styles," *ELH* 35 [September 1968]: 448).

8. CSmH HM 924. Passages from worksheets (HM 924) are reproduced by permission of the Huntington Library, San Marino, California.

9. CSmH HM 924.

10. Shanley, *The Making of "Walden"*, p. 182.

11. All passages from the fourth and fifth versions are from CSmH HM 924.

12. Nathaniel Hawthorne, "Preface," *The Marble Faun*, ed. Roy Harvey Pearce et al. Vol. 4 of *The Centenary Edition of the Works of Nathaniel Hawthorne* (Columbus: Ohio State University Press, 1968), p. 3.

3

Comparative Demands

The principal successor to *Walden*'s concern with enterprise, economy, and the art of life, is Thoreau's "Life without Principle." "Ah,
how I have thriven on solitude and poverty!" Thoreau entered in his
Journal as he prepared himself to write his first completed literary
work after seeing *Walden* through press. "I cannot overstate this
advantage. I do not see how I could have enjoyed it, if the public
had been expecting as much of me as there is danger now that they
will" (1906 J 7:46). The work he was about to commence was the
drafting of his first version of "Life without Principle," a lecture
that he liked to refer to by the title "What Shall it Profit" or "What
Shall it Profit a Man."[1]

Thoreau began "What Shall it Profit" in October 1854, drawing
heavily on his Journal of the last four years. A recent entry in his
Journal provided him with his germinal passage, one that echoes
the language of vocation and self-culture in *Walden*:

> The lecturer must commence his threshing as early as August, that his
> fine flour may be ready for his winter customers. The fall rains will make
> full springs and raise his streams sufficiently to grind his grist. We shall
> hear the sound of his flail all the fall, early and late. It is made of tougher
> material than hickory and tied together with resolution stronger than an
> eel-skin. For him there is no husking-bee, but he does it all alone and by
> hand, at evening by lamplight, with the barn door shut and only the pile
> of husks behind him for warmth . . . and he goes to bed happy when his
> measure is full. (1906 J 6:486–87)

The New Testament Gospel of Mark (8:36) furnished him with topic, title, and opportunity for language play: "What shall it profit a man if he gain the whole world, and lose his own soul?" One synonym for the Greek word for "soul," Thoreau knew, was "life." In reworking the lecture over the next several years he incorporated more recent Journal passages. In 1859 he prepared a new lecture version, for which he drew from his Journal of 1855–59. He also referred to his lecture by a new title, "Life Misspent," a title that retained the moral/economic nature of his earlier title but dispensed with the biblical quotation and the appearance of a text for a sermon.[2]

Thoreau's carefully chosen titles for his lecture versions of "Life without Principle" accurately reflect the keynote of these addresses, "profitability"—the comparative profitability of gaining what in the opinion of many Americans is both much and most desirable and of gaining what to most is undesirable but which to the economist of higher economic principle represents the irresistible voice of plenitude. Both "What Shall it Profit" and "Life Misspent" feature comparative demands concerning labor and investments well spent and misspent. The reciprocal annoyance of Thoreau and his Lyceum audience over his address in Concord on "What Shall it Profit" probably had something to do with Concord's continuing participation in the national economic transformation. More germane to the negative reception of the lecture, however, was Thoreau's own development and the content of his lecture. By the mid 1850s his views on American enterprise had become increasingly negative and unyieldingly oppositional. Moreover, "Life without Principle" and its lecture versions feature a more directly contestatory approach than *Walden*, a strategy wherein comparative demands are placed in an opposition in which Thoreau's demands sharply contest the demands of cultural belief and practice and in jeremiadlike fashion call for a cultural renewal.

It is as though in turning to his new writing project Thoreau was looking for a way to take up the challenge of the morally suffused McGuffey *Reader*, since the 1830s America's passport to literacy, and thereby to raise the intellectual, moral, and linguistic ante of literacy (including economic literacy) of the champions of business enterprise, most of whom had learned their reading through McGuffey. In calling into question the current craze for profit, the

Reader invoked the piety of the forefathers and elders discredited in the "Economy" chapter of *Walden*: "If in our haste to be rich and mighty, we outrun our literary and religious institutions, they will never overtake us." A similar moral vein is mined on another page: "Can we not so order our habits, and so fix our principles, as not to suffer the luxuries of our days to choke, and strangle, with their rankness, the simple morality of our fathers' days?"[3]

In his way, and very much in the mid-nineteenth-century American grain, Freeman Hunt had taken up the same challenge. For him the simple pieties of both the fathers and the McGuffey *Reader* were a point of departure. One did not repudiate them; one merely went beyond them. Hunt, owner/editor of perhaps the most widely read and highly respected American business serial in the forties and fifties, assured his readers that despite the many manifestations of greed and narrow self-interest, the impulses of modern America and the traditional republican and Christian teachings by which he had been reared could be reconciled. His magazine, as well as his books *Worth and Wealth* and *Lives of American Merchants*, unabashedly celebrates virtuous private enterprise while acknowledging the importance of moral character and ethical practice. A man who professed education, civilized refinement, moral sense, and religious belief, he expressed regret over the fact of life in the new American society that "gradations of social position are measured by stock-certificates, rent-rolls, and bank accounts." A New Yorker, he sought to challenge the powers in his city with the power of his position when he warned against "the really wicked personal extravagance, which at present forms the most prominent social feature of our Eastern cities." Because the extravagant and fashionable are becoming role models of achievement, he complained, "they are thus enabled practically to give a tone to society at large." Incessant change of employment in the hope of advancement, blind speculations, and geographic promiscuity encouraged by dreams of sudden wealth were especially repulsive to Hunt. Yet in a typically ambiguous passage he noted that "peculiar vice of our age and country to put a false estimate on the mere acquisition of riches."[4] The weasel word here, as elsewhere in *Worth and Wealth*, is "mere," an adjectival qualifier that allows for acquisition of riches but also leaves an indeterminate amount of room for talk of private virtue and public responsibility.

Not surprisingly, Hunt argued that the same scriptural "authority which requires man to be 'fervent in spirit' also commands us to be 'diligent in business,'" a point made repeatedly by the American success manuals for young men, a popular kind of publication in the time of Hunt and Thoreau. "Religion and business, therefore, are both right, and may essentially serve each other."[5] Although Hunt stops short of equating the two, indeed, pointedly criticizes the religion of business, the "Father's business" that Jesus invokes at his bar mitzvah and to which Hunt professes loyalty is somehow tied to American business enterprise, certifying and stabilizing it with a residuary of piety and moral principle. *Worth and Wealth* repeatedly distinguishes between honest labor and speculation, between legitimate enterprise and reckless greed, and between wealth that adorns character and riches that further degrade the huckster. Yet his business wisdom assumes that economic success is ultimately a generative force able to strengthen individual and collective virtue while itself flowing from character and virtue. In his thinking, enterprise, principles of enterprise, and principled enterprise are conflated.

Contrary to Hunt and many of his contemporaries, including most Concordians, the Thoreau of the post-Walden years rejected the doctrine of economic progress that linked the special destiny of the children with the piety of the fathers by means of the economic enterprise of the present. Such a cultural teleology was, to his way of thinking, a rationale for enterprise without principle, by which he meant the getting of a living without the economy and "*extra vagance*" of the higher economic/moral law that governed his view of vocation and that helped him to define and continuously redefine his career. Like Hunt, however, he readily employed the vocabulary of *free labor* for his observations on worthy and unworthy enterprise. He appropriated the current terminology of *free labor* from political economy, politics, and Northern trade and commerce to justify his practice of vocation and to criticize Northern and New England economic preoccupations and values.

I

By the time Thoreau published *Walden* and began to draft "Life without Principle," "free labor" theory and idiom were associated not only with laissez-faire principles of production, distribution, and trade, but also with slavery and the issue of forced labor. In appropriating the terminology, therefore, he transformed for his own purposes a concept and terminology that by the early 1850s had become attractive to Conscience Whigs and Free Soilers and that soon became the core of the thinking of the new Republican party. Republican ideologues characterized their society as tied together by edifying labor relationships of autonomous, enterprising citizens, all citizens performing their freely elected labor for personal profit and social progress. Through these relationships between free laborers and various kinds of free labor, the individual would satisfy his or her economic, moral, and social needs. Moreover, wholesome cultural values would be promoted, and collective intellectual and moral progress would be a concomitant of economic progress.[6] Thoreau's opinions in the 1850s on enterprise and the views of "Life without Principle" recall but also go beyond the demand in "Reform and the Reformers" for "pure labor" and the unorthodox application in the second paragraph of "Resistance to Civil Government" of the newly popular doctrine of laissez-faire economics. Although Adam Smith's views (which Thoreau admired), other modern definitions of free labor and marketplace, and Concord's rejuvenated economy appear to be at stake in the opening paragraphs of "Resistance to Civil Government," what is more fundamentally at stake is the desire and right of the speaker to cultivate his life without interferences. Thus the freedom at issue in his castigation of legislators who create a dangerous road for trade and commerce (like felons who place obstacles on the tracks in order to derail the train) is the condition that permits him to practice self-culture and to develop his vocation outside the power of any attempts narrowly to confine either. The argument on freedom and free labor culminates in the well-known declaration, "If a man is thought-free, fancy-free, imagination-free, that which *is not* never for a long time appearing *to be* to him, unwise rulers or reformers cannot fatally interrupt him" (*Reform Papers*, p. 86). What has been written of Thoreau in another context is particularly applicable here; the speaker of "Resistance to Civil Government" seeks to articulate a "moral and esthetic counterpart of the ideal free entrepreneur."[7] In order for the "laws of nature" to prevail in economic life, barriers in production, distribution, and trade would have to be removed. In "Resistance to Civil Government" and, for that matter, in *Walden*, Thoreau appropriated this "let-alone" principle as a law of vocational definition and practice. The activities of the speaker should constitute labor free of any form of peonage or coercion and should be governed solely by the demands of his vocation.

In the 1850s, this understanding of "free labor" still served Thoreau as a basis for observations on worthy and unworthy forms of enterprise. Cape Cod fishermen, for example, exemplified the principle of free labor. By freely elected and economical means they got much life while getting a living. The narrator admires the citizens of Provincetown for their alliance with nature in their efforts to produce and consume the necessaries of life. In this strategic point on the highways of enterprise, where hundreds of boats ply the harbor waters on a normal day, swamps are turned into cranberry meadows at minimal cost of money, labor, and natural alteration, and seamen may be found fishing for turtles in the freshwater ponds. In the winter Cape Cod fishermen do "nothing but go a-visiting, sit about and tell stories,—though they worked hard in summer. . . . Almost every Cape man is Captain of some craft or other,—every man at least who is at the head of his own affairs."[8] Those affairs, described with affectionate detail in *Cape Cod*, contrast sharply to the mean and sneaking lives anthologized in *Walden*, whose guidebook wisdom depends on its contrast between the narrator, a master of many occupations and captain of his vocation, and the desperate and complaining mass of men, who cannot understand what it is to be in charge of their own affairs, and who cannot comprehend that "a man is rich in proportion to the number of things which he can afford to let alone" (*Walden*, p. 82).

Although Thoreau did not abandon his laissez-faire principle, a shift in emphasis in the 1850s, evident particularly in a work like "Life without Principle," suggests another version of his free-labor principle, one that served as basis for his noticeably more negative critique of his society. The language of slavery and freedom in *Walden* represents a different appropriation of free-labor terminology, one that complicates the argument of *Walden*, sounds a note recurrent in Thoreau's writings of the 1850s, and reminds us of the rapidly increasing cultural tensions that tested the political and economic stability of the nation and threatened its survival. Reformers in the North had transformed free-labor language into a sociopolitical platform of free individual and corporate enterprise and abolition of slavery, the twin guarantors, it was presumed, of a free government and free institutions. Since all labor is work performed for one's own living, another's profit, or both, free labor, the argument went, resists exploitation of the laborer and rejects forced labor. Furthermore, free labor promotes individual enterprise and character rather than class differentiation. One might say, then, that the free-labor doctrines of the first generation of Republicans represented a jerryrigged (anti-South) effort at restoring a moral dimension to economic vernacular and practice.

"Chesuncook," which Thoreau began in 1853 and published in *The Atlantic* five years later, is an indication of how receptive Thoreau was to the political reformers' new adaptation of the language of free labor. Whereas the desperate entrepreneurs and speculators of *Walden* are depicted as victims of perverse investments and slaves to oppressive labor, the aggressively enterprising Americans of "Chesuncook" are "villains" who "grub" up whatever they can, "poaching on our own national domains." They are the North's equivalent to Southern slave masters, and their villainous enterprise threatens the free labor of others and seriously impoverishes the prospects of these others. In the Maine wilderness, the civilized citizen of Massachusetts, using words "in the ordinary sense, with his ideas and associations, must at length pine there," that is, languish there, or learn the language of the pine. Or he will turn Maine into a Boston and Concord commonplace of high profits while impoverishing others. The land of Lake Chesuncook and Mount Katahdin will, perhaps, "soon be where Massachusetts is. A good part of her territory is already as bare and common-place as much of our neighborhood." And, close to home,

what are we coming to in our Middlesex towns?—a bald, staring town-house, or meeting-house, and a bare liberty-pole, as leafless as it is fruitless, for all I can see. We shall be obliged to import the timber for the last, hereafter, or splice such sticks as we have;—and our ideas of liberty are equally mean with these. The very willow-rows lopped every three years for fuel or powder. . . . As if individual speculators were to be allowed to export the clouds out of the sky, or the stars out of the firmament, one by one.[9]

The legacy of the poachers and grubbers is already becoming clear: exploitation is touted as free labor, material and intellectual resources are wasted, and new patterns of economic dependency and peonage are emerging. Let political reformers pretend to restore the moral to the economic; in Thoreau's view, the prevailing impulses in American life conformed to what Tocqueville had predicted two decades earlier. "When the taste for physical gratification among them has grown more rapidly than their education and their experience of free institutions," the notable French observer of the energetic young American republic had written, "the time will come when men are carried away and lose all self-restraint at the sight of the new possessions they are about to obtain. In their intense and exclusive anxiety to make a fortune they lose sight of the close connection that exists between the private fortune of each and the prosperity of all."[10]

The view of American enterprise expressed in the concluding pages of "Chesuncook" resembles that of "Life without Principle." The attempt by the ideologues of the new Republican party to make vigorous economic progress morally legitimate by uncovering and calling to mind the moral element in economic vernacular and principles and by geographically identifying their moral renovation of enterprise with the North made no discernible impression on Thoreau's convictions, but the moral presumptions of this ideology presented him with an opportunity to transform new reform principles and apply them close to home. Slavery takes many forms, Thoreau was convinced, and slavery was as endemic to Massachusetts as to the South. For this reason, in large part, he refused to countenance the argument of moralists, including a number of transcendentalist and Unitarian ministers and abolitionists of the Northeast, that the economically booming North was reestablishing itself on moral law and that consequently no further compromises should be made with the immoral socioeconomic system of the South.

David A. Wasson, Conscience Whig, radical transcendentalist minister and reformer, skillful defender of transcendentalism in the 1850s and 60s, and acquaintance and admirer of Thoreau, sought to ground the economic doctrines of the Republican party and the North on what he understood as fundamental transcendentalist principles, thus reconciling, indeed melding, Republican moral pol-

itics and "higher law." In the early spring of 1863, this "diligent
writer, chiefly on Ethical and Philosophical themes, on the border
land of theology"[11] and occasional contributor to *The Atlantic*,
wrote a Civil War piece on the morality of economics and the
economics of morality which editor James T. Fields, who had been
holding Thoreau's "Life without Principle" for more than a year,
immediately published in *The Atlantic*. Since Wasson's "Shall We
Compromise?" was, among other things, war propaganda in the
form of a moral tribute to the enterprise of the North and a moral
indictment of economic practice in the South, its speedy publication is understandable. Yet Fields' editorial decision, one suspects,
involved more than the need for high-toned moral justifications of
the Union war effort. Wasson subscribed to the Republican party's
deep commitment to business enterprise, the nation's most important ledger of progress. His article assumes that economic behavior
needs to be suffused by mature moral awareness. He argues, moreover, that such awareness had diminished in the North but had
recently been recovered. Moral awareness, however, is still conspic-
uously absent in the South. Above all, he is certain that the victory
of the North will have a morally renovating effect on American
economic enterprise, individual and corporate, because the reinvig-
orated conscience of enterprise in the North will preside over the
activities of the entire republic.

Wasson's tropes, as much as his declarations, identify him as a
citizen of his era and region. "Shepherds who make compromises
with wolves sell their mutton at an exceedingly cheap market"—this
is his maxim to a readership that is mindful of profit lines. Or, to
switch metaphors, as he does, "Will you sell the elective franchise
itself into slavery, and take for pay barely the poltroon's price . . ?"
To conduct business with the South or to conduct it in the manner
of the South is to "give over civilization to the bowie-knife, with the
mere hope of so making money out of Southern trade." Such a
capitulation is what Wasson's South expects; "so far as we are base
bargainers and unbelievers, they can tolerate us." But to adapt to
the economic policies of the South is to take "stock in human
degradation" and to declare "dividends upon enforced ignorance
and crime." The South has waited for the North to concede, to
announce to the South, "'We submit; do what you will; we are
shopkeepers and cowards; we must have your trade . . .'" Such a

concession would have been fatal to America's economic and moral life. "One step more in that direction, and we had gone over the brink and into the abyss."[12]

A voice for the uneasy conscience in America's muscular economic development, Wasson circumscribed his moral concerns about enterprise by projecting on the South what disturbed him about modern economic practice—enterprise without moral law. By assigning the South the role of scapegoat, he could declare the war to be the supreme sign of a national recovery of economic life with principle. James T. Fields no doubt found Wasson's argument attractive since it supported the war, business, and conscience.[13] "Life without Principle," which would have to wait much longer at *The Atlantic* for its turn, attributes grasping, run-for-luck, amoral economic pursuits to the entire American culture, but particularly to the North and West, the regions of the most vigorous economic activity (the latter identified as a child of New England). The tireless, greedy pursuits cited are depicted as examples of losing one's freedom and life in getting a living, of enterprise without "principle," of aggressive economic activity without any rationale or sanction other than the desires and behavior it generates and reinforces. In "Life without Principle" the demands of such an enterprise are countered with different sanctions and with unlike demands.

II

At a lyceum, not long since, I felt that the lecturer had chosen a theme too foreign to himself, and so failed to interest me as much as he might have done. He described things not in or near his heart. . . . The greatest compliment that was ever paid me was when one asked me what *I think*, and attended to my answer. . . . Commonly, if men want anything of me, it is only to know how many acres I make of their land,—since I am a surveyor,—or, at most, what trivial news I have burdened myself with. . . . I take it for granted, when I am invited to lecture anywhere,—for I have had a little experience in that business,—that there is a desire to hear what *I think* on some subject, though I may be the greatest fool in the country,—and not that I should say pleasant things merely, or such as the audience will assent to.

So begins Thoreau's "Life without Principle" (*Reform Papers*, p. 155). This self-styled economist will join the occupants of the

Middlesex Hotel porch in saying some unpleasant things, unpleasant even to the porch sitters and their proprietary notions about progress. His comments are more unsparing in the final version of the address than in "What Shall it Profit," which does not include the confrontational pronouncement, "As the time is short, I will leave out all the flattery, and retain all the criticism. Let us consider the way in which we spend our lives" (p. 156).

Unlike Emerson in a recent address in Concord on a theme "foreign" to himself and Thoreau, this speaker "will give them a strong dose of myself" (p. 155). The "I" will be everywhere present, and this "I" is thoroughly oppositional. "Life without Principle" is less tolerant than *Walden* of appropriation by means of parody since the assumptions, activities, and language of enterprise have been found to be quite inhospitable to the speaker's vocation and idea of culture. There can be no temporizing with the current spirit of American enterprise or the language of enterprise. If his time is short in the Lyceum hall, the time for the culture is even shorter. "I think that there is nothing, not even crime, more opposed to poetry, to philosophy, ay to life itself, than this incessant business" (p. 156). In one respect, at least, Daniel Roger's allusion to Quixote in his observations on Thoreau is apt: the metaphor of Thoreau shaking a spear "at one of the most formidable windmills of mid-nineteenth-century opinion" features an instructive pun in its equating of "windmill" and prevailing American "opinion."[14]

The polemicism of "Life without Principle" is more a function of its relation to an imagined audience, however, than an uncompromising sword-and-spear attack on windmills. The essay assumes an obtuse reader/listener who should be taken by the shoulders and jostled with a set of unfamiliar demands. Since no coterie of sympathetic, enlightened audience is imagined, the speaker and his language take on an exclusivity, a unique order directly challenging an order that, by its agreement and his, excludes him. His is the voice of principle, and it is presumed to be both superior and normative. In seeking to disqualify the order it opposes, individual and cultural life without principle, this voice is identified with conspiracy, but not a "conspiring with" that the term "conspiracy" usually implies. Indeed, the speaker is fastidious about the kind of belief, language, and practice with which he will associate. His fastidiousness presumably does not include the single-mindedness he imputes to his

audience. He disparages, insults, harangues, cajoles, humors, pro-
scribes, prescribes and, like the prophet Isaiah, is willing to reason
on the basis of his assumptions; but he is not hopeful of meeting
many on his terms. The difference in the respective understandings
of what is meant by getting a living and the difference between the
two when measured on his moral scale leave him no alternative but
to work in opposition, and to expropriate rather than appropriate
that which is salvageable and valuable to him. His oppositional
spirit appears to be inhospitable to "many a 'bran new' theory of life
. . . which combined the advantages of conviviality with the clear-
headedness which philosophy requires" (*Walden*, p. 268).[15] Yet, as
unflattering as the speaker is to his audience, he is more than ready
to talk to those invalided by their belief in the fall of man. He is
ready to reason with them, that is, if they acknowledge that as fallen
people they are prostrate and that they might be willing to get up.

There is nothing roundabout in the propositions of this essay.
The American scene "is nothing but work, work, work" (p. 156).
The panting of the citizens after money is like the panting of the
locomotive that awakens the speaker almost nightly. The speaker
has trouble sleeping because business and commerce about him
refuse to sleep. Tireless pursuit of tiresome employment is based on
the belief that labor will help to regulate life while making one rich.
Such regulation is, in the speaker's view, "the police of meaningless
labor" (pp. 156–57). Yet those who trouble his sleep look on him as
an idler, and in the moral ledger of American enterprise the loafer is
evil, the speculator good. Abhorrence of idleness has become the
ironic cultural emblem for the futility and worthlessness of work
performed merely to make money, and more money. Money is the
omnipresent factor. The notebooks he purchases for the purpose of
keeping his Journal are ruled for dollars and cents. He much prefers
to rule his own Journal. When he enters field notes into these
notebooks, he is assumed to be calculating his wages. Aside from
the money produced by work, there seems to be no way to evaluate
work. Above all, there seems to be no emblem signifying the importance of excellent work, excellent performance in one's work, or the
moral/aesthetic economy in which work gratis or paid for is intrinsic to one's vocation. Yet in his scale of things, work and reward
have meaning only in relation to calling, and humans are called to
elevate the aim of their life, if ever so slightly, and not be "satisfied

with a level success" (p. 161). Unfortunately, the "ways by which you may get money almost without exception lead downward" (p. 158).

The strongest evidence that America is not minding her business well is the lack of useful literature on the subject of getting a living. In the popular press and popular current publications on the subject of getting a living, especially those that offer advice on success, Lord Timothy Dexter[16] and the California gold rusher are American heroes and the mother lodes of California the newest promised land for those eager to succeed. Religion, science, philosophy, politics, and literature offer nothing more memorable than the forty-niners. "It is so hard to forget what it is worse than useless to remember" (p. 172). All of this suggests a lopsided economy, a vigorous production in a system without intellectual/moral investment, and which merely mimics its mythic success figures rather than examining the principles of its economy. "We are provincial, because . . . we are warped and narrowed by an exclusive devotion to trade and commerce and manufactures and agriculture and the like, which are but means, and not the end" (pp. 174–75).

The several successive versions of "Life without Principle" are a record of an increasingly "strong dose of myself" (p. 155), that is, a self in stronger opposition to America's "provincial" and "exclusive devotion." Thoreau registers his culture of enterprise only to resist its power, contesting demands with demands, and increasingly calling on his language and structural organization to conduct his contestatory challenge. The conventional homiletic maneuver in "What Shall it Profit" of announcing a biblical text is set aside and replaced with an imperative that succinctly announces the business at hand: "Let us consider the way in which we spend our lives" (p. 156). The single most important of Thoreau's alterations, however, was his deletion of paragraphs seven to thirty from later versions of the address. The artistically self-conscious, apologia-like passages and the purely additive principle at work in the succession of loosely connected anecdotes in the paragraph sequence present problems for an essay that strives to "come a little nearer to the facts."[17] With the removal of these paragraphs, the paragraph noting "the comparative demand which men make on life" is moved forward from number thirty-nine in "What Shall it Profit" to number fourteen in "Life without Principle." Both deletion and moving forward of elements account for the thematic focus, structural principle of opposition, and the strong wariness that characterize "Life without Principle."

III

Although replete with quotable propositions, "Life without Principle" is not contained or containable by them. Life with principle and life without principle serve as opposites in this essay of structural, rhetorical, and logical oppositions. The contestatory principle that serves as the essay's main strategy is explicitly named as the "comparative demand which men make on life" (p. 161). This "comparative demand" identifies the structuring principle of the essay, in which a key assumption is that the American culture of enterprise has no such structuring principle. "The ways in which most men get their living" indicate "mere make-shifts, and a shirking of the real business of life" (p. 162). The essay is an intricate play of opposition in which the contrast is invariably reciprocal. Juxtaposition and opposition explore the "comparative demands" of the essay, but opposition is also a feature of the makeshift school of thought with its popular, makeshift ways of getting a living. The assumptions, language, and conduct of the mass of enterprising Americans contradict themselves as well as the speaker's values.

Two finishing schools offer admission to the speaker. Speaking for himself and his address he declines the offer from the most popular school: "I prefer to finish my education at a different school" (p. 157). Two schools of thought, two kinds of students, two ways of finishing one's education and oneself serve as actors on this stage of contradiction. By means of the processive and constantly shifting reciprocity of oppositions or contrasts in the early pages of the essay (155–61), the two schools of living are introduced.

Neither of the opposing schools can be singly or unequivocally named. Their significance issues from difference, from an ongoing contrast by means of accumulative and shifting illustrations. The saunterer in the woods is antithetical to the speculator who shears off those woods. The surveyor's angle of the speaker is at odds with a surveying merely for money or for the enlargement of one's land by questionable means and degrees. The confusion of "good" and "well" in the vulgate of the nation of enterprise is unconfused by the grammar and semantics of the speaker, who distinguishes between getting a good job and performing well a certain work regardless of monetary reward. The paradox of having little, if any, mind at stake in one's employment (a condition conceivably helpful to progress in its susceptibility to change) is subsumed by the irony "that a little money or fame would commonly buy them off from their present pursuit . . . as if activity were the whole of a young man's capital" (p. 159). This condition, in turn, is contrasted, by means of a new metaphor, to the speaker's vocation as seaman and the several ports of call in his unusual voyage. Part-time labors that furnish both a livelihood and the opportunity of "minding *his own* business" are ledgered opposite the industrious man consuming his life in trying to get a living, the speculator selling "inefficiency to the highest bidder," and the plight of the individual of inherited wealth who is not born rich into this world but is "still-born" (pp. 159–60). The school of obsessive, money-making enterprise finishes (closes off) life; the speaker's school of life with principle finishes (matures and completes) the individual. The "money-making fellow in the outskirts of our town," an industrious man admired in Concord for his enterprising ways, is "undertaking" a new land stabilization project along the edge of his wet-lands, a project designed to yield substantial profits yet no more recommendable than "many an enterprise of our own or foreign governments." The speaker is devoted to labors "which yield more real profit, though but little money" (pp. 156–57).

The mutual oppositions of the two schools of the essay are confusing only to those who practice life without principle, but then these people are confused in any case. Thoreau's grammar lesson on "good" and "well" (p. 159) is a case in point: one should expect these terms to be confused in the vernacular of American enterprise. And one should not be surprised that the speaker's entries in a private journal notebook are confused as calculation of wages. Nor is it odd by Concord's demands that the town's moral and economic equivalent of Timothy Dexter has sought to develop a pretentious estate but has turned it into a clutter that aptly registers his intellectual and moral confusion. And his maneuvers in bankruptcy courts are an indication of his financial confusion. Although not a contradiction in terms, life without principle is the source of much contradiction and, under the scrutiny of the speaker, is itself thoroughly contradictory. Many of the aphoristic statements and series of such statements within a paragraph serve a repetitive and additive function in demonstrating the inherently self-contradictory and confused nature of life without principle. Yet "one would suppose that [practitioners of such a life] were rarely disappointed" (p. 160).

The confused but non-reflective behavior of the popular school is cited as both cause and effect in the speaker's complaint that there exists "little or nothing to be remembered written on the subject of getting a living." The literature on success in getting a living has separated "getting" from "living" and assumed that in addressing the business of "getting" one need not disturb the other term. A typical confusion of means and ends, the speaker notes. Not only has "getting" become identified as the end of "living"; the confused thinking that fails to recognize it as means also fails to acknowledge that means have a way of directly harnessing ends to means, thus determining, defining, and limiting ends. "As for the means of living, it is wonderful how indifferent men of all classes are about it, even reformers" (p. 161). An additional reason why the speaker is full of wonder is identified. In the disparaging statement on the literature devoted to getting a living, the qualifier "to be remembered" reminds the reader that much has been written, that what has been written is not memorable, indeed, is a "nothing," that writers who have been getting a living by writing these nothings are exemplars of life without principle, and that "Life without Principle" can justify itself only if it is more than "little or nothing," and thus a memorable response to the "little or nothing" prolifically published and distributed.

This latest writing on getting a living will contradict the unmemorable writings on the subject of success and put to nought the advice of the supposedly wise authors of these unremarkable writings. Presumptive guides to the enterprising not only have written much counsel on how to succeed in getting a living but also have placed much of their advice under the heading of "wise." Yet the "title *wise* is, for the most part, falsely applied." A rapid succession of nine contrastive questions form and re-form possible yet frequently contradictory definitions of wisdom or of wise advice for those interested in success (p. 162). What emerges from the rhetorical interrogation is cumulative and contrasting versions of wise counselors and foolish counselors presuming to be wise, of make shifts and reliable entrepreneurs, of carefully minding one's business and mindless business, of those well grounded and those who dig where they did not plant.

The metaphor of digging in soil that is not the digger's, another in Thoreau's arsenal of tropes for life without principle, prepares the textual ground for one of his most extended metaphors—the California gold rusher, one of the "inviting and glorious" types in popular lore and literature. This much ballyhooed speculator/hero serves a positive function here only insofar as he, a displaced person, is a notable example of the most powerful impulse in current American culture: "many are ready to live by luck, and so get the means of commanding the labor of others less lucky, without contributing any value to society! And that is called enterprise!" (pp. 161, 162). Unlike the gold rusher, the speaker has not gone "to California for a text." The new national prospect of the forty-niner "is the child of New England, bred at her own school and church." Panning one's luck in an alien ground. Scrambling for pennies. "The world's raffle." Enterprise. Grains of golden sand but intellectual poverty and moral bankruptcy. These speculators prospect "farther and farther away from the true lead, and are most unfortunate when they think themselves most successful" (pp. 166, 163, 165). The play on "lead" reminds the reader that this speaker does not assume himself to be amiss in his signals, or the essay amiss in following them. By contrast, the gold-rush lottery is amiss in presuming to provide the alchemist's secret to success. Panning for gold cannot transform "getting" into "living."

Both principle and life are notably absent from those sources customarily mined as wise advice on success: religion, science, philosophy, politics, and journalism. Especially the newspapers. On getting a living, on what is truly profitable, on whether they themselves are profitable, or on what is memorable, newspapers are unmemorable. People of the present generation, eager for success, "lumber their minds" with "rubbish," and the "worse than useless" rubbish is a presence which, like stories of gold nuggets in California hills, is "so hard to forget" (pp. 171–72).

In the failure of these presumed sources of wisdom, "Life without Principle" can establish its principle of success. Through a series of contrastive semantic and moral maneuvers with terms important to both schools and their comparative demands, for example, the speaker can reclaim these terms, making them serve legitimate demands, demands lumbered with principle. Like speculators who use the property of others for their own purposes, and like miners who dig in alien soil for personal gain, he expropriates for the purpose of his address terms that are public property, but which have been devalued and inefficiently employed by an age of enterprise without principle. I have in mind a number of terms deployed in the first part of the essay (on "the comparative demand which men make on life") and the demands made on these terms by the essay as a whole: terms such as "get," "living," "undertaking," "enterprise," "industry," "work," "labor," "toil," "services," "money-making," "wages," "pay," "income," "money," "stock," "capital," "profit," "interest," "bankruptcy," "valuable," "serviceable," "mind," and "minding." Words can be organized by principle, and made valuable by the principle while enhancing the value and serviceability of the principle.

The oppositional strategy and its redefinitions of failure and success are also featured in structural juxtapositions. Usually, the opposition features a juxtaposition in which a manifestation of enterprise opposed by the speaker is cited first. The speaker initiates his litany of contrasts with two paragraphs dominated but not exclusively controlled by examples of the opposing school. The third paragraph, on the other hand, is headed by an example from his school. Successive paragraphs are headed sometimes with an example from one school, sometimes with the other. Moreover, the degree to which the opposition is present and makes its presence felt varies from paragraph to paragraph and contrast to contrast. The effect in these pages is not that of a definitive ledger or a series of symmetrically arranged, precisely consistent and additive versions of a single paradigm but of a clarifying juxtaposition, a process of ongoing contradiction and reciprocal definition.

Juxtaposition and reciprocality serve as the principle of organization within each paragraph that follows upon the imperative presented politely as an invitation: "Let us consider the way in which we spend our lives" (p. 156). They are also the principle of organization and relation between and among paragraphs. The first paragraph following the invitation introduces the "comparative demand" and registers considerable exasperation over the fact that the demands he makes on himself, and makes in this address, are not only interrupted but also effectively opposed by the demands of "this incessant business." The next eight paragraphs conduct a comparison and contrast of opposing ways of spending one's life. The second paragraph in this drama of opposition begins with an example whose logical relation to the conclusion of the preceding paragraph is indirect but whose link to the opening sentence of the preceding paragraph is direct since it offers a specific example of that opening pronouncement, "This world is a place of business" (p. 156). Except for that linkage, the paragraph has a self-contained, independently finished quality, and thus represents a unit whose borders separate rather than unite it with contiguous paragraphs. It seems to be as randomly related to the paragraph that follows as to the one that precedes it—we shift from the speaker's declaration that he prefers to finish his education at a school unlike that of the "boisterous money-making fellow" to the new topic sentence, "If a man walk in the woods for love of them half of each day, he is in danger of being regarded as a loafer." The brief paragraph that follows contrasts this walker to lumber merchants and a town whose interests coincide with the lumber merchant. Then comes another rather abrupt shift with the beginning of another paragraph: "Most men would feel insulted, if it were proposed to employ them in throwing stones over a wall, and then in throwing them back, merely that they might earn their wages" (pp. 156–57).

Yet, to regard the shift from the paragraph on the boisterous moneymaker to the one that follows it or from that one to the next one as an unfortunate rupture would be to impose on the "comparative demand" of this essay rhetorical and logical demands that reduce the oppositional principle of the essay. Life with principle and life without principle are mutually resistant, indeed, discontinuous. The issue for the reader is what to expect from a thematic antilogy that insists on incompatibility and that raises questions of relation only to subject them to the contestatory nature of the antilogy. Thus the division between one paragraph and another (and not infrequently between contrastive elements within the paragraph), the connections between topic sentences, and the ties between alternate and even more widely separated paragraphs all indicate a dual principle of relation, repulsion and attraction or the discontinuous and the continuous. This structure of oppositions, of which the speaker himself is quite aware, rejects the assumption in traditional dialectic that opposition is the means to a synthesis that accommodates the comparative demands and proceeds beyond them.

Thus opposition rather than continuity and reconciliation is the impression created by the shift from one paragraph to another. On the other hand, since the antilogy features two schools of life, paragraphs whose propositions, examples, and word plays are devoted largely to the articulation of one of the two orientations are related to each other. The paragraphs beginning, respectively, "There is a coarse and boisterous money-making fellow" (p. 156), "Most men would feel insulted" (p. 157), "The ways by which you may get money" (p. 158), and "It is remarkable that there are few men so well employed" (p. 159) have a common bond in that their main accomplishment is to present a contradiction-filled picture of life without principle. They form a sequence of sorts, even though, with one exception, they are alternate paragraphs. The paragraphs beginning, respectively, "If a man walk in the woods" (p. 157), "The aim of the laborer should be, not to get his living" (p. 159), and "The community has no bribe that will tempt a wise man" (p. 159) are similarly related to each other by likeness (articulating life with principle) and to intervening paragraphs by opposition. This oscillation not only shifts the focus back and forth in the contrast of comparative demands but implicitly underscores the moral argument that life with principle has a coherence and integrity, that it is what one should always return to if one has been separated from it, but that the division between the comparative demands is so profound as to raise the possibility of no return.

The play of opposition is an index of how and to what extent Thoreau has stacked the deck in the moral dealings of the speaker. In claiming principle, the speaker can claim moral integrity for his position, and the integrity of moral law gives his position the upper hand. The many questions punctuating the essay do not question principle or the possibility of living life with principle; rather, the questions serve to define principle while issuing rhetorical and moral protests against life without principle. Illustrations participate in the same process as the interrogation—to offer hints and examples that answer questions in behalf of principle and resist answers that the culture considers requisite. Although principle is never precisely and essentially defined, the essay provides numerous hints about interpreting its meaning.

Thus, the term *principle*, which like its earlier version *higher law* is rooted in a metaphysics of transcendence, is constituted, reconstituted, and above all certified by personal and cultural experience. The forces that prompt and organize the oppositions of the essay are forces at work in Thoreau's America, forces that prompt the indirect question at the outset of the essay of how "we spend our lives," a query that initiates the comparative demands of the address. Many fragmentary answers are provided to the question of how we spend our lives and its concern to know which of these ways represent principle and thus are connected by principle. The answers do not add up to a comprehensive and definitive clarification but to a contest of communications, the one representing the speaker's economics and the one issuing from America's frenetic enterprise.

The "same ear is fitted to receive both communications," the speaker advises his listeners. "Only the character of the hearer determines to which it shall be open, and to which closed." Immature and parochial persons live by "the profane and stale revelation of the bar-room and the police court" (pp. 172–73). There are "those who style themselves statesmen and philosophers who are so blind as to think that progress and civilization depend on . . . the activity of flies about a molasses-hogshead." Yet rum will not draw out the best in the mind and "artificial wants" will not draw out "the great resources" of the culture (pp. 176–77) and what is valuable in its "communications." Nor will the rum trade, or any other such lucrative enterprise. What these have drawn out is unwariness, a non-reflective willingness to be "profaned by the habit of attending to trivial things," or (to join the speaker in drawing in another metaphor) to be so leveled and paved in one's mind that the wheels of America's culture of enterprise can roll over it without friction. The popular culture is quite capable of macadamizing "our very intellect," as reading "the Times" confirms: both the one who reads "the Times" for wisdom and the content of "the Times" have been leveled and paved (p. 173). There is a lack of "wariness" on all sides; wariness requires attentiveness on all sides.

The alternative proposed by the essay, and offered as its last definition of principle, is "wariness and devotion to reconsecrate ourselves, and make once more a fane of the mind" (p. 173). Wariness is not identified with protest, opposition, better advice, or fuller hearing as such; rather, it is presented as the principle underlying these, the condition for discriminating between different kinds of "communications," for drawing out the several kinds of implications, for drawing conclusions, and for making decisions. The speaker, himself an example of the wariness he recommends, draws out the resources of the term "wariness." In urging wariness, he calls for circumspection, that is, attentiveness on all sides to circumstances and demands. But this exceedingly wary speaker and essay also urge the importance of being on one's guard against deceptions and mistaken conclusions. Attentiveness, then, also carries with it the idea of vigilance—a watchful mind opposed to being assimilated by the culture of enterprise and appropriated for its purposes. Since one of the meanings of the term wariness is the well-considered person, the wary speaker will not allow that potentially narrow meaning to be warped out of shape by the culture. Only well-considered judgments can certify a well-considered person. Wariness means to be on guard, but also to be an effective guardian of one's mind, as the speaker pointedly notes in his prescription of the remedy for his culture (p. 173). Thus his resourceful definition of "wariness" draws in a meaning still found in nineteenth-century usage but already somewhat archaic in Thoreau's time: wariness as watchfulness in expenditure, thriftiness, and circumspection in one's economy.

Although most Americans are unwary and do not hear what they are capable of hearing, the speaker's appeal to wariness is based on several assumptions that justify the writing of "Life without Principle." First, the life of the mind is not moribund in America. Second, wariness has transformative power. Third, wariness is capable of opposing cultural siren calls and clearly hearing the communications of life with principle. "Life without Principle" offers the reader both communications and the wariness to deal with them. Listeners whose minds have not been "permanently profaned" will recognize the incompatibility of the two communications in the essay and within themselves. Moreover, they will identify one as life with principle and the other as cultural "conventionalities" which are "at length as bad as impurities" (p. 173). Conventionalities are assimilated at the cost of the mind; they must be resisted by the wariness recommended and exemplified by the essay.

Whereas the source of the speaker's resistance is wariness, its basis is his principles of economy as distinguished from the culture's conventions and his sense of the intellectual/moral disparity between the two. Thus everything associated with convention is weighed by the scale of the essay, in which principle is the weight on one side of the balance. Virtually every paragraph becomes a weigh station; even near the end of the essay we see the speaker at the scales: "What is called politics is comparatively something so superficial and inhuman, that, practically, I have never fairly recognized that it concerns me at all." Or, later in the same paragraph, "as I love literature, and, to some extent, the truth also, I never read [newspaper] columns at any rate. I do not wish to blunt my sense of right so much" (p. 177). What he represents as a contest between conventions and "true culture and manhood" (p. 174) is a confrontation between conflicting assumptions and values. We observe him warily identifying conflicting claims and practices and making moral choices. The authority of unquestioned rightness that accompanies his position, especially his call for wariness, does not conceal the fact that he is choosing between relativisms. On the other hand, the nature of the contest does not invalidate his choice. Wariness, he is convinced, will empower those not completely macadamized by their culture to distinguish between character and manners, freedom and slavery, metropolitan awareness and provincial culture, vocation and moneymaking, "the gizzard of society, full of grit and gravel" and a dyspepsia-free opposition to that grinding, "*eu*peptics" and tellers of "bad dreams," economical demand and "exorbitant demand," principle and the "lack of high and earnest purpose" (pp. 173–79).

IV

The demands of his address, the speaker of "Life without Principle" recognizes, are as exorbitant to the dyspeptic champion of American enterprise as the demands of that enterprise are to the speaker. His principle of wariness will be at least as confusing to the unwary as the marketplace is to the Indian basket maker in *Walden* and at least as unsettling as life in Concord has been to Joseph Hosmer, Jr., who chose to settle in the grit and gravel of the new city of Chicago, and who years later characterized the author of "Life without Principle" as an acquaintance who followed no business and who failed to find a useful place in his culture, who sought specie of real value and died leaving no signs of having succeeded in his quest.

Hosmer's assessment of Thoreau's economics was a sign of things to come. In this respect Sherman Paul's *The Shores of America*, far and away the most comprehensive examination of Thoreau's writings, is typical of the history of Thoreau scholarship: whereas "Autumnal Tints," "Walking," and "Wild Apples" (three of the four essays Thoreau revised on his deathbed for publication in *The Atlantic*) are closely analyzed, "Life without Principle" (the fourth essay) receives a few sentences that by comparison would have to be characterized as perfunctory. In Walter Harding's view, a century of scholarly neglect of "Life without Principle" called for redress. "This essay," he argued, "epitomizes in a few pages the very essence of Thoreau's philosophy. It is his essay on self-reliance, and asks his audience to get down to fundamental principles. . . . It is pure Transcendentalism, a plea that each follow his own inner light." Yet the most recent biographical study uses dismissive statements to return "Life without Principle" to the traditional scholarly judgment of inconsequentiality: the essay is "largely a negative, Persius-like attack on business. . . . With its biblical text and sermonic tone, it is . . . a jeremiad directed against both the Protestant ethic and the spirit of capitalism." As such, it is "polemical" and "uncompromising"; it has "a new vehemence, a new one-eyed fixity." It is a "diatribe unsupported by his own life and circle of acquaintances." And, finally, the most formal of disqualifications: "the prevailing tone is stiff."[18]

The editorial privilege that Fields of *The Atlantic* invoked with Thoreau's essays was a clear indicator of how Thoreau's views on enterprise would fare in a postbellum America and what kind of Thoreau would be privileged by future scholars. Early in 1862 Thoreau, aware that he was dying, revised for publication and, over a five-week span, mailed to Fields "Autumnal Tints," "The Higher Law," "Walking," and "Wild Apples," respectively. "Walking" appeared that June, about a month after Thoreau had been buried.

"Autumnal Tints" was published in October, and "Wild Apples" in November. "The Higher Law" did not appear until October 1863, and then under another title. Fields had objected to Thoreau's title, and before Thoreau died had negotiated with him on a new one; they agreed on "Life without Principle." Fields' reasons for delaying the publication of "Life without Principle" are not clear, but obviously not only Wasson's piece but also Thoreau's three nature essays took precedence over an essay on the kind of enterprise that "Life without Principle" describes as besetting the minds and revealing itself in the behavior of the American citizenry. Perhaps Fields was unaware that in accepting for publication "Life without Principle" he would be printing the most frequently delivered address of Thoreau's career. Thoreau had presented versions of this, his most concentrated statement on American enterprise, at least eight times, almost twice as often as his other most popular lectures of the 1850s, "Walking" and "Autumnal Tints."[19] The decision of *The Atlantic* and the influential versions of Thoreau that Emerson and Channing subsequently promulgated suggest that the importance Thoreau attached to "Life without Principle" and the hot/cold reactions of various audiences to his lecture versions of this work would have been dismissed by Fields in any case.

In the longer run of postbellum cultural developments, the question of the relative pertinence, accuracy, and moral authority of "Life without Principle" or of Wasson's "Shall We Compromise?," for that matter, was largely moot. Freeman Hunt's arguments were a closer link than either of them to the verdict of the next generation, which left both Wasson's and Thoreau's assessments in the past, as part of a discourse and debate that had had resonance in Thoreau's time but evoked only weak responses in a later nineteenth-century America in which, as prewar signs had presaged, wealthy businessmen displaced ministers, lawyers, and politicians as role models and accumulation displaced maturation as the most pertinent individual and collective end. To be sure, the language of "Life without Principle" contained Thoreau's culture as much as any of his other writings and anticipated imminent developments in his culture more than most of them. Nonetheless, "in this day of wonderful prosperity, when the differences between political parties [were] so slight; . . . when self-interest, the accumulation of wealth, the desire for prominence, the quest for fashion and luxury, [had] full sway over the whole civilized world,"[20] it was difficult for the new generation of Americans to imagine the debate in the 1840s and 50s over the astonishing growth of business enterprise and wealth. It was even more difficult to find pertinence in Thoreau's case for a system of valuation other than that of the gold standard.[21]

Yet Thoreau's words were neither canceled by the emerging economic culture nor reduced simply to signs of the times. The next three chapters acknowledge the pertinence (to *Walden*, Thoreau, literary historians, and criticism) of the speaker's declaration in *Walden* that although time is the stream he goes "a-fishing in," he "would drink deeper" (p. 98).

Notes

1. In identifying "Life without Principle" as an immediate and important successor to *Walden*, I raise some questions about the special status William Howarth has conferred upon Thoreau's "Moonlight" lecture manuscript, a hastily prepared address that Thoreau presented to a small circle of friends in Plymouth and then set aside. Howarth's high view of this essay is based on considerable conjecture about Thoreau's intentions in preparing a lecture on moonlight, deference to the tradition that privileges Thoreau's nature writings, and the assumption that when Thoreau wrote at the end of the summer of 1854 about the threshing on Concord farms and his desire to do his own threshing he was pointing to his "Moonlight" project. Thoreau's Journal talk of threshing is the substance of the first two paragraphs of his "What Shall it Profit" lecture. See Howarth, "Successor to *Walden*? Thoreau's 'Moonlight—An Intended Course of Lectures,'" *Proof* (1972), pp. 89–115.

2. Bradley Dean has ingeniously reconstructed reliable versions of Thoreau's lectures "What Shall it Profit" and "Life Misspent." See "The Sound of a Flail: Reconstructions of Thoreau's Early 'Life without Principle' Lectures," (Master's thesis, Eastern Washington University, 1984), 1:132–245. A somewhat altered version of this reconstruction has appeared in *Studies in the American Renaissance 1987*, ed. Joel Myerson (Charlottesville: The University Press of Virginia, 1987), pp. 285–364. Other titles attributed by Thoreau scholars to the lecture versions of "Life without Principle" are probably misnomers resulting from a confusion between general characterizations of the content of the address by reporters in attendance and the actual program title of Thoreau's lecture.

3. William Holmes McGuffey, *The Eclectic Fourth Reader* (Cincinnati: Truman and Smith, 1837), pp. 57, 129.

4. Freeman Hunt, *Worth and Wealth* (New York: Stringer & Townsend, 1856), pp. 182, 482, 484, 293.

5. Ibid., p. 60.

6. According to Republican party documents in the 1850s, "labor was separate from and superior to capital. Labor embraced the working as well as middle classes and Republicans emphasized mobility from wage-earning to a manner of economic independence—the ownership and management of one's own business. Moving into middle class business was the prime goal of Americans, in this view, and keeping the avenues of mobility open was a prime task of government. Party ideologues stressed social mobility as defusement of class conflict; with abundant resources and opportunity to exploit them, there was no need to take from one class to give to another" (Earl J. Hess, "Liberty and Self-Control: Republican Values in the Civil War North," [Ph.D. diss., Purdue University, 1986], p. 70). From its inception, the Republican party was a strong champion of business enterprise, but prided itself in promoting enterprise with a conscience, unlike Southerners and cowardly Northerners.

7. R. Jackson Wilson, *In Quest of Community* (New York: John Wiley and Sons, 1968), p. 22.

8. *Cape Cod*, ed. Joseph Moldenhauer, in *The Writings of Henry D. Thoreau* (Princeton: Princeton University Press, 1988), p. 203.

9. *The Maine Woods*, ed. Joseph Moldenauer, in *The Writings of Henry D. Thoreau* (Princeton: Princeton University Press, 1972), pp. 156, 155, 153, 154.

10. Alexis de Tocqueville, *Democracy in America* (1835; reprint, ed. Phillips Bradley, New York: Alfred A. Knopf, 1945), 2:149.

11. Octavius B. Frothingham, *Transcendentalism in New England: A History* (1876; reprint, Gloucester, Mass.: Peter Smith, 1965), p. 349.

12. David A. Wasson, "Shall We Compromise?" *The Atlantic* 11 (May 1863): 649–50, 652, 652, 653, 652, 653, 654.

13. In ranking Thoreau's "Life without Principle" below "Autumnal Tints," "Walking," "Wild Apples" and Wasson's "Shall We Compromise?" in publishing priority, Fields was undoubtedly influenced by more than a single factor. Whig loyalty to American business interests had for years characterized the Ticknor and Fields publishing house. On the other hand, as new editor of *The Atlantic* Fields rejected manuscripts from some of his leading contributors (e.g., Emerson and Bayard Taylor) because he did not consider the work up to his standards and theirs. Thirdly, he was sympathetic with the argument of Northern moralists who viewed the South as morally bankrupt and who believed that moral bankruptcy would eventually spell economic bankruptcy.

14. Daniel Rogers, *The Work Ethic in Industrial America* (Chicago: University of Chicago Press, 1974), p. 1.

15. That reference in *Walden* to "'bran new' theory" is, of course, Thoreau's pun on Sylvester Graham's graham-cracker-barrel theories of health and well being, parts of which impressed Thoreau from time to time.

16. "Lord" Timothy Dexter (1747-1806), cited in Thoreau's Journal (21 April 1852) as well as here in "Life without Principle," was born in poverty, received a limited education, and became wealthy in the early federal period as a result of numerous shrewd dealings in depreciated continental currency. He lived the remainder of his life in conspicuous and eccentric affluence in Newburyport, Massachusetts, where he purchased a High Street mansion and engaged a ship carver to make more than forty painted, life-size statues of great personages, including saints, presidents, Adam and Eve, and Dexter. On his statue was inscribed, "I am the first in the East."

17. "What Shall it Profit," ed. Bradley Dean, "The Sound of a Flail," 1:139. All references to "What Shall it Profit" are to Dean's edition of the text.

18. Sherman Paul, *The Shores of America* (Urbana: University of Illinois Press, 1958); Walter Harding, *The Days of Henry Thoreau* (New York: Alfred A. Knopf, 1965), p. 342; Robert D. Richardson, Jr., *Henry Thoreau: A Life of the Mind* (Berkeley: University of California Press, 1986), pp. 332-33. Richardson's characterization of "Life without Principle" as an attack on the "Protestant ethic and the spirit of capitalism" recalls one of the most important studies of Thoreau's economic views, Leo Stoller, "Thoreau's Doctrine of Simplicity," *New England Quarterly* 29 (December 1956): 443-61. Stoller is sympathetic, however, in his treatment of what he regards as Thoreau's unsuccessful years-long effort to reconcile his doctrine of simplicity and the new economic order. Thoreau's critique, in Stoller's view, finally elevates the simpler economic order of an earlier Concord. What Thoreau identifies with, Stoller assumes, is the self-sufficiency of a pre-industrial past. Basing his conclusions almost entirely on *Walden*, Leo Marx espouses a similar view of Thoreau in *The Machine in the Garden* (New York: Oxford University Press, 1964), especially pp. 242-65. I find little evidence to support this oaken-bucket view of Thoreau.

19. On Thoreau's addresses and his presentations of his lecture versions of "Life without Principle," see Walter Harding, "A Check List of Thoreau's Lectures," *Bulletin of the New York Public Library* 52 (February 1948): 78-87; idem, *The Days of Henry Thoreau*; *Reform Papers*, pp. 369-71; and especially Dean, "The Sound of a Flail," 1:5-30. Dean notes several erroneous assumptions and errors of fact in Harding and *Reform Papers*.

20. Alfred T. Andreas, "Women and the Rebellion," *Military Essays and Recollections: Papers Read Before the Commandery of the State of Illinois, Military Order of the Loyal Legion of the United States* (Chicago: A. C. McClurg, 1894, 2:423-24).

21. Although my use of "gold standard" is figurative, it might be observed that after the Civil War America gradually turned to the gold standard in its monetary life, officially adopting it through federal legislation in 1900, after having observed it de facto for some years. Inherent in most of the gold standard proposals was the assumption of real value, as opposed to apparent and substitute value, the equation of specie with real meaning, as opposed to

provisional and relative exchange meaning, and therefore the possibility of a precise and highly stable exchange. The major challenge to the gold standard toward the end of the century came not from people with fundamentally different assumptions but from the silverites, most of them populists and a number of them directly or indirectly tied to silver mining regions. A silver standard was assumed by its champions to be fair, truly democratic, and free of moral corruption. Had Thoreau lived to old age, he would no doubt have contested the assumptions shared by the economists of gold and silver standards and the defenders of literary naturalism. His challenge would have been what it always was: what is real? what is natural? what is equivalent? what is valuable? Each "what" here also implies a "why." For a provocative discussion of several aspects of the relation of "real value" monetary economics to the premises of literary naturalists see Walter Benn Michaels, *The Gold Standard and the Logic of Naturalism* (Berkeley: University of California Press, 1987), pp. 137–80.

PART II

Walden and the Guidebook for Young Men

4

The Young Man's Guide

Some months after the publication of *Walden* George Eliot observed in her laudatory review that Thoreau's book is "animated by that energetic, yet calm spirit of innovation, that practical as well as theoretic independence of formulae, which is peculiar to some of the finer American minds." The most remarkable aspect of her assessment is that it is the only one of its kind in the first generation of notices and reviews. Two decades later Alexander Japp expressed a similar view in his *Thoreau: His Life and Aims*. Thoreau, he proposed, had moved to Walden Pond to prepare himself, "as far as he could, for the artificial conventions on which society necessarily rests." The account he gave in *Walden* reveals a gusto for administering "what Emerson calls 'shocks of effort.'" Yet American readers have regarded Thoreau as a "morbid solitary," and too many Englishmen have either adopted this view or conceived of the author of *Walden* as a "semi-wild man of the woods," one whose rare instincts "made him influential with the lower creatures, but divorced him from human society." Contemporary impressions of Thoreau, then, are akin to the *Walden* narrator's view of Alek Therien, without Therien's gregariousness; and Japp took issue with such a view. "Thoreau," he contended, "instead of being divorced from the spirit of his day, in a special way interpreted it. He would not spend time in trying or experimenting with conventions, which he held had been already sufficiently tested. . . . The teeming wealth of a new and illimitable country must ever, in the outset, oppose itself to the assertion of the individual genius, and essay . . . to break it down to its own level. . . . Society in such conditions in no slight measure exists by the very reaction it breeds. . . . Hawthorne, Emerson, and Thoreau have all used this reaction in favor of true progress."[1] Notwithstanding Japp's narrow and somewhat arcane view of cultural and literary conventions, he and George Eliot, both English, were on to something: *Walden* is marked by its immediate ties to its American cultural milieu and the culture's necessary conventions, its familiarity with and impatience with received conventions, and its independent formulae. Moreover, conventional and independent practice implicate each other and neither is separable from the spirit of the culture.

A century later Joseph Moldenhauer remarked in a study of the rhetorical nature and devices of *Walden* that, among the forms of American literary documents, "sermons, essays, addresses, and exemplary autobiographies" have remained on the margins of critical inquiry.[2] The observation was accurate then and is apt today. No doubt the persisting predilection of scholars to regard such forms as something other than literature or as a lesser kind of literature has something to do with what Japp perceived as a dogged unwillingness to see *Walden* as participating in its culture and the discourse of that culture. In studies of eighteenth- and nineteenth-century literature a similar prejudice against cultural criticism and in favor of particular recent institutional doctrines of literary canon probably accounts for the scant attention accorded the conduct book and one of its popular species, the guidebook for young men. In the history of Thoreau scholarship the prejudice probably accounts for the absence of studies that consider the rhetorical performance of *Walden* for its ideological significance and its links to the guidebook for young men and its American descendant, the success manual. Like *Walden*, the guidebook incorporates features of the sermon, essay, lecture, and autobiography and could be characterized as a compound of these elements. *Walden* is linked to these guidebooks for young men, and the scholar interested in examining the connection will have to follow Thoreau's lead in his beanfield undertaking and cultivate new acres.

The next three chapters track the hints of Eliot, Japp, and Moldenhauer by pursuing several kinds of exploration: (1) the guidebooks for young men in Thoreau's personal library; (2) the emergence of a popular, lucrative species in the publishing enterprise of Thoreau's day, the success manual for young men; and (3) Thoreau's proclivity for parody and *Walden* as a parody of the guidebook for young men, a species of conduct book also known as copy book, and by Thoreau's time, as success manual (in America) and self-help manual (in Britain).

Thoreau recognized that many of the conventions and concepts of the guidebook for young men had been and were being applied in an increasingly essentialist and narrowly profit-oriented way by his culture and its discourse. Precisely therein lay his opportunity—to accept, contest, and reconstitute conventions that could serve several masters. Thus the *point d'appui* of *Walden* is a playful, serious, pointedly ambiguous announcement: "Let us consider for a moment what most of the trouble and anxiety which I have referred to is about, and how much it is necessary that we be troubled, or, at least, careful" (*Walden*, p. 11). To understand the "uncommon success" of *Walden* in these terms—a success that relies at least in part on Thoreau's familiarity with guidebooks for young men and his effort to write another guidebook that acknowledges and displaces aspects of these guidebooks—requires that we examine the genre of the guidebook, especially the works and conventions within Thoreau's ken.

I

Guidebooks for young men were familiar to Thoreau. His personal library included four such works: *Addresses to Young Men* by the eighteenth-century Scottish Presbyterian minister James Fordyce; *Letters Addressed to a Young Man, on his First Entrance Into Life* by the self-educated, popular, and aggressively anti-modernist turn-of-the-century English author Mrs. [Jane] West; *Lectures Addressed to the Young Men of Hartford and New-Haven* by early nineteenth-century Hartford Congregational (Trinitarian) minister and pastor Joel Hawes; and *The Life of Dr. Benjamin Franklin*. The last title is not to be confused with Franklin's *Autobiography* as we know it. The *Life* consists of a section of Franklin's memoirs and a "continuation" (after Franklin's death) by a co-author represented as "one of [Franklin's] intimate friends" (Franklin, p. 82).[3] Thoreau's library also included the British Baptist minister John

Foster's extraordinarily popular *Essays in a Series of Letters to a Friend*, a work of four parts, the first section of which discusses in self-conscious and almost endless literary flourishes the possibilities of writing a book of guidance in the form of a selective memoir of one's growth and maturation for those entering the modern world. Such a moral/aesthetic guide would use an autobiographical mode of address and "first-person superlative" voice as a superior method of instruction.[4]

One traditional literary genre familiar to Fordyce, West, Franklin, and Hawes is the conduct book, which emerged as an important species in middle-class literature and commercial publishing in seventeenth- and eighteenth-century Britain, and which proliferated into several species over these years. One such species of conduct book offered young men advice on general moral principles, religious belief and practice, and, above all, practical virtues, civilized manners, and professional success. These guidebooks usually took one of three forms: a collection of loosely connected essays, lectures, or letters; a more tightly integrated treatise on a range of conventional topics; or a manual of manners.[5]

Certainly the favorable reception of Fordyce's and West's guidebooks in America is not unrelated to the emergence of a similar guidebook as a profitable and widely imitated publication in the United States during the period of initial railroad construction, publishing house consolidations in major eastern cities and Cincinnati, the publishers' development of a national market, and the unprecedented growth of trade and commerce. Many of the economic and cultural shifts in Britain in the latter part of the eighteenth century occurred in different versions in Thoreau's America.

It is not difficult to understand why Thoreau's brother, John Thoreau, Jr., was presented with an American edition of West's *Letters Addressed to a Young Man* in his twentieth year, one suspects on his birthday.[6] (The work probably came into Henry's possession after John died in 1842.) Nor should we be surprised that Thoreau's library included three additional guidebooks for young men and John Foster's *Essays in a Series of Letters to a Friend*. Fordyce, West, Franklin, and Foster could be found in the major circulating libraries of New England, and Fordyce and Foster were listed in the holdings of the Concord Social Library in 1836. Hawes was not as widely disseminated. None of these books appeared on the reading lists for Harvard's approximately 400 students when Thoreau attended college. Not that these books would have been condescendingly associated with the muddy streets and barnyard conditions around the college. These books simply could not be accommodated by an inflexible, rote-learning curriculum of a small number of courses.[7] But the guidebooks enjoyed an infinitely greater authority of presence in the homes of moderately and well-educated families than at Harvard. If the Thoreau family was an indication, the success of the British works in America was owing at least in part to their perceived instructional value in the family. Thoreau's copy of Fordyce bears his father's signature, which is to say at some point the book passed from father to son. And it is quite likely that the parents were the source of the gift of West's *Letters* to Thoreau's brother, John, Jr. All five works (Foster, Fordyce, West, Franklin-Stuber, and Hawes) appeared in numerous editions and, with the exception of Hawes, can be included on a list of perennial strong sellers at that time. The Franklin *Life*, for instance, was reissued by numerous presses during its first decade, at the rate of approximately one "edition" per year. (Additional background information on the guidebook for young men and descriptions of the guidebooks in Thoreau's library are provided in the Appendix.)

More pertinent to Thoreau's experiments in *Walden* than the presence of Fordyce, West, Franklin and Hawes in his library and his society are the topics, voices, and rationales of those guidebooks. The blending in the guidebook of school, church, lecture hall, reading room, and private library is at once literary ploy, religious statement, paternalistic moralist's gambit, and experienced professional's training workshop. Fordyce announces that "partly to impress upon the youthful mind, sentiments of piety and worth, partly to warn it against the mischiefs to which it is most exposed in a state of public manners highly corrupt and seducing, was my chief endeavour" (Fordyce, p. vii). His inventory of "mischiefs" includes "bad companions, bad books, bad fashions, false ridicule, or continual flattery; often from the blandishments of worthless, but artful women; often from the worst examples in the nearest relations; often from rank and affluence; and alas! how often from an education deplorably neglected, or grossly mistaken!" (p. 15). By encouraging and specifying the "intellectual, moral, and religious improvement" of young men, his guidebook will oppose the cynical, "fantastic, effeminate, conceited" forces at work (pp. 15, 75). Transcending the modesty he recommends to youth, the speaker inquires rhetorically and authoritatively, "Have not all the best minds, and most virtuous nations, ever taken a deep interest in the sentiments, tempers, and manners of young men?" Indeed, by paying attention to the intellectual, moral, religious, and social needs of young men, he is merely following the example of "many of the inspired writers" of "scripture" (p. 14). "How deeply society will be affected by the connexions which Young Men shall form, and by the conduct which they shall hold, as they advance, it is not difficult to imagine; nor can it be necessary to prove, that, as the behaviour of individuals in their early days gives for the most part a turn to the rest, so from the character of our Youth in general, we may prognosticate . . . concerning our own times" (p. v).

Just as these passages recall similar pronouncements and rationalizations in West and Hawes, so West's prophylactic program rings true for the others: "My admonitions will not be confined to your present errors, and immediate wants; preventive remedies form a noble branch of medicine; and it is both easier and wiser to preserve the constitution [of the individual and the culture] in a healthful temperament, than to restore it to vigour after it is become diseased" (West, 1:19). Her inoculations against the contagions of a corrupt and diseased modernism come in threes—"economy, industry, and subordination" and (a reconstituted version) "prudence, industry, and good management" (3:349–50). Hawes prefers a simpler and more commonplace classroom metaphor: he will present young men "a substitute in something that shall interest their hearts and minds, and engage them in a course of intellectual and moral improvement" (Hawes, p. 60).

But Hawes' plainer metaphor also reflects a somewhat humbler tone, more clearly defined audience, stronger trust of his readers, and simpler style. In offering young men a desirable substitute he does not devote lengthy chapters to a defence of his enterprise as Fordyce and West are wont to do. He takes for granted not only a conventional rationale of the guidebook for young men but also his rationale for writing his book for particular young men in New Haven and his hometown of Hartford: "I propose . . . to address myself directly to the young men of this community. I feel that in doing so, I attempt a service for a most interesting portion of society" (p. 6). He assumes that "*the virtue and intelligence of its youth—especially of its young men*" (p. 5), are the factors in Hartford and in the new American republic that most favor his undertaking, and that guidebook instruction, if judicious, will confirm that virtue and intelligence. "As matters now are," Hawes observes of New England and urban centers south of it, "our young men of business usually finish their education, at fourteen, or fifteen years of age,—at the very time, when their minds are most susceptible of improvement;—when they are most exposed to temptation, and most need the protecting and guiding influence of judicious instruction" (p. 60).

Hawes' emphasis on the "judicious instruction" of "men of business" and the possibility of continual "improvement" is also characteristic of the Franklin-Stuber *Life*. For example, the speaker reports that he ordered a gravestone cut and inscribed for his parents some years after they had died—a marble marker for which he composed the epitaph: "They lived together with reciprocal affection for fifty-nine years; and without private fortune, without lucrative employment, by assiduous labour and honest industry, decently supported a numerous family, and educated, with success, thirteen children, and seven grand children" (Franklin, pp. 14–15). West's trinity of "prudence, industry, and good management" is etched as theme on what must have been a large gravestone. But Franklin's epigraphic profile—exemplification of honorable individual enterprise in a culture that rewards such enterprise—apotheosizes improvement and the possibility of extraordinary improvement. In the name of the parents' values and example of improvement the son surpasses the parents. "From the bosom of poverty and obscurity, in which I drew my first breath, and spent my earliest years, I have raised myself to a state of opulence, and to some degree of celebrity in the world." And why should a thematically selective and ideologically focused narrative of his improvements be useful? To the extent that his descendants (however one defines his metaphor of family and sustaining bosom) share his interests and accept his theme of improvement, they will "be desirous of learning what were the means of which I made use, and which, thanks to the assisting hand of Providence, have proved so eminently successful. They may also, should they ever be placed in a similar situation, derive some advantage from my narrative" (p. 5).

The translator's choice of the term *advantage* here in rendering the French text (it appears recurrently in Fordyce, West, and Hawes and in later American success manuals) is precise and fitting in the Franklin-Stuber *Life*. In the time of Franklin, as in the time of Thoreau, *advantage*, when understood as a result or effect, carried the general meaning of improvement and the more specific meanings of personal progress, promotion to a position of better circumstances, and pecuniary profit. It also referred to the condition that produced such improvement: the condition of being ahead of others intellectually, morally, politically, economically, and so forth, improved circumstances that in their nature would produce even more advantageous circumstances, and (by then an archaic but not discarded usage) a better place of vantage, that is, a better prospect and, therefore, better prospects.

Why guidebooks should be written (to promote improvement) is a consideration implicated in a more fundamental question: To what end has humankind been formed? In the Catholic and most Reformation catechisms, including the Westminster Confession (the catechism of New England Congregationalism), the cardinal question concerns the end for which man has been created. The formative purpose of the guidebook is to provide a finite supplement to the work of creation; that is, the guidebook serves the rationale of why the guidebook recipient has been created. Creating humankind and forming or reforming the young man share the same purpose—"security" and "glory," to quote Fordyce (Fordyce, p. 17). To what end the human has been created is the unabashed question behind numerous pious assertions in the first four paragraphs of the Franklin-Stuber *Life*. It is also the question that shapes the narrative in "Honest John" Bunyan's *Pilgrim's Progress*, a work that Franklin admired and, in a serious way, parodied for his own ends. Like Bunyan, Franklin appropriates catechetical features (catechetical terms, phrases, propositions, and the rhetorical/pedagogical mode of right answers for basic questions) which a critic, with reference to Thoreau, has described as the conventions of "'the minister, the school-committee,' and even Christ's scheme."[8] The use of the catechism is even more pronounced in Fordyce, West, and Hawes than in Franklin. Questions concerning the nature and purpose of humankind and the guidebooks' ready answers offer a link, of sorts, between theology and social philosophy, timeless verities and particular circumstance, principle and practice, past and present, imitation and innovation, the community and the individual, divine economy and making a living.

In each of the guidebooks the author simply counts on the reader's familiarity with the catechism and tradition, the latter two linked by conventional principles of authority and assumptions about a healthy society. This catechetical bond between guide and guidebook recipient is both acknowledged and used against itself in the first chapter of *Walden*: "'So thoroughly and sincerely are we compelled to live, reverencing our life, and denying the possibility of change. This is the only way, we say; but there are as many ways as there can be drawn radii from one centre" (*Walden*, p. 11).

The instructions of the guidebooks press on their readers rules of living and getting a living which, if followed, promise the security of moral, intellectual, religious, and professional advancement. As West observes, her remedies are offered in the form of "admonitions," which are actually a mortar-and-pestle compound of general assessments and encouragement, helpful hints, specific instructions and illustrations, authoritative imperatives, and censure, all for the sake of the young man's advancement. Admonitions of these kinds are ubiquitous in all four guidebooks and readily apparent in the vocabulary of "rules," "laws," "principles," "precepts," "prescriptions," "proscriptions," "instructions," "experience," "wisdom," "guidance," "advice," "correct guides," dependable "information," "correction," and "improvement." Each offers admonitions in conventional areas and does so with a conventional rationale toward the conventional end of improvement. The guidebook convention of instructing youth does not imply identical assumptions about the culture or the recipients of the advice, identical admonitions, or a uniform mode of instruction. Nevertheless, the convention of instructing youth so as to secure their future invariably calls on a number of shared conventions.

II

The ubiquitous concept of culture-building in Thoreau's guidebooks is itself a major component and definition of *culture*, a term whose meanings include: to subject to culture, to cultivate, to rear, to advance toward maturity, to improve, to refine by education and training. Without its major component of culture-building, culture is seriously deficient; without its major component of education, culture-building is seriously incomplete. Understood thus, education is the chief form of cultivation in the culture of self and society. As one would expect, the guidebooks view education as intrinsic to culture-building and virtually synonymous with it. Consequently, education is a topic discussed at great length. Moreover, the guidebook presumes to be an important factor in that education.

In an era in which literacy was rapidly spreading through the middle class, especially among males, and even into the lower class, the principle of sufficient education was extended to the young man's so-called leisure time, not only in the form of advice on how to use leisure time to one's advantage but also in the doctrine that leisure time constituted an opportunity for further schooling. Reading figured prominently in this doctrine since reading was viewed not as an adjunct to education or an escape from it but as a promising means to moral, intellectual, and professional improvement for the literate. A sign of education was the ability to read; a sign of proper education was the habit of reading profitable books. Fordyce, for example, warns against the intellectually and morally pernicious influence of immoral works such as popular romances and atheistic treatises and the enervating effect of trivial books. West, who devotes two lengthy chapters to the topic of reading, advocates historical literature for its relevance and usefulness to young men, but she also recommends natural philosophy, biography, travel literature, "and whatever tends to elucidate the human character" (West, 1:152).

As for literary art, although the "cultivation of literary taste" will be "a most useful and pleasant companion in your journey through life" (3:125), it is better to do nothing in one's leisure time than to seek after new publications with "insatiable eagerness" (3:124). In West's opinion, an unchecked appetite for the new literature is responsible for "a species of reading which engenders a vicious enfeebling sensibility, and a proud, or, I should rather say, a conceited self-confidence, which stores the imagination with false images and bewildering ideas, but leaves the mind uninformed, and the heart uncorrected" (3:132). Examples in her campaign against scandalous, seductive, bewildering, and enfeebling literature are close to inexhaustible: the sentimental novel, works of courtly love and chivalry, works that entertain "an extravagant admiration of the fair sex" (3:144), Goethe, Sterne, back-to-natural-state authors, politically and socially liberal treatises, atheistical and pagan literature, newspapers, pamphlets, literary criticism, juvenalia, Rousseau, almost anything French, almost everything modern (including the modern novel), and unquestionably everything romantic. Her censures of "puerile" and "garbled compositions" (1:150) are governed not by a wariness of aesthetic literature or aesthetic sensibility but by a desire to elevate certain popular and didactic middle-brow forms to the level of respectable literature. In short, the other side of devaluing much of modern literature while joining her culture in reifying and valuing the aesthetic is the desire to elevate the guidebook both by keeping ends and means in proper relation and by making her guidebook resemble a literary work. Instinctively she knew the formula for co-optation, for serious parody, for reaching and influencing readers who read the kinds of writings she disdained. In this respect she was simply more forthcoming and explicit about the aim of her treatise on reading than were Fordyce and Hawes: to compete aesthetically as well as morally, and above all politically, for potential readers and so to redistribute the power of the printed page.

Hawes' *Lectures* remind the reader that good reading improves "taste," cultivates respect for nature, art, and social order, and creates a habit of using leisure time well. The young man is thus indirectly reminded that in reading Hawes' encomium to good reading he has, in fact, practiced good reading. And Franklin's part of the *Life* concludes with a description of how the protagonist founded a lending library in order to encourage good reading and to make useful books accessible for everyone. Such a reading program is deemed a significant factor in the maturation of a republican-minded people. Dr. Stuber continued the story of Franklin's contributions so as to complete and publish it, thus making it available to readers, including the patrons of lending libraries.

The best educated, to quote West, "are, generally, the most amiable and deserving" representatives of the culture (West, 3:50). The difficulty of defining the best educated is resolved with remarkable ease by the guidebook; indeed, the apparently vacuous generalization provides an opportunity for the speaker to fill areas of deficiency and emptiness in modern education with a substantial and, it is assumed, effective mentor, the guidebook. The guidebook always sees itself both as an alternative school and a finishing school. Speaking with the magisterial plurality of a school principal, Fordyce explicates the relation between his *Addresses* and higher education: "we would not now send you back to academies and colleges, for a system of morality, founded on deep speculation, wrought out by slow deduction, or supported by laborious argument." In fact, "curious speculations, learned inquiries, philosophical disquisitions, or the distinctions of a metaphysical divinity, did not enter into my design." Rather, *Addresses* will commit its students "to the care of conscience" and the "school of Christ" (Fordyce, pp. 20, vii). His advice will conform to universal and uniform moral sentiment, to the Greco-Christian tradition, and to the standards of the principal of all true schooling, Christ. Too often modern education makes men "fantastic, effeminate, conceited" (p. 75).

West, too, seeks both to supplement and replace modern education. If education "is so entirely confined to the aim of becoming a good linguist, that, in ascertaining the derivation of words, the nature of things is wholly neglected, I will own that I do not see how the understanding, the temper, or the heart, can derive any advantage from an accumulation of mere *verbal* knowledge" (West, 3:130). The "advantage" gained in understanding "the nature of things" is partially clarified in a passage that calls on parents and schools to follow the speaker's example in considering "the sphere of life in which [young men] will probably be called to move" and in endeavoring "to inculcate such *habits*, and to bestow such *accomplishments* and talents, as are fit and *appropriate* to their expected stations. A course of instruction thus directed, I call a good education" (3:373).

The education Hawes recommends "for the special benefit of young men" conflates the school of Christ with the practical schooling of Franklin, the "man of business," and urges that these be supplemented with "courses of instruction" established by town and city associations (Hawes, pp. 58, 13). By presenting his *Lectures* as formal public addresses in an "easy and familiar manner" before publishing them as a guidebook, Hawes was using the pulpit as a kind of Lyceum lectern needed in the cultivation of a Christian, republican, and practically skilled American society. His version of "intelligent and useful members of society," however, is notably more conservative than Franklin's, especially in its emphasis on the role of church and society in determining "intelligent" and "useful" conduct and occupations (p. 59).

In the thorough cultivation necessary for culture, distinctions between the topics and the marks of proper education are quite blurred. For example, the cultivation of respectability is a function of education in both respects: it is an important topic in education, but it is also the sign of the educated person. The same is true of terms housed by respectability: manners, fashions, civility, and chastity. To varying degrees the authors seek to ground respectability in immutable principle to prevent counterfeit conduct. By *prevent* I mean anticipate, recognize, and oppose with something better. Here again the aim of co-optation is very much in evidence. West, in her own words, will "define, welcome, and adopt" the "rage of being genteel" (West, 3:53). It is hardly coincidental that her major treatise on reading appears in her third volume, which is devoted to morals and manners. Hawes, like Franklin, understands respectability chiefly as reliability, more specifically a personal reliability that bespeaks *virtus* and virtue while also fostering them in others. "If young men could once be convinced," Hawes moralizes, "that the patronage and favor of the respectable part of the community, and consequently their success in life, depend on their possessing a fair, unimpeachable character, it would have the happiest influence on their morals and habits" (Hawes, p. 61). Hence his advice "to fulfil the duties which you owe to society" while at the same time taking "the most effectual measures to promote *your own respectability*" (p. 27).

One of the preeminent avatars of respectability is chastity. Like other manifestations of respectability, chastity is a condition of true learning, a course in one's education, and a respectable course of action, that is, a sign of the properly cultivated person. As condition, chastity is understood as purity of intellect, moral sense, and aesthetic sensibility. In Fordyce and West the theme of chastity is centered by discussions of chaste love and the passions, "a subject too often treated with levity" (Fordyce, p. 78). Chaste love of the woman and womanly spirituality (for the young man this love is the main sign of his chastity) is explicated by terms such as "purity," "reverence," "respect," "self-respect," and "perfection." As sign and seal of proper cultivation chastity is a synonym for perfection. *Perfection*, in this context, conveys the notion of completion that figures in the Greek term it presumably translates. The chaste person is governed by the highest laws. Fordyce defines chastity by its absence, in the examples of "profligate poets, prostitute novelists, artful debauchees, and ignorant boys" (p. 95). Hawes uses a somewhat similar maneuver when he distinguishes between the "principle of pleasure" and principles of purity, but his discussion of "principles" is governed throughout by his advocacy of an "*elevated*" life based on "*established*" transcendent principles or immutable divine laws (Hawes, pp. 68, 41–42, 54, 65–66). The life of higher laws rejects as "subversive of right" the assumption that "*it is right to do whatever is sanctioned by common usage and public sentiment*" (p. 78). In Franklin higher laws and the school of authoritative tradition are displaced by moral pragmatism and moral utilitarianism, respectively. In its origins, the chastity promulgated by the guidebook is linked with a noble-mindedness strong enough to defend itself in a dangerous modern world; in its effects, it is linked to good health, deserving professional success, and legitimate economic returns.[9]

At the heart of the guidebooks by Fordyce, West, Franklin-Stuber, and Hawes and of their emphasis on education as means to moral culture is the problem of modernism. All agree with Fordyce's call for "intellectual, moral, and religious improvement" in an increasingly complex and dangerous world. In harnessing purpose to key terms and concepts, each guidebook presumes to be doing its part in providing stability in the unstable modern world.

Consider, for instance, the question of the past (ancestors, elders, tradition, the common law of accumulated experience). "If we consult the English history," Fordyce asks with the assurance of one who assumes history to be on his side, "what do we learn there?" (Fordyce, p. 194). He learns that his father, principal of Aberdeen University, was right in recognizing the past as the story of the great Greco-Christian tradition, the western tradition that Fordyce's appeals "to observation, to history, to poetry, to philosophy, to the united intelligence and accumulated wisdom of ages" valorize (p. 39). That tradition, both historical and fabular testimony to "the magnanimity and triumph of conscious worth"

(p. 40), will resist the evils and excesses of the modern age. Not surprisingly, the tradition this Scottish Presbyterian appropriates reveals no tension between Elizabethan England and the Cromwellian Republic but honors both. Like West and Hawes, he calls for "deference," which includes a deferring to "truth." His truth includes the legacy of the more complete Protestant Reformation and, in line with that completion, Presbyterian doctrine. To submit to the "wisdom of ages" is to "choose the good part," and to choose thus is "the only path of security and glory" in this world and the next (pp. 39, 17).

West and Hawes also decry what Fordyce calls "disrespect to authority, to age, to experience, and a contemptuous rejection of wise and pious advice" (Fordyce, p. 283). Although a conservative New England Congregationalist clergyman, Hawes is less sharply censorious in noting "the restless desire of independence and self-control" and a concomitant "disposition to throw off the restraints of parental counsel and authority" (Hawes, p. 36). "With respect to this contempt for prescription, parental authority, experience, or even this insolent ridicule of hoary age," West thunders in contrast, "I defy them to shew a nation or a period of time in which the voice of a father, an elder, a chief, or a priest, was not *listened* to with *reverence*" (West, 3:364). Her announced purposes answer the desperate need to counter the many recent and current publications that "tend to subvert that first principle of order and subordination, on which the very existence of society depends" (1:xviii), to unmask "contempt for all preceding ages," "restrictive authority," and "prescribed forms," and to censure "swaggering self-importance" which is fashionably styled "a free independent spirit" (1:xix).

Predictably, the authoritative past that West invokes repudiates "republican despotism," which she refers to as an "iron yoke" (West, 1:81). The accounts of "the *professed partizans* of democracy" betray that which is being praised by the extravagant and evil defenders of republicanism. "What a strange disgusting mixture! the name of republicanism, and the manners of the haram" (3:333). In contrast, Hawes, who in his encomium to "venerable fathers" (Hawes, p. 7) appears to echo the Anglican West's declaration that "our ancestors deserve the epithets of *brave* and *wise*" (West, 3:365), speaks as a conservative republican and invokes a nonconformist republican past, principally its American version.

Republicanism, zeal for improvement, and success are linked in his thinking as a kind of natural law. He is steeped in a tradition of American conservative republican discourse, in its categories and idiom.

Franklin's narrator is left more "alone with America"[10] not because he lacks a past or must cut himself off from it but because he is a type of the modern mind criticized by Hawes for its presumption "to think and act for itself" (Hawes, p. 36). Although Franklin does not withhold the epithets *brave* and *wise* from some of his ancestors, their bravery and wisdom cannot offer him a program of improvement that he will recommend to his descendants as his own or as suitable for them. This "youngest son of the youngest branch" of a nonconformist family "counting five generations" (Franklin, p. 8) extends the principle of nonconformity beyond the Roman Church or the Church of England and, for that matter, well beyond religion. Above all, he is a committed new-world republican whose version of republicanism is not centered on the Cromwellian experiment for its historical rationale and who vigorously defends revolutionary republicanism in America and France.

Respect for the past and tradition is, for three of the guidebooks, a condition for the building of one's culture, since culture-building is inconceivable without culture-saving. In the face of modernism, in Franklin's case on behalf of modernism, building the culture is the supreme duty of its members. Fordyce identifies the cultivation and invigoration of "moral culture" (Fordyce, p. 31) as the obligation of each generation, an obligation inadequately acknowledged in his time and nation. By *moral culture* he means the nurturing and constant renewing of a morally mature society that, in turn, encourages an individual regimen of self-culture in the service of moral culture. His moral culture is centered by "ancient virtue," not by "modern honour" (p. 33). Indeed, the "ardour of enterprise" will blend untutored passion with vice as easily as with virtue (p. 36). Neither an enterprising spirit nor success is the exclusive property of the meritorious; yet the Christian meritocracy of the wary Fordyce discriminates enterprise worthy of emulation.

While offering similar views, West examines another side (in her view *the* other side) of moral culture: proper manners. In this respect she combines a treatise on moral authority, principle, and conduct with the courtesy book and its code of manners. Her purpose in emphasizing manners, she notes, conforms to other contemporary conduct books: "I am not singular in affirming, that, next to morals, manners is a subject highly worthy of your attention" (West, 3:36). Indeed, "established forms claim your concurrence; if not from that deference of opinion which so well becomes youth, at least from that regard to the means of promoting your future advantage, without which ambition is but a meteor light" (3:37).[11] Hawes, on the other hand, contends that the surest promotion of moral culture is "an *unbending regard to rectitude and duty*" (Hawes, p. 81). Thus he establishes a virtual identity between moral culture and "*established principles of action*" (p. 65). In his view these principles have been established by divine revelation, the wisdom of a duty-minded Protestant community, the practical evidence of individual moral and intellectual advancement, and the record of divine blessing in the realm of "*temporal interests*" (p. 85).[12]

Although as dedicated as Fordyce, West, and Hawes to culture-building, both the Franklin and Stuber narrators of the *Life* find the lexicon associated with "moral culture" problematical because traditional thinking does not adequately acknowledge the culture at hand, especially its most recent traditions, new experiences, and current exigencies. Franklin's narrative presents a persona who learns through doing what his duties are and what rectitude means in a life lived in his time, place, and circumstances. Stuber's narrative continues Franklin's moral line of thought. Without invoking an eternal verity or perdurable tradition to establish his moral lexicon and, for that matter, without defining the term *moral*, Stuber describes the moral activities of his hero.[13] These activities contribute incrementally to the definition of the term *moral*; they also continually re-present in yet another version the meaning of *moral*. In this narrative of definition and redefinition through action, the conventions of the courtesy book and the appeals therein to decorum, politeness, deference, and inducements to civil and generous behavior are particularly serviceable.

Equally important to the *Life* is self-culture, a theme subordinated in Fordyce and West to a social definition of moral culture and in Hawes to the community of the orthodox Protestant faithful. Franklin elevates the theme by presenting self-culture as a crucial means of building a republican culture and as an important end in itself. Both the *res publica* and the *res privata* are affirmed in their own right, yet they are reciprocally linked. Serving as cause and effect in Franklin's affirmation of the public and private order is the reification of the individual and an insistence on the individual's centrality in the guidebook's drama of moral, as of economic, advantage and advancement.[14]

III

Despite the professed aim of these guidebooks of strictly subordinating economic to moral (and in Fordyce, West, and Hawes, religious) considerations and of seeking to cultivate intellect, upright character, and pious heart in the eyes of God and men, the intellectual/moral enterprise is no more free of the economic enterprise than subject is free of object in a transitive verb construction. To pursue the analogy one step further, often the relation of one enterprise to the other is rather like that of interchangeable predicate nominatives on the two sides of a copula verb. The same point must be made about *Walden*, as we shall see. If distinctions are to be made, they must rest on the content of the mutually defined terms, not on the mutuality with its implied identity. Certainly Franklin's and West's treatises on industry and idleness depend on a reciprocal and mutually dependent relationship between the two enterprises. The clearest indication of the interdependence, however, is in the lexicon. The same basic terms and metaphoric expressions serve the discussion of either, and the language of business enterprise is not inappropriate in discussing individual character and moral culture. Consider, for instance, the principle of likeness, indeed virtual identity, at work in a key passage in Hawes: "Character is like stock in trade; the more of it a man possesses, the greater are his facilities for making additions to it. Or, it is like an accumulating fund,—constantly increasing in value, and daily acquiring to itself fresh accessions of stability and worth" (Hawes, p. 109). The shifts in the extended simile could go on and on, of course, confirming both the vigorous strength of business language as general vernacular and its efficacy in discussions of virtue and a healthy culture.

What is clear early on in each of the guidebooks in Thoreau's library is that regardless of differences in reciprocity between guidebook and its culture, all four guidebooks feature a reciprocity between culture as cultivation and improvement as moral, social, and economic advancement. Good nurture and training build and sustain culture. Culture-building is understood as an *enterprise* in the positive sense of that term. Enterprise includes economic considerations, and *oeconomy* is both one of the moral virtues and a practical means of success. As for *success*, it is notable both for its omnipresence as theme and for the reciprocity it assumes among inner (moral/intellectual) rewards, social benefit, and economic advantage. In the various guidebook equations, *enterprise* is a term associated with a cluster of related terms, concepts, and *doxas* that serve as nexus in the equations. For instance, Fordyce, West, Franklin, and Hawes all treat the theme of enterprise in relation to the individual and collective good and note, to use Fordyce's terms, the inner "fortune" and "riches" (Fordyce, p. 102) that come with proper maturation of the individual and the group, the necessity of "oeconomy" and "industry," the importance of both appearance and actual practice of economy and diligence, and the professional and financial rewards of praiseworthy enterprise. Comparatively speaking, Fordyce marks the narrowest boundaries for the ambiguous terms *fortunes* and *riches*; yet even his intellectual, moral, and spiritual meanings slip beyond the purely inner and ideal to suggest economic considerations.

The imperatives to participate in the divine economy and to practice what West refers to as "oeconomical habits" and "frugality" (West, 1:94–95) at times are distinguished by their connection to distinctly different categories and at times are indistinguishable. The less distinguishable these imperatives, the more demystified the divine economy. Moreover, in West and Franklin, and to a lesser extent in Hawes, there is a tendency to link the divine economy and successful human economical practice in a way that detranscendentalizes the former. To offer an example, *extravagance* in West's guidebook refers not to an unwarranted crossing of divine boundaries per se but to "*extravagant*" social and economic expectations and behavior (West, 3:134). As for Hawes, since "the field of enterprise is unbounded" (Hawes, p. 44), the extravagant young man becomes the counter of an economical young man whose discipline includes strict management, limitation, stability, and prudence. The same binarial idea and contrastive argument are crucial to Franklin's *Life*.

Morally sanctioned "oeconomical habits" include the appearance of being economical. "I took care not only to be *really* industrious and frugal," Franklin's speaker confides, "but also to avoid every appearance of the contrary" (Franklin, p. 78). Thus both one's regimen of economy and the rewards of economy will be supported by others if the practice of economy is evident and manifestly proper. West, mindful of the nature of the world in which one must seek success ("in every line of business you must have many competitors"), encourages her son to manage his life so as "to excite greater attention in the minds of those who can assist you" (West, 3:22). The assistance envisioned here is help in one's professional advancement because one deserves the help. It is honest industry that attracts the external assistance so important to "*allowable* ambition" and "*moderate* success" (3:21). Franklin reports in some detail his failure with the politicians and politics of the British Empire in order to argue that reliance on corrupt forms of external assistance is fatal; nonetheless, he welcomes assistance that stimulates moral and economic improvement, and he recounts how such assistance was a factor in the advancement of his several careers.

Guidelines for the improvement of the individual and the cultivation of culture consistently assume a link between culture-building and professional success. "While I thus speak," Fordyce declaims in a passage that has its counterparts in the other guidebooks, "I fancy that I see you shooting up into fathers, masters, men of business, teachers, tutors, guardians of youth, physicians, lawyers, divines, magistrates, judges, legislators, or, to say the whole at once, into useful members of a mighty State, through all its variety of departments, which you may in the progress of life be called to fill" (Fordyce, p. 13). This litany of professions in the opening pages offers a vision that spans his subsequent chapters. One might be called to fill more than one office at one time or in the course of one's life; Fordyce, for instance, professes divinity, pastoral care, and the office of "guardians of youth," the latter ranked with the other noble professions and therefore marked with an imprimatur of some distinction. Presumably the production of his guidebook will perpetuate the highly regarded profession of guardian of youth by encouraging the author in his endeavor and the readers to seek after this profession. But all of the offices in his inventory, if filled by what West calls men of "industry, fidelity, attention," will serve as guardians of youth. Rather than recommend a particular trade or profession, West endorses what for her is the only legitimate "independence," the young man's "ability of honestly providing for his pecuniary wants, of ceasing to be a burthen to his friends, and of obtaining by his own exertions a respectable rank in society" (West, 1:35).

Hawes addresses a similar recipient of and concern with success: "The various departments of business and trust, the pulpit and the bar, our courts of justice and halls of legislation; our civil, religious and literary institutions; all, in short, that constitutes society and goes to make life useful and happy, are to be in your hands and under your control" (Hawes, p. 8). But he also assumes among his readers a somewhat less elite auditory of would-be professionals. To them he announces that "if a young man complete the time of his apprenticeship, or clerkship, with good principles and a fair character, he is made for life. His reputation is better to him than the richest capital" (p. 112). Franklin suggests, however, that one not ignore the importance of capital; his frugality, penuriousness, and prudential investments built up the capital that made possible important professional advancements. Capitalizing on one's opportunities requires capital.

In the lexicon of these guidebooks, *enterprise* and *economy* are terms that imply each other and that touch on every definition and example of success. West and Fordyce repeatedly offer tributes to "diligence," "industry," "labour," and "determination"; Franklin and Hawes add "perseverance," "resolution," and "persevering exertions" to this vocabulary of industry. Prudent "economy," Franklin asserts, is marked by "unwearied industry" (Franklin, pp. 72, 37). And Hawes pronounces that "in the formation of character, personal exertion is the first, the second and the third virtue" (Hawes, p. 96). Lack of this virtue is designated by a nest of related terms, always used censoriously: "idleness," "dissipation," "apathy," "time-killing." The common basis for censure is moral principle; "industry" is consistently described as a "virtue," whereas the "idleness," "boredom," and "profligacy" of what West calls the "lack-a-daysicals" reveal lack of moral development. Conflating practice and appearance in her pessimistic assessment of her son's generation she opines, "honest industry is a virtue that is sadly out of fashion" (West, 3:300). In Hawes' view, industry guards against

"a treacherous confidence in external advantages" (Hawes, p. 97).
Yet the reputation of a young man created by industry *"makes
friends; it creates funds; it draws around him patronage and support; and opens for him a sure and easy way to wealth, to honor
and happiness. . . .* The field of successful enterprise will be open to
you; friends and patrons will rise up to encourage your efforts and
advance your interests" (pp. 112–13).

Hawes' guidebook is replete with language of this kind, notwithstanding his warnings against the pursuit of wealth, which, "to the
almost entire exclusion of other subjects," causes "the intellect and
the heart" to be "shrivelled up to the little dimensions of dollars and
cents" (pp. 45, 46). Although similar lexical and tropic behavior is
readily discernible in Fordyce, West, and Franklin, the business/
enterprise terminology and analogies in the former two are more
limited, more discreet in the sense of modest, and more illustrative.
Yet, while Fordyce's and West's guidebooks undoubtedly are more
representative of British productions of this species in the late
eighteenth and early nineteenth centuries than Franklin's and
Hawes' are, the important consideration here is the demonstrable
fact that in their language in general and moral discourse in particular the two British authors anticipate major features in the two
American guidebooks and that Franklin and Hawes, in turn, pro-
leptically feature major characteristics of the American success
manuals of the 1830s to 1850s.[15]

IV

The success of the guidebook's inculcation of "successful enterprise" depends on how the instruction is received, and the latter
depends on how the speaker is received. Just as Thoreau links the
credibility of the account in *Walden* to the "I"-persona, the fortunes
of the guidebook rest with its persona and the enterprising mode of
the persona with the reader. Indeed, a particular kind of persona
inhabits the guidebooks, a presence linked to the agenda of the
book. As a number of the quotations from Fordyce, West, Franklin, and Hawes have disclosed, the speaker is, without exception, at
least a generation older than the internalized reader, and thus well
on his or her way to being identified with ancestors, tradition, and
the preponderant lessons of experience. Claiming the authority of

an experienced elder, however, might create the impression of a large generational gap between persona and reader, an impression at cross purposes with the aim of finding and augmenting a coterie of young readers. Hence the expression of a familial need to share one's possessions (in this case wisdom) with those in whom one has confidence. Hence also the persona's reminder that he or she, too, was once young and ambitious, that he or she is familiar with the aspirations and pitfalls of the young. Pointedly mentioning one's own faults (Franklin prefers to call them "errata") enhances the credibility and authority of the persona while at the same time bringing speaker and reader into a relationship of close affinity.[16]

Clearly the most striking and compelling quality of the persona is the speaker's mode of address. Within the first few pages, each guidebook identifies and establishes a first-person narrator who presides as narrative center throughout. West's *Letters* feature a circuitous and verbally inflated forty-seven page introduction of third-person address and balanced sentences as though to demonstrate her neo-classical proclivities. Yet in the opening sentence of the first chapter she shifts to a first-person exposition. The significance of this convention of the persona speaking directly and personally will probably be underestimated if one divorces the persona from the guidebook's agenda. What Lawrence Buell has described in another context as "the sense of a persona as opposed to a mere editorial voice" is evident in all of these guidebooks.[17] This "sense of a persona" is a sense (illusion) created not of a life story but of a companionable, autobiographical voice. (In Franklin's *Life* the content is also largely autobiographical in the first section.) Repeatedly invoking the word *character*, the guidebooks depend heavily on a person-as-character in both the moral and dramatic sense of the word *character*. The first-person narrative creates the sense of a distinct, unique, and verbally present speaker whose personal witness impinges on and represents the reader's experiences. Such a persona can be separate from his or her readers yet identify with them, encourage them as a reliable friend yet pontificate over them.

In no case does the persona identify himself or herself by name as the author, but without exception the personae identify themselves as authors in a statement of purpose. As a rule this apologia for one's literary enterprise features both humble admission of inade-

quacy or narrowness and presumption of authoritative information. In the context of the persona's purpose with his or her recipients, these two aspects of the apologia are not incompatible. In
Fordyce the speaker begins his apologia by submitting his credentials: (1) he has already written a guidebook for "Young Women,"
no small task since the "dispositions and manners" of young women
are more complicated and formidable than those of young men;
(2) his addresses to young women received a "generous reception"
by persons "whose judgment I must ever respect"; (3) he has been
encouraged in his new undertaking by "repeated and animating
calls of kindness" from mature and honorable acquaintances as well
as from virtuous young men; (4) he has successfully tested his book
as a series of lectures from the pulpit; (5) he had meant all along to
publish these lectures. His credentials establish his right to the
territory despite the apparently self-deprecating and apologetic in-
flections that "I could add but little to the large stores of moral and
religious instruction, with which Young Men disposed to use them
were already furnished," that "the attraction of novelty was gone,"
that "many would expect something better than what preceded,"
and that readers might be disappointed "without any blameable
defect on the part of the writer" (Fordyce, pp. v–vii).

The persona in West's *Letters* has throughout "endeavoured to
preserve the reverence of a Christian and the humility of a novice."
She is "happy to find" that her opinions coincide "with the most
respectable authorities." Thus she will seek shelter "under the
strength of those authors whose talents and learning are equal to
the important subjects that they have discussed" (West, 1:xvii,
1:xxxiii).[18] While admitting inexperience and weakness, she claims
that all-important word *authority* and metaphorically characterizes
her approach as "the wisdom of a physician prescribing a wholesome regimen, as the mean of eradicating the seeds of a mortal
disease," and as "the benevolence of a superior intelligence, warding
off evils from a blind defenceless being" (1:xlvi). Not one to take the
easy road, she has undertaken her book with diffidence, secure in
the success of her former writings and undeterred by "the numerous
publications, on education and morals, which daily issue from the
press" (1:ix).

Franklin's apologia to his son and to the reader in the opening
four paragraphs of the *Life* is well known to the reader of the

Autobiography. No doubt Franklin's ploy was one of the many reasons why Thoreau admired the *Life*. Beginning with an apology for succumbing to the tiresome habit of old men to talk about themselves and their earlier years, Franklin's narrator concedes that his ramblings satisfy his vanity only to discredit his vanity with the observation that he owes his successes and happiness to providence. Yet he assumes that in offering his life story to others, the successful means described therein will be found fit to be imitated. As for Hawes, both the tone and the particulars of his apologia are closer to Fordyce and West than to Franklin. He begins his *Lectures* with an epigraph from a Johannine epistle in the New Testament—"I have written unto you, young men, because ye are strong" (Hawes, p. 5)—and explains to this strong and "interesting" auditory that he will merely "attempt a service." Yet he immediately offers a three-fold justification for preparing his lectures: a Christian, republican community; the example of "all wise and benevolent men," who "have always felt a deep and peculiar interest" in youth; and the example of the Christian Bible with its "prominent . . . concern for the youthful generations of men." And heading an important paragraph in his apologia is the declaration, "How entirely this accords with the spirit of inspiration, it is needless to remark" (Hawes, p. 6).

Also in accord with the first-person address and its spirit of inspiration is the hortatory voice, prominently featured on almost every page in Fordyce, West, and Hawes. This hortatory voice is a particularly useful response to the need to establish a convincing and authoritative speaker. Examples range from argumentation by a succession of rhetorical questions for the "you" in Fordyce to a timpany roll of warnings in West to the practical, proverb-like directives in Hawes to the use of aphorism,[19] testimonial witness, and oracular insights in all three. Although two of the three authors were clergymen, that fact alone does not satisfactorily explain the strong presence of the hortatory voice, which is present but less noticeable in Franklin. The hortatory voice is a rhetorical convention of persuasion. Aware of the power of rhetoric to deceive and mislead as surely as the power of logic can, the speaker of the *Life* uses his suspicion of rhetoric to make himself all the more persuasive with suspicious readers. Thus prudence and caution enhance his authority without enhancing dogma or imposing the weight of unsuitable traditions. Despite this difference, in all four guidebooks the hortatory is linked to the issue of authority, an issue that is really a nest of issues, one of which is whether the instruction will be received in the spirit in which it was given or, to rephrase this point, whether the assumed recipient will, in fact, be receptive. The hortatory voice provides the hearer with some reassurance about the authority of the instruction in that the persona can be aloof as a schoolmaster, urgent as a prophet, and affectionate as an elder friend.

Both the apologia and the hortatory voice contribute to a fundamental strategy of the guidebook—constituting speaker and audience and the relationship between them. In large part the persona is created through the persona's incessant references to his or her audience. To put this another way, the creation of the persona depends on, yet also contributes to, the creation of an audience, and the creation of an audience depends on, yet contributes to, the identification and definition of the persona. In Fordyce the listeners/readers are mentioned at least every few pages. The protocol of address, although pulpiteering, serves the speaker's purposes: "we," "you," "sir," "sirs," "you" (both singular and plural), "my brothers," "my young auditors," "my fellows," "my young friends," "ye sons of virtue," "my honoured hearers." Those who have ears are hearing, the speaker assumes. The aim appears to be to establish a coterie of readers, enlarge that coterie through periodic additions, and strengthen the loyalties of the reader to the persona and his message. "We naturally expect to find in young men, a lively fancy, a ready understanding, a retentive memory, a resolute spirit," the speaker proclaims, inviting the young men in attendance to find themselves in his audience.

Additional appeals widen the net: the speaker acknowledges his hearers' "quick sense of honour and disgrace, an irresistible love of action and enterprise, an ambition to be admired and praised, especially for their probity, their manhood, their generosity . . . and other virtues of that order" (Fordyce, p. 14). In an appeal to their "lively fancy" and "ready understanding" he encourages them to join him as author in "pictur[ing] to yourselves a pious and virtuous youth." The attention will turn chiefly on his principles, his temper, his passions, his motives of action. Additional suggestions are offered the "lively fancy" of the audience: "upright designs, good affections, a devout spirit, and useful life, the testimony of his own mind, and the friendship of a few people like himself" (p. 56). Speaker and audience join in providing a recognizable picture of "pious and virtuous youth" for the frame created by the speaker's general evocations.

Invitations to the reader to "consider," "imagine," "picture," "attend," "observe," and "perceive" abound in Fordyce. Not only is the reader encouraged to "picture" a type that the speaker helps him to "conceive"; the reader is also encouraged to picture himself in the frame provided by the speaker. (No distinction is made between internalized reader and the actual purchaser and reader of the volume.) To join the speaker in picturing virtue and piety in terms of their absence is a supposedly more daunting exercise; even the speaker acknowledges the difficulty of painting the presence of virtue by its absence: "But who can paint the meanness or the misery of such a character [a man of appearances]? Who can enumerate the sacrifices of sincerity, conscience, spirit, independence, real dignity and solid fame, that are daily offered to the idol of vulgar popularity?" (Fordyce p. 58). Yet his expressed doubts concerning his feat are merely rhetorical: the cumulative sequence of rhetorical question, parallel clauses, and catalogue of particulars in this passage discloses a strategy used repeatedly in the book, one that is similar to Virgil's in Book IX of the *Aeneid* ("Rome in the Absence of Aeneas"), where he defines Aeneas' virtue and piety by removing him from the scene. To define virtue by its removal is, in Fordyce's work, another act of collusion between speaker and reader that draws in the reader, establishes his credentials, and makes him part of a joint venture. This twin program of inclusion and collusion is also served through acts of exclusion: "I only except the hypocritical bigot," the speaker informs his coterie, "the profligate infidel, and the malevolent detractor. For them I profess no zeal; on them I can stamp no impression" (p. viii).

No one who has joined the speaker in picturing virtue or painting its absence is threatened by exclusion here. In fact, the exclusion confirms the reader's inclusion. On them the speaker can and does "stamp" the "impression" of virtue, respectability, and success. The metaphor of stamping here seems to refer to the minting of coins rather than the printing of an edition. If so, it is a particularly appropriate image, recalling one of the seventeenth- and eighteenth-century meanings of *patron* and its etymological and semantic sibling *pattern*. The inseparability and reciprocal relation of these two terms nicely capture the persona/reader relationship.

In West and Hawes the persona also works effectively to create a readership, to establish the speaker's presence and authority of presence, to convince the coterie of the principle of mutual identification and loyalty, and to engage their attentive and collaborative readers in an authorized joint undertaking. Readers are asked to join the speaker in considering, contemplating, recognizing, acknowledging, imagining, conceiving, and agreeing. While the impression of the stamp is not identical to Fordyce's, the stamping is strikingly similar.

The metaphor of coinage with is implied patron and pattern is less appropriate (in the sense of serviceable) for the Franklin-Stuber *Life* than metaphors of literary and printing-house composition. The persona who explains and illustrates in numerous vignettes the expertise he developed in editing manuscripts, setting type, and producing attractive, correct, and highly regarded products also recounts his arduous efforts over a period of years to increase his vocabulary, to improve his word choice, images, and analogies, to enhance the sound of his sentences, and to strengthen his argumentation. Although as deliberate as Fordyce, West, and Hawes about creating and augmenting a readership that will collaborate in the persona's enterprise, Franklin's speaker refrains from pontificating and from authorizing any authority other than that of experience, circumstance, perceptiveness, anticipation, courage, and prudence. The reader is encouraged to accept the roles of author and compositor, to join the speaker in shaping, correcting, and otherwise improving one's life as one does a composition, and to make the composition as accomplished as possible. "We see, in every page," the "Preface" to the 1796 *Life* notes, "that the author examined his subject with the eye of a master" (Franklin, p. iii). The "Dear son" salutation, then, is a statement of relationship that addresses the internalized reader as much as Franklin's son William. As master of his text, the speaker is also master of the internalized reader. Yet the reader's participation in composing and editing is a schooling in the art of mastery and testimony to a joint business. That relationship, and the success it envisions and promotes, is the heart of the enterprise in each of the four guidebooks.

Understood as a guide to ambitious young men in a culture perceived to misrepresent and confuse *advantage* and *advancement*, the guidebooks and their conventions examined in this chapter are aptly described by several key phrases Perry Miller and Sacvan Bercovitch use to characterize the jeremiad: for Miller a form that makes "sense out of [the community's] unique experience," and for Bercovitch "a mode of public exhortation . . . designed to join social criticism to spiritual renewal, public to private identity, the shifting 'signs of the times' to certain traditional metaphors, themes, and symbols."[20] By appropriating features of a ritual and therefore acceptable form of public instruction and correction in Britain and young America, Fordyce, West, Franklin, and Hawes can decry the degeneracy or note the dangers of the times, emphasize individual and cultural character, advocate responsibilities and duties (including the overriding responsibility of building a moral culture), counterbalance censure and dismay with a vision of success and with pointed advice on how to improve—all this without alienating the recipient of the instruction.

Notes

1. George Eliot's review is in *Westminster Review* 65 (January 1856): 302–3. Japp published his book on Thoreau under the pseudonym, H. A. Page. See *Thoreau: His Life and Aims* (Boston: James R. Osgood & Company, 1877), pp. 109–11, 113.

2. Joseph J. Moldenhauer, "The Rhetoric of *Walden*," (Ph.D. diss., Columbia University, 1964), p. 1.

3. The guidebook editions in Thoreau's library were: James Fordyce, *Addresses to Young Men*, 2 vols. (Boston: Manning & Loring, 1795; first published in England in 1779); Benjamin Franklin [with Dr. Stuber], *The Life of Dr. Benjamin Franklin* (Salem, Mass.: Cushing & Carlton, 1796); Joel Hawes, *Lectures Addressed to the Young Men of Hartford and New-Haven* (Hartford, Conn.: Oliver D. Cooke, 1828); Mrs. [Jane] West, *Letters Addressed to a Young Man, on His First Entrance into Life, and Adapted to the Peculiar Circumstances of the Present Times*, 2 vols. (Boston: Samuel H. Parker, 1803; first English publication in 1801 in 3 vols.). For a record of Thoreau's library see Walter Harding, "A New Checklist of the Books in Henry David Thoreau's Library," *Studies in the American Renaissance 1983*, ed. Joel Myerson (Charlottesville: The University Press of Virginia, 1983), pp. 151–86.

It should be noted that the Franklin not a few scholars have seen as challenged or rejected by Thoreau is the protagonist of the complete *Autobiography* that appeared six years after Thoreau's death (edited by John Bigelow). Whether Thoreau ever read the initial but incomplete edition of the *Autobiography*, published by Temple Franklin, is unknown. The Franklin to whom Thoreau alludes, and whom he admires, recommends, and quotes is the hero of the Franklin-Stuber *Life of Franklin*, a work closer to guidebooks in its topics, emphasis, and professed aim than to the *Autobiography* as we know it. The two parts of the *Life* on Thoreau's shelves consisted of a translation, from the French, of Franklin's memoir to 1730 (the first of the four installments in the complete *Autobiography*) and a "continuation" by "the late Dr. Stuber of Philadelphia" (Franklin, p. 82), who not only continued the narrative into Franklin's later years but who did so along the lines of the guidebook for young men.

For his part, Franklin had acknowledged the genre in deciding to write an account for his son that would finally explain to a son still requesting financial assistance in his middle years how the father, in a time of fewer advantages, had been successful in advancing himself through his own discipline, industry, resourcefulness, and appearances. William Franklin, Governor of New Jersey, who had never had to fend for himself and could not claim, "I have raised myself," was transformed by the father into an attentive and worthy recipient of guidebook wisdom, more for the sake of the *Life*, one has to assume, than for the sake of family relations.

Thoreau cites Franklin in his Journal, *A Week*, "Resistance to Civil Government," *Walden*, "A Plea for Captain John Brown," and his correspondence. In a letter to B. B. Wiley in 1857, Thoreau recommended the *Life of Franklin* as essential reading. This recommendation is preceded by the observation: "Books can only reveal us to ourselves, and as often as they do us this service we lay them aside" (*The Correspondence of Henry David Thoreau*, ed. Carl Bode and Walter Harding [New York: New York University Press, 1958], p. 478).

4. In his defense in the opening paragraphs of *Walden* of the obtrusive "I" and the autobiographical mode of the work, Thoreau may have parodied parts of Foster's opening essay. See John Foster, *Essays in a Series of Letters to a Friend* (Boston: J. Loring, 1833). Thoreau owned this edition. My characterization of Foster's voice borrows an expression from Lawrence Buell, "First Person Superlative: The Speaker in Emerson's Essays," in *Emerson's Relevance Today*, ed. Eric Carlson and J. Lasley Dameron (Hartford: Transcendental Books, 1971), pp. 28–35.

5. See the Appendix for additional information on the guidebook for young men as a species of conduct book.

6. John Thoreau, Jr., signed the book in 1834, presumably when he was presented it. According to his father's record in the family Bible, John was born 14 July 1814, not a year later, as incorrectly inscribed on his grave marker some years after his death. The edition which John received was published in 1803 by Samuel H. Parker of Boston in a two-volume format.

7. Foster's *Essays* represents a quasi-exception in that this book, the most inflated and anti-intellectual of the lot, was recommended in an alternative reading list anonymously published by student reformers in 1832 and treated by many as a Bible in the years when Thoreau attended Harvard. See Kenneth W. Cameron, *Transcendental Apprenticeship of Henry Thoreau* (Hartford: Transcendental Books, 1976), pp. 268–99; especially p. 291.

8. Henry Golemba, "The voices of *Walden*," *ESQ* 31 (4th Quarter 1985): 249. On Thoreau's use of the catechism, an appropriation of what I see as a conventional guidebook feature, the reader should consult Sargent Bush, Jr., "The End and Means in *Walden*: Thoreau's Use of the Catechism," *ESQ* 31 (1st Quarter 1985): 1–10.

9. The advice of the Quaker woman to the speaker in response to his social and sexual interest in her two female servants constitutes a short parental treatise on chastity and women in this guidebook addressed to a son. "'Young man,'" she lectures him, "'I am in pain for thee. Thou hast no parent to watch over thy conduct, and thou seemest to be ignorant of the world, and the snares to which youth is exposed. Rely upon what I tell thee: those are women of bad characters; I perceive it in all their actions. If thou dost not take care, they will lead thee into danger'" (Franklin, p. 38).

10. Perry Miller, *Errand into the Wilderness* (Cambridge, Mass.: Harvard University Press, 1956), p. 15.

11. While according morals and manners equal rank, West refuses to dissociate one from the other as Hamlet seems to do in his advice to his less-than-exemplary parent to "Assume a virtue, if you have it not." Moral culture is inconceivable without "honour," and manifestations of honor, to wit proper station, behavior, and decorum, are viewed both as principals and agents in culture-building.

12. Mindful of rapid changes in the youthful American republic, Hawes must emphasize the "auspicious bearing of [established] principles on the formation of your characters" (p. 65). Furthermore, by "associating with the virtuous, the wise and the good, we bring to bear on ourselves, a most powerful influence of assimilation" (p. 42). Association produces two related kinds of assimilation—the assimilation of the individual by the virtuous group and the assimilation of principle by both. His pedagogical approach to inculcating principles reflects a rationalist Protestant assumption that correct principles will in a natural chain of cause and effect produce moral culture and correct individual conduct. He also sounds another note, which is paradoxical, to say the least, given his high regard for the role of God and Christian community in guarding and promoting established principles of action as these apply to the group and the individual: "While you aim to fulfil the duties which you owe to society, you take the most effectual measures to promote *your own respectability*" (p. 27).

13. The individual initiatives of Stuber's culture-designing hero include founding a seminary of learning that will "promote and establish [the students],

whether in business, offices, marriages, or any other thing for their advantage" (Franklin, p. 97); helping to found a hospital and dispensary; helping to reorganize the colonial postal service into an efficient and profitable organization in contrast to the incompetent British service in the Canadian colony; proposing a plan for military, political, and economic union of the colonies; calling for representative government; defending the doctrines of republicanism at home and abroad; defending America's republican revolution; and serving as president of the Abolition Society (which expressly aimed to stop both slave trade and slavery).

14. The *Life* contrasts sharply to West's law of the subordination of the individual to the cultural order and moral interests. "If the good of the individual and that of the public come in competition, the *latter* must predominate," she reminds young men dedicated to success. Hence her imperative to "learn to have a deference for others, and early acquire habits of proper subordination" and her rejection as "absurd" of the suggestion "that it is even possible for you to rise to any *high station* in life. Such ideas would be very improper for any parent to inculcate" (West, 3:301, 3:21).

15. On the whole there exists a greater temporal lag in Britain than in America between the inauguration of a vigorous business economy and the full impact of that vigor in the vernacular of the culture and in the guidebooks and success manuals in particular.

16. Franklin's speaker requests the authorial privilege of correcting "in a second edition, certain errors of the first" (Franklin, p. 6), a privilege that incorporates several requests, all of which turn on the infinitive "to correct" and the richly ambiguous reference to a "second edition." Errors in life will be corrected in the *Life*, and the fable will be a corrected (properly altered) version of the unedited mass of the lived life. But "second edition" and the prospect of useful correction also brings to mind the son as announced recipient of the memoirs and the readers, who will glean both knowledge and wisdom from the narrative.

17. Buell, "First Person Superlative," p. 30.

18. West's apologia also justifies her role as a female author. Her honorific acknowledgment of male masters and mentors appears to be, among other things, a shrewd strategy for claiming her place in the sun.

19. Aphorism (or apothegmatic rhetoric) is not unique to Hawes; indeed, aphorisms are much in evidence in all four guidebooks. Franklin, however, does not treat aphorism as an uncaused cause and undebatable word. He admires the mixture of narration and dialogue he has noticed in writers like Bunyan, Defoe, and Richardson. In them, the aphorisms are a function of narration and dialogue, not vice versa. Thus he hopes to make the aphorism a natural part of the speaker's experience, that is, subject it to the same test of validity as the record of experience in which it appears. In Fordyce, West, and Hawes, however, aphorism is a form of argument in which rhetoric and logic meet. At times the persona is the aphorist whose sententiae are his or her basic

units of composition and articulation, at other times we are presented with a speaker whose repertoire includes the apothegm with its ingenious turn. An example of the former in Fordyce is the epigram: "I pretend to no influence but that of persuasion, and to no authority but that of truth." An example of the latter is the question/answer proverb so common in the biblical Psalms: where are "temptations" most "strengthened and multiplied?"—"in rich and populous cities" (Fordyce, pp. 9, 16). Some of West's most interesting paragraphs turn on aphorisms, and her most memorable sentences are apothegmatic: "If we must all be men and women of fashion, let us not, in the name of common sense, rest content with pantaloons and muslin drapery" (West, 3:52); or, to the well-read and richly experienced person, "solitude is so far from being an inconvenience, that he never is more occupied than when alone" (3:126); or, those who are devoted to killing time, "though they most effectually contrive to murder him day after day, yet they find the invincible monster alive again" (3:292). In his version of "Time is but the stream I go a-fishing in," Hawes remarks of the Pilgrims and all true pilgrims that "they labored, not for themselves, but for mankind; not for time, but for eternity" (Hawes, p. 20). And echoing the wise teacher in the biblical Proverbs, Hawes' speaker epigrammatizes, "He who cares not for others, will soon find that others will not care for him" (p. 19). We also get more than echoes: Fordyce likes to quote Roman aphorists, Franklin quotes Dryden, among others, and West repeatedly conscripts Pope.

The reader will notice echoes of West and Hawes in several aphorisms in *Walden* that Joseph Moldenhauer identifies as Thoreau's original inventions. They surely are original in their new versions; in working to transform guidebooks for young men Thoreau, not surprisingly, reworked maxims he found in his guidebooks. The most complete and reliable inventory of aphorisms in *Walden* is Moldenhauer's "The Rhetoric of *Walden*," pp. 362–409. Several months after the publication of *Walden*, when consulting his recently complete Journal notebook for material for a new lecture (the first version of "Life without Principle"), Thoreau chided himself in a note on the paste-down endpaper of the notebook for "Using current phrases and maxims, when I should speak for myself" (1906 J 7:8).

20. Perry Miller, *The New England Mind: From Colony to Province* (Cambridge, Mass.: Harvard University Press, 1953), p. 31; Sacvan Bercovitch, *The American Jeremiad* (Madison: University of Wisconsin Press, 1978), p. xi. What Miller calls "unique experience" has a twofold meaning for the guidebook as it does for Miller: the perception of a unique historical and cultural development, and the perception that immediate circumstances are unique.

5

The American Success Manual for Young Men

By the time that Thoreau drafted his first version of *Walden*, the success manual for young men had become a form of acceptable, indeed desirable, redundancy, especially with, but not limited to, economically growing and entrepreneurially vigorous publishers in the major publishing centers. This lucrative form of repetitiveness, plagiarism, and inventiveness offered publishers one means of filling new regional and national markets opened by the railroad, of consolidating production and marketing, and of increasing profits. Thus, even if Thoreau had not been familiar with Fordyce, Franklin, West, and Hawes, the spate of contemporary success manuals advertised in Boston and New York serials, the widespread dissemination of these works in homes, circulating libraries, church libraries, and bookshops made them a familiar item in the community and a continuing factor in the story of both production and distribution of the times.[1]

If one adds Foster's *Essays* to the four guidebooks on Thoreau's shelves, three of the five works were written by ministers, one was produced by a professional writer who relied on the income from her publications for her livelihood, two were written by non-establishmentarian ministers (Foster was an English Baptist and Hawes worked in a state that had disestablished its clergy some years earlier), and both Foster and Hawes supplemented their income through their writing. Moreover, four of the authors were inclined toward belles-lettrism (Fordyce, Franklin, West, and Foster), two were minor publishing poets (Fordyce and West), and two moved in circles of acquaintances and friends that included major literary figures (Franklin cultivated the acquaintance of several French and British authors and Fordyce befriended Dr. Johnson and James Boswell). Nor should one overlook the success of works by these five writers as confirmed by the numerous editions of their guidebooks and the popularity of the British works in America.

Consider the following statistics on the American success manuals of the 1830s to the 1850s. Of the sixteen titles I have found that appeared from the time that Thoreau entered Harvard to his final revisions of *Walden*, ten are by clergymen. Most of these ministers updated the age-old Christian imperative to cast one's bread upon the waters while expertly acting out their own advice. Seven of the authors (including several ministers) regarded themselves as professional writers, several (including at least two ministers) practiced belles-lettrism, several published poetry, two were prolific producers of romances and tales, and a few, including at least two ministers, cultivated literary acquaintances. Five of the authors frequently contributed to journals and magazines, and several of them served as editor of one or more serials. Four of the authors were largely self-educated; an equal number, including one of the self-educated writers, were educators; and each noted the educational value of his advice for young men. As for the sixteen guides to success, the majority of them went through multiple printings and editions, and virtually all of them vastly outsold the two books Thoreau published in his lifetime (*A Week* and *Walden*).[2]

Whether one focuses on the guidebooks in Thoreau's library, the plethora of success manuals that appeared in America in the 1830s to the 1850s, or both, the results are similar. The reason is not mysterious. As the first section of this chapter demonstrates, the American guide to success, one of the several kinds of popular success literature in Thoreau's time, offers a template of behavior and advice on how to succeed morally and socially (hence "copy book"). Above all, this success, as section II explains, is exemplified as professional and economic success (hence "success manual"). Like Fordyce, West, Franklin, and Hawes, American guides for young men represent themselves not as philosophical treatises but as pedagogical guides in a joint venture. And more emphatically than their predecessors they apotheosize the young man since with him lie the fortunes of the nation's future and of civilization. In the third section, I examine the nature of the persona and its role in the apotheosis of the young man, the manual's convention of joint undertaking, and the largely writ theme of success.

I

Although I do not presume to have identified and examined all of the success manuals of the twenty-year period under consideration, I offer a representative roster of titles and large sampler—sixteen guidebooks in all. These are listed in the alphabetical order of the authors and with the year of first publication: John S. C. Abbott, *The School-Boy; A Guide for Youth to Truth and Duty* (1839); William A. Alcott, *The Young Man's Guide* (1833); idem, *Familiar Letters to Young Men* (1849); Timothy Shay Arthur, *Advice to Young Men on Their Duties and Conduct in Life* (1847); Henry Ward Beecher, *Seven Lectures to Young Men, on Various Important Subjects* (1844; later retitled *Lectures to Young Men, on Various Important Subjects*); Nathan S. Beman, *The Claims of Our Country on Young Men* (1843); Charles Butler, *The American Gentleman* (1836); Dorus Clarke, *Lectures to Young People in Manufacturing Villages* (1836); John Frost, *The Young Merchant* (1839); idem, *The Young Mechanic* (1843); William T. Hamilton, *The Responsibilities of American Youth!* (1851); John Todd, *The Student's Manual; Designed, by Specific Directions, to Aid in Forming and Strengthening the Intellectual and Moral Character and Habits of the Student* (1835); idem, *The Foundations of Success* (1844); idem, *The Young Man. Hints Addressed to the Young Men of the United States* (1844); William Howard Van Doren, *Mercantile Morals; or Thoughts for Young Men Entering Mercantile Life* (1852); and Daniel Wise, *The Young Man's Counsellor; or, Sketches and Illustrations of the Duties and Dangers of Young Men* (1850). By printing and sales norms of the time, most of these guidebooks were successful, some were exceedingly successful.

Regardless of whether the manuals are titled *Lectures to Young People, Lectures to Young Men, Advice to Young Men*, or *The Young Man's Counsellor*, their shared features prompt me to offer *The Young Man's Guide* by William Alcott as an appropriate collective title. Neither college trained nor, like the majority of the authors of the sixteen manuals, a member of the clergy, this cousin to Bronson Alcott was nonetheless living proof of successful self-education in his efforts to improve the education of others, especially youth. His numerous roles in life included teacher, missionary of reform in public education, pioneer in physical education, physician, farmer, and author. His writings, including his early treatise *The Young Man's Guide*, were means of disseminating his views, of making a living, and of influencing young men and their interested elders on the linked subjects of improvement and livelihood.[3]

Manuals focusing on steps to success in a single trade and not governed by the general themes of moral culture and self-culture are not included in my list, although such works are relevant to the discussion.[4] Also missing from my list are manuals limited to manners per se, such as Margaret C. Conkling's *The American Gentlemen's Guide to Politeness and Fashion* (1857),[5] which is quite devoid of Butler's sense of sin, virtue, self-culture, moral culture, and national ideals. It is simply a manual on how to cultivate desirable appearances, a work that, while not irrelevant to the discussion, belongs to the literature on manners criticized by Fordyce, West, and several of the sixteen guidebooks discussed in this section. The most prolific warren of titles not included in my sampler, yet as much a sign of the times as the popularity of the young man's guide to success, is the book of wealth, with its three principal subspecies: biographical or autobiographical profiles of exemplary men who amassed wealth in particular fields of enterprise, surveys of the accumulation of wealth and of accumulators as a group, and the "Way to Wealth" treatises aptly described by the title of a book by Asher L. Smith and J. W. Hawxhurst, *How to Get Rich; or, a Key to Honest Wealth* (1866).[6]

Beman's and Hamilton's manuals and Todd's *Foundations of Success* have been included partly as a reminder of the oratorical/ rhetorical nature of the guides to success, and partly as evidence that lectures and addresses on the popular theme of the young man's success often proved to be as popular as their theme and that some of these texts were published in booklet form. The subtitle of Hamilton's fifteen-page text is "An Address Delivered at Orrville, Dallas County, Ala., Before the Students of Orrville Institute, June 26th, 1851"; the subtitle of Beman's thirty-six page manual is

"An Address Delivered Before the Literary Societies in Hamilton College, on the evening of July 25, 1843"; and the lectern-sized subtitle of Todd's address is "An Oration Pronounced Before the Philomathaean and Phrenakosmian Societies of Pennsylvania College, Gettysburg, Sept. 19, 1843." The other thirteen works are booklength productions, some of them multiplied versions of these three addresses, that is, series of lectures connected by theme, topics, and mode as in Fordyce and Hawes. One should not infer from the three subtitles listed here that students were the sole or principal recipients of the guides to success. Nor were the manuals limited to a particular social class, religious group, or geographic region.

These manuals vary assortments of conventional themes such as modernity and its considerations, *sub voce*, of the past; the hallmarks of a superior culture; the ideal political system; the building of a moral culture; the importance of education; private and public virtue; the perils of ignorance; the dangers of the city; ideal social arrangements; the duties and opportunities of the individual; and the primacy of industry, discipline, and love of success. The typical format, especially in the booklength manuals, consists of a series of six to ten chapters devoted to topics and subtopics such as: the ultimate end of living, noble goals, concentration of purpose, economy (of time, resources, and effort), effective training, reading and study, conversation, diet and drink, the claims of society, deference and respectability, women (in several manuals mainly the "strange woman" of the city), and business—especially business. Business enjoys a noticeably stronger claim on the overall emphasis in these manuals than in the guidebooks in Thoreau's library. The repertoire of evils includes "idleness," "sloth," "extravagance," "waste," "fashion," "drunkenness," "fornication," "oversleeping," unproductivity, greed, lack of respect for God, lack of piety, disregard for the church, disinterest in the nation's special destiny, and (in the pro-Jacksonian manuals) antirepublicanism, antiegalitarianism and antiequality of opportunity.

These manuals, too, offer advice, prescriptions, examples of successes and failures, and jussive exhortation; they create images of stability against a background of instability; they rely on familiar affective and logical appeals in moral argument; they encourage participatory response through the use of a companionable persona with generous offers of joint enterprise and promises of success. Behind the generous offers is more than the paternalism and desire for influence so obvious in these works. The authors of the success manuals are impressed by the uniqueness of the times and their opportunity. John Todd's observation reveals a typical assessment: "The circumstances in which the American youth is now coming forward in life are so very peculiar, the age in which he is to act is so marked,—the social organization with which he is to be united is so constructed,—and the responsibilities which rest upon him are so heavy, that I may be excused if I feel that he needs and deserves the best hints, the clearest counsels, and the wisest instructions which can be given." Thus Todd accepts equally heavy responsibilities: the young men's unique opportunities and his counsels will conspire in behalf of the future and America's special destiny. Timothy Shay Arthur sees a similar destiny as manifest, but his assessment of the present makes his writing of a guide to success all the more urgent: "There are a very large number of young men, just entering upon life, of good minds, but deficient educations, who, from this cause, are kept back."[7]

II

"The *thing* which the student desires above all others in this life is SUCCESS," Todd intones at the outset of his *Foundations of Success*, "by which [the student] means, obtaining an influence among men—or, the power to influence men. . . . I place myself in the situation of the student."[8] Proper economy, of course, puts everything into perspective, including the means and ends of success. As Alcott notes in "Economy," a chapter of *The Young Man's Guide* replete with precepts, prescriptions, exhortations, and aphorisms: "There is a false, as well as a true economy. I have seen an individual who, with a view to economy, was in the habit of splitting his wafers. Sometimes a thick wafer can be split into two, which will answer to a very good purpose; but at others, both parts fall to pieces. Let the success be ever so complete, however, all who reflect for a moment on the value of time, must see it to be a losing process. . . . Economy in time is economy of money—for it needs not Franklin to tell us that time is equivalent to money."[9]

Clues as to the orbit into which the concept *enterprise* was being

drawn by cultural developments are found in many chapter head-
ings in three of the earliest published of the sixteen guidebooks,
Butler, Alcott, and Abbott, which explicate enterprise in telling
forms: "Hints to Those Who are Designed for a Mercantile Life,"
"The Merchant," "The Young Should Determine to Rise," "Time is
Money," "Commencing Business," "Rules for Doing Much Business in Little Time," "On the Management of Business," "Application to Business," and "Money Getting." Daniel Wise's heading for
his sixth chapter, "Industry the Highway to Success," belongs to the
storehouse of winsome clichés of the time; his definition of *industry*, however, has little of the cliché and will not have put his
reader at ease: "Industry implies regular and habitual devotion to a
useful pursuit. It is covetous of *moments*, and guards them as a
miser his grains of gold."[10]

An altered distribution of emphasis in which a substantially
larger proportion of the book is devoted to economic enterprise is
perhaps the most obvious difference from earlier guidebooks for
young men. Discussions of business, for example, rest in some cases
four square on moral principles, in others on no clearly identified
verities. In still others, the appearance of moral ground is appearance only, and is cultivated, it would seem, out of deference to
convention or to satisfy certain demands of readers and publishers
that grow out of deference to convention. The significant characteristic here is not the nature of the linkage of business to morals,
however, but the greater prominence of a concern with successful
economic enterprise as reflected in the chaper topics and subtopics
and in the network of topical repetition within the volume as a
whole. In reading through these American guides to success, one is
struck by the increased vigor of the language of enterprise and its
increased influence on the guidebook as a whole. Indeed, the language of business activity is a suggestive and useful source of
expression in discussing any subject, including faith, morals, and
respectability.

What this evidence testifies to is an increasingly specific understanding of *economy* and *enterprise*. To be sure, repeated tributes
to these terms and what they stand for suggest both older and newer
meanings. In the case of *enterprise*, for instance, all of the authors
praise a venturesome spirit, the shrewdness and diligence to conceive a design and follow through with it, and the courage to take a

calculated risk. Nonetheless, as the lexicon of economic improvement discloses and the chapter titles confirm, a number of key terms, whose multiple applications and rich associations in Fordyce and West allowed them highly specific applications as well, were now being rapidly transformed into narrow signifiers associated with business and with unprecedented and thoroughgoing change in American culture. Whereas in Fordyce's and West's understanding of *oeconomy* economic considerations are framed by what they see as stable moral tradition, religious doctrine, and social philosophy of "virtue," in these success manuals *economy* as religious duty is invoked largely for moralistic purposes and functions as nostalgic idea and ritual expression. Rarely in the manuals is *enterprise* separable from economic considerations; indeed, it has become a key term in the lexicon of economic improvement. The same can be said of terms like "commerce," "business," "profession," "industry," "diligence," "profit," and "loss." *Profit*, a religious, moral, aesthetic, and economic term in the guidebooks in Thoreau's library, shed much of its religious and aesthetic meaning, and hitched moral considerations to economic ones. In conservative, traditional republicans like Butler and Abbott, and to a lesser extent in Beman, Todd and Wise, older and newer conceptions of *enterprise* and *profit* contend for ascendancy. Furthermore, to some extent all sixteen of the guides habitually fall back on old religious and moral precepts. Yet the alchemical change of the lexicon of *enterprise* is unmistakable.

This harnessing of traditionally general terms with moral and in some cases biblical associations to economic purpose, a process which turned traditional terms into vigorous new signifiers in a discourse of economic enterprise, is already very much in evidence in the two earliest published of the sixteen manuals, Butler and Alcott. What Butler, an entrepreneur in his own right, has to say about *commerce* is said by other authors in a similarly laudatory fashion about other business activities:

> In a country whose situation has rendered it naturally commercial, it is good policy to place the mercantile profession in an honourable light. It has not usually held a very high place in the esteem of the world; because, in most countries, it has been disgraced by covetousness and circumvention. Its primary object, the accumulation of money, has never

appeared with any peculiar lustre in the eyes of those who have seen the beauty of disinterested patriotism and heroic generosity. But, at the same time, it is certain that a mercantile life affords scope for the display of many good qualities, and of virtues which, from their sublime and difficult nature, may constitute the merchant a practical philosopher.[11]

In the first two chapters of Alcott's *The Young Man's Guide* (one-half of his book), terms such as "profession," "industry," "diligence," "trust" (noun and verb), "entrust," "profit," "loss," and "ruin" are his major functionaries in a discussion governed by enterprise in its contemporary American and economic context. In his *Guide* as a whole, Alcott's illustrative use of Jesus anticipates a number of characteristics and values much more fully worked out in Bruce Barton's 1925 best-selling life of Christ, *The Man Nobody Knows*, a profile of Jesus as the great prince of enterprise by one of the pioneers of Madison Avenue advertising.[12]

Although piously distinguishing between the business of Christianity and the young nation on the one hand and American business on the other, the practical effect of the large majority of the guidebooks is to link the two and blur the distinctions between them.[13] In endorsing the new age of enterprise, these guidebooks also envision a harmonious and prosperous society composed of independent, self-reliant, self-motivated, gentle, and civilized businessmen amassing economic returns by virtuous industry.

The ascendancy and semantic narrowing of the language of enterprise in the success manuals reveal not only a shift in moral assumptions but also a new moral rationale for *enterprise* as discussed and exemplified in the manuals. A new watchword of the times is *prosperity*, a term that has largely displaced *oeconomical habits* and *frugality* and that is linked to spiritual fulfillment and moral well-being. One notices fewer warnings against the amassing of wealth and a stronger approval of economic security as a favorable condition of higher development. Even luxury is rarely condemned when understood as the natural sign of prosperity and thus an outward expression of an inner commitment unsullied by waste and extravagance. Luxuriousness (profligate reveling in luxury) is a dissipation, but wealth is a sign of industry and reward. Whereas a writer like Thoreau refuses to distinguish between wealth and luxury, painting them both as corruptive in their effects, the success manuals distinguish between the two either to honor wealth as the reward of enterprise or to discriminate between legitimate and illegitimate luxury. Godliness is prominently factored into the equation of success. *The Young Man's Counsellor* offers a rather typical pronouncement: "The *temporal* advantages of an early religious life are not sufficiently considered by most young men. They blindly conclude that success in this life is the exclusive heritage of the worldling. . . . *Godliness is profitable* FOR ALL THINGS." But the Reverend Wise allows that religious piety is not "the *only* road to temporal prosperity and social superiority."[14]

If qualifications and warnings do not fundamentally challenge the activities and energies associated with enterprise, they do challenge what the authors see as enemies of virtuous enterprise. Butler, for instance, in citing "envy," "violent passions," "deceit," "intemperance," and selfish disregard of the public interest as evils that will undermine enterprise, articulates a version of republicanism more at home linguistically and morally in the early national era than in Jacksonian and post-Jacksonian America. Todd's and Van Doren's warnings against the burning desire for sudden growth (wealth and character should be the result of gradual growth) inform us of a contemporary cultural phenomenon, the widespread enthralment with the dream of making money as quickly as possible. Arthur, likewise, registers a widespread prejudice of his culture, but he conscripts it without reservation in his "clear and strong presentation of the real truth" in order to illustrate the relation of good minds, noble purpose, and persistent industry to civilization: "The want of an adequate purpose is what makes a man indolent. The Indian will spend days and weeks in slothfulness and inactivity, and to an observer seem the most inefficient and powerless of human beings; but let the war-whoop sound, or a deer go bounding past his wigwam, and he is instantly as full of fire, strength, and endurance as a war-horse."[15] Arthur's point is clear enough; what is not clear is who or what is the enemy of American enterprise—the American Indian, or certain widespread habits best illustrated for his readers by the example of the Indian. Perhaps both are the enemy, and perhaps in Arthur's mind they are one and the same enemy. On the other hand, it is clear that the reform-minded Arthur did not write his manual to reform the Indian or to extend to him the rewards of enterprise. On this point, his view is akin to Todd's, who envisions one to two billion enterprising Saxon people in the United States by the middle of the twenty-first century.[16]

If definition and illustration of virtuous enterprise and its enemies form a bond of similarity in these guides to success, both the polysemous character of *virtue* and historical and cultural developments in which the language of virtue had to participate inevitably assure differences between the guides. The adherence of Abbott, Beman, and Butler to an earlier version of republicanism that was being crowded out by social, economic, and political shifts in the nation is a case in point. A noticeable impulse in their guides is to retain contact with a passing order by ritualizing some of its principles and values. They invoke conservative republican values and lament the degeneracy of the times. In their view, enterprise is virtuous if it redeems the present by placing it under the superintendence of principles tested and proven by the past, especially by the national experience of nation-building. One can document the shift in the republican temper by comparing Butler's guide with Van Doren's. Both offer the views of a commercially minded man familiar with the large city and its commerce. Butler is pre-Jacksonian in his orientation whereas Van Doren is clearly post-Jacksonian. The majority of the authors, and virtually all of the authors after the early 1840s, are much more akin to Van Doren than to Butler. They seek to redeem the time in the economic sense of redemption. In other words, they encourage the development of productive business habits as a means to moral development and as a sign of a virtuous character. Alcott's first chapter, "On the Formation of Character," consists of four sections, titled, respectively: "High Standards of Action," "Industry," "Economy," and "Indolence." Chapter two is titled "On the Management of Business." The perspective in Alcott anticipates most of the manuals of the 1840s and 50s. Entrepreneurship is assumed to be the normal activity, business enterprise the normal state of things, and shrewd planning and the right habits of paramount importance.

The shifts in habits of thought and usage just noted are epitomized in John Frost's *The Young Merchant*, the first two chapters of which are devoted to the "Intellectual Qualifications of the Merchant" and "Moral Qualifications." Under the latter Frost classifies *economy* with traditionally designated moral virtues, a classification that echoes the past rather than the present, yet a past that reaches close to the present, as the treatment in Fordyce, West, and Hawes confirms. Such a housing of the term *economy* in moral philosophy is not in keeping with most American success manuals, however, especially those of the 1840s and 50s. Nor is it in keeping with the rest of *The Young Merchant*, particularly when Frost turns to subjects such as "Setting up in Business," "Principles of Commerce," "The Merchant's Duties," and "The Merchant's Conduct Under Reverses." In effect, Frost invokes a convention of the past, appears to give it authority, then shifts to contemporary associations of the term as the exigencies of his discussion shift.

Another sign of the times is the shift from the preeminence of the *res publica* (Butler's view, which he shared with other traditional republicans and with guidebook authors like Fordyce) to the exaltation of self-culture. But self-culture as viewed by the manuals is not a unitary concept. The different ends of self-culture necessarily imply different conceptions of self-culture. For Alcott and Hamilton, for instance, self-culture is the keelson of culture. While Wise accepts such a view, he is more dedicated to a view in accord with his perfectionist theology—self-culture as Christian perfection, that is, self-culture as culture. For the majority of the authors, self-culture is the basis of individual economic success, which, in turn, enhances the prospects of self-culture. "I know that we are too covetous, and too greedy of gain, and too reckless in its pursuit," Todd concedes, "but I know that there is something vastly more valuable than wealth, in the estimation of our country—and that is *character*." By itself this passage will probably misrepresent Todd, who repeatedly underscores the symbiosis between vigorous enterprise and the building of individual character, and who can declare with assurance: "Left to ourselves here, we work off a small part of our restlessness in such small enterprises as subduing forests, filling valleys, levelling and tunneling mountains, sending the canal boat through the heart of a continent, or starting the deer by the snort of the iron horse as he scours over the plains, or by the panting steamboat."[17]

As the manuals reveal, the linkage of "secure economic position" to the "life of self-development" that Daniel Howe identifies with Harvard moralists and Unitarian Whigs of the region was hardly limited to Cambridge or to New England Whiggery.[18] It is not at all surprising that New Englander Todd warns the young men in his enterprising America against indulging *"in the reveries of imagina-tion,"* an aesthetic self-indulgence that is wasteful, extravagant, obstructive, and immature. Better to pursue money recklessly than indulge the imagination. "Even in business, where one would think it [imagination] harmless, it must be kept in strict subjection, or you are unfitted to succeed. A young man in setting out in business . . . may have an honest heart, and yet if the imagination is suffered to hold the reins, he will certainly build castles in the air, which are as baseless as the element in which he builds them."[19] Todd's under-standing of success as a competence of material goods (outward development) and the growth of a disciplined Christian character (inward development) is the most common one in the success manuals, which are national in their sampling.

A poignant example of the major shift represented in the guides to success is offered by the Beechers, father and son. Henry Ward Beecher, the son (1813–87), an evangelical reformer, staunch advo-cate of American enterprise, and defender of prosperity, wrote a guidebook that envisioned a productive nation that would peren-nially honor God in its production. Adequate self-culture, in his view, both legitimized and dignified enterprise. Beecher's guidebook was itself an example of successful enterprise in that its many editions produced handsome profits for publishers and author and allowed him to live well, in part by the immediate aid of effectively promoted and well-received books. The father, Lyman Beecher (1775–1863), born a few months after the battles of Concord and Lexington, preached a version of Christianity and republicanism that was intol-erant of concentration of wealth, sharply distinguished between God and Mammon, and stressed the impossibility of serving two masters. When the disestablishment of the clergy in Massachusetts became imminent, he warned that after disestablishment Congregational min-isters would become "slaves to the worst of masters." For more reasons than one, then, the dedicatory note in Henry Ward Beecher's *Seven Lectures* provokes ironic responses in today's reader: "To/ LYMAN BEECHER, D.D./To you I owe more than to any other living being. In childhood, you were my Parent; in later life, my Teacher; in manhood my Companion. To your affectionate vigilance I owe my principles, my knowledge, and that I am a Minister of the Gospel of Christ. For whatever profit they derive from this little Book, the young will be indebted to you."[20]

III

The rights to Beecher's dedicatory note are held by the speaker, of course, who presents himself as an American and Protestant Elisha draped in the mantle of his mentor and embodying his purpose and influence. But as a student able to approximate the master and thus carry forward his work into the next generation, Beecher identifies with his readers. Their relation to him will resemble his relation to his illustrious father, that is, if *Seven Lectures to Young Men* proves to be as effective in its tutelage as the father supposedly was in his. Thus already in the first-person dedicatory note the speaker is both instructor and student, master and colleague, elevated authority and companion. The double identity and dual role are both a function of the first-person mode of address and its certification as the most strategic form of negotiation in the guide to success. In more ways than one, then, the guide to success is a joint enterprise that, in most cases, relies for its success on the first-person address of the speaker.

The capacity of the speaker to identify with the student in a way that encourages the student to identify with the speaker is central to Todd's introduction of his undertaking in his *Student's Manual*: "As I look back upon the days when I was a 'student,' I can see that here I went wrong, and there I mistook; here I missed a golden opportunity, and there I acquired a wrong habit, or received a wrong bias; and as I sometimes walk past a college, as it is lighted up for evening-study, I pause, and sigh, that I cannot go back and begin life again, carrying with me my present experience. I think, too, I can see, that if there had been such a book as I am now attempting to write for students, put into my hands at an early period, it would have been of incalculable advantage to me."[21] The ample register of terms like "golden opportunity," "students," "study," "experience," and "incalculable advantage," finds its rhetorical equivalent in the persona as teacher, who is also student, inquirer, and friend. The topical heading for the page just quoted reads simply: "Want of experience in the student."

Usually this speaker is encountered in the opening paragraphs of the first chapter, but in Beecher's *Lectures* he announces himself in the two-paragraph "Preface" and, in the second edition, in a short new "Preface" as well. These prefaces and their self-justifying

"I" suffice in subsequent editions, in which the front matter is supplemented not by additional prefaces or expanded apologia but by notices that advertise the excellence and usefulness of this guidebook. Van Doren and Frost are exceptions in their preference for the "we" over the "I." But in Van Doren a rather traditional editorial "we" addresses readers directly in the second person, singular and plural. Only in Frost's two guides is the "you" understood but not named. When the reader is addressed, he is referred to in the third person, the same person in which the pedantically egocentric speaker refers to himself. In the other thirteen guidebooks the speakers fix their eye on their audience as though to encompass the entire auditory while also seeking out the individual reader-listener with the fitting word of advice, criticism, and encouragement. (Arthur's preliminary remarks in his first chapter are replete with "we" and moral saws, but he, too, shifts within a few paragraphs to the first person singular.) Speakers try to take possession of the reader not by altering convictions and habits but by valorizing a select number of them (the ones most compatible to the speaker's purposes), and by making these an important part of the bond between an entirely reliable "I" and a well-meaning, ambitious "you." In most cases the "I"/"you" exchange is rated as an exceptionally valuable bond because of the unique and rare qualities of the subjects selected as most important for the "you." "I Address you, Young Men of my country," the speaker declares in an extraordinarily long introductory paragraph in Todd's *The Young Man*, "not because others have not given you many and wise counsels; but because, so far as I know, no one has occupied the ground which I have selected, nor said just the things which I am wishing to say."[22] In several of the guidebooks another ingredient in the bond is the literary/dramatic voice that appeals to the "you" through metaphors on stage, so to speak. If one has little tolerance for nineteenth-century pulpiteering, theatrical melodrama, rhetoric of moral suasion, or John Foster's *Essays*, several of the speakers will quickly be dismissed as mawkish overactors. Daniel Wise is probably the most notable, if perhaps not quotable, example of "I"/"you" bonding through mawkish theatrical address. His first chapter opens with the following: "Give me your hand, my dear young friend, and I will lead you to the dark passages and the rugged steeps whose forbidding shadows fall gloomily on the highway of life."[23] Beecher's speaker also offers his hand, although with less excessive invitations.

The self-proclaimed commitment of the guidebook to promote the young man's prospects for success forms a significant part of the persona's apologia. Beecher's persona explains: "I felt an earnest desire, if I could, to raise the suspicion of the young, and to direct their reason to the arts by which they are, with such facility, destroyed. . . . I only claim the place of a companion; and that I may gain his ear, I have sought to present truth in those forms which best please the young."[24] And Van Doren, who titled chapter six of his *Mercantile Morals* "The Young Merchant needs a Guide," places persona and inexperienced young man alike in "this dark world of doubt and perplexity, of deceit and ignorance," and identifies the exchange between them as "a guide equally infallible, easy, and safe."[25] Wise offers a similar sentiment, in his characteristic prose: "Open your heart to my counsels! I will teach you how to escape the teeming dangers, which, like troops of ill-omened phantoms, wait in the 'slippery places' of youth, seeking his destruction. I will unfold to you the secrets of success and of eminence in this life, and the sure means of winning a crown of glory in the next!"[26] Clarke spares the reader overloaded metaphors, loading all of the importance of his task on the undertaking itself. His series of lectures was prepared, he notes in the "Advertisement," "with the desire to promote the intellectual, moral and religious improvement of the young people of the author's pastoral charge" and "at the solicitation of the young men before whom they were delivered."[27] The pastoral charge is limited by the distribution of *Lectures to Young People*, but the dangers and opportunities facing the young man in manufacturing centers are unlimited.

The commitment of the speaker to promoting the success of young men in the young and enterprising nation is supported by the assurance of successful advice. Alcott's speaker announces, "I believe you will try to follow my advice; for I take it for granted that none will purchase and read this work but such as are willing to be advised. I repeat it, therefore—I go upon the presumption that my advice will, in the main, be followed. . . . In this view, I submit these pages to the youth of our American States."[28] Sounding a common note in the guide to success, Hamilton's speaker concludes his counsel to young men with a clarion call both for a guide to success such as his and for the age: "From the ranks of American youth must arise those who are to be the counsellors of their country in the hour of deliberation, . . . the patterns to her sons yet unborn. . . . Thus resolve, and act out your resolution, and you are a true patriot!"[29]

The "true patriot" is exemplified in the economically enterprising man. Honesty and piety will be his nature; these virtues will be engendered and strengthened by his undertakings and by his environment of vigorous enterprise. The pattern for the sons yet unborn is the life of self-development through economic enterprise. Like Bunyan's Pilgrim Christian, the patriot can all too easily go astray. As Todd warns his readers, if the enterprising young man is to succeed, the imagination must be kept in check. To disregard the advice of the success counselor, and to indulge the life of the imagination, is to "build castles in the air . . . as baseless as the elements in which he builds them."[30] The conventional wisdom of the American manuals for young men, the designs of the speakers, and the aggressively second- and third-rate authorial minds represented more than the faith and works of the culture in which Thoreau lived. To him, they represented an opportunity for serious parody.

Notes

1. The publishing story is touched only lightly by John Cawelti's contention that for publishers "the production of formulaic works is a highly rationalized operation with a guaranteed minimal return as well as the possibility of large profits for particularly popular individual versions." Cawelti sees "an inevitable tendency toward standardization . . . if only because one successful work will inspire a number of imitations by producers hoping to share in the profits" (*Adventure, Mystery, and Romance* [Chicago: University of Chicago Press, 1976], p. 9). The term *imitations* is an invitation to caution here. Many degrees and kinds of imitation are possible. Although American success manuals can be described as formulaic and imitative, these manuals changed considerably in the brief span of the 1830s to the 1850s. Moreover, related forms developed alongside success manuals in these years (e.g., guidebook romances, courtesy books, profiles of self-made men, surveys of wealthy citizenry, and so forth). This proliferation was probably a larger factor in the phenomenal increase of profits than was careful adherence to formulas. A powerful capitalist development in the booktrade is unquestionable. Cawelti's explanation, however, cannot satisfactorily account for the increase in American publishers'

profits from half a million dollars in 1820 to twelve and one-half million dollars four decades later.

2. In a few instances the information on publication and sales is too skimpy to support an unqualified generalization. A few of the manuals, it would appear, enjoyed only modest success.

3. Guides to success that are devoted to a narrow set of trades and professions, the two by Frost and the work by Van Doren, did not fare as well in the marketplace as the popular general guides did (for example Alcott, Beecher, and Todd). Concentrating on a narrow range of trades and professions, Frost and Van Doren nevertheless offer advice on moral principles, cultural values, national destiny, individual behavior, self-culture, and the building of a stable social order. Thus they participate in the same general undertaking and seek similar success with pretty much the same kind of readership.

Van Doren's *Mercantile Morals* did not fare poorly, however, and it sold better than a book he had published two years earlier—*Novels, Useless and Dangerous*—a war-on-the-novel publication (especially the modern novel) whose arguments are repeated in *Mercantile Morals*, where they constitute chapter XI. His argument was largely wasted on an American readership that either viewed the literary world as dangerous or useless (in contrast to business enterprise) or regarded literature as useful and entertaining when understood in terms of popular romances and tales by a new generation of American authors. Not a few of these popular works were fashioned around the topics, motifs, and values of the guidebook for young men. I have in mind, for instance, extraordinarily popular volumes such as Timothy Arthur's *Riches Have Wings; or, a Tale for the Rich and Poor* (1847); *Rising in the World: a Tale for the Rich and Poor* (1847); *Lessons in Life, for All Who Will Read Them* (1851); and *Leaves from the Book of Human Life* (1853); and Louisa Tuthill's *I Will Be a Gentleman: a Book for Boys* (1844); *Onward! Right Onward!* (1844); and *Reality; or, The Millionaire's Daughter. A Book for Young Men and Young Women* (1856). Other authors whose tales or some of whose tales suggest the young man's guidebook turned into romance include Jacob Abbott, Charles F. Briggs, Timothy Flint, Emily Judson, Sylvester Judd, Hannah Lee, Sarah Mayo, Catharine Sedgwick, Elizabeth Buckminster Dwight Sedgwick, Susan Livingston Ridley Sedgwick, Thomas H. Shreve, J. N. Smith, and Alexander L. Stimson, and in the next generation the most notable of them all, Horatio Alger. No doubt Margaret Fuller included many of the romances and tales of this kind in her protest against popular moral tales: "Now that everybody who wants a new hat or bonnet takes this way to earn one from the magazines or annuals, we are inundated with the very flimsiest fabrics ever spun by mortal brain. . . . the sale-work produced is a sad affair indeed and 'gluts the market' to the sorrow both of buyers and lookers-on" (*Margaret Fuller: American Romantic*, ed. Perry Miller [Gloucester, Mass.: Peter Smith, 1969], p. 214).

4. The following list offers examples of manuals devoted to a single profession: James W. Alexander et al., *The Man of Business Considered in His*

Various Relations (1857); James Turnbull, compiler, *Advice to Young Trades-men, on the Formation of Business Habits, Calculated to Form the Character on a Solid Basis, and to Insure Respectability and Success in Life* (1835); and Louisa Tuthill's 1850 trilogy, *Success in Life, The Lawyer; Success in Life, The Mechanic;* and *Success in Life, The Merchant.* The several functions of *calculated* in Turnbull's title summarize the perspective of these works.

5. Published under the pseudonym of Henry Lunettes. Also absent from my list, yet, like the gentlemen's manual offering illuminating insights into the social and literary contexts of the guidebook for young men, is the courtesy book for "young ladies," about which Ann Douglas has cogently observed: "Etiquette books of the day make it amply clear that women were to cultivate domestic piety behind closed doors while their male counterparts were to face, and if possible conquer, the competitive world of commerce. . . . The lady's preoccupation is to be with herself: her clothes, her manners, her feelings, her family. . . . The 'Young man' is warned against the sins of the world . . . the 'Young woman' against the sins of the soul" (*The Feminization of American Culture* [New York: Alfred A. Knopf, 1977], pp. 66–67). In eighteenth-century Britain, the courtesy book for young women, like the young man's guide, is an identifiable species of conduct book. According to Mary Beth Norton, American manuals for women "must be seen . . . for what they were: expressions of social norms formulated largely by men, outlining ideal types of female behavior. It is possible to understand the impact of the roles laid out for white women in nineteenth-century America only through detailed studies of how individuals and groups of women were affected by the role expectations" ("The Paradox of the Women's Sphere," in *Women of America: A History*, ed. Carol Ruth Berkin and Mary Beth Norton [Boston: Houghton Mifflin, 1979], p. 141). Norton's terminology "largely by men" is to be understood in at least two ways: (1) the majority of the courtesy books for young women were written by men; and (2) the norms and values expressed were those of a middle- and upper-middle male-oriented society. I would quibble with this assessment only if it obscures the fact that a number of women (e.g., Catharine Beecher, Sarah Hale, Mrs. L. A. C. Sanford, and Louisa Tuthill) wrote courtesy (women's success) books and that their books, although similar in some respects, are also unlike each other. A major premise of one of these female authors, Sarah Hale, both supports and qualifies Norton's view. Hale remarked in a review of a domestic economy text titled *The Frugal Housewife* that "there is a spirit in the work . . . like the economical maxims of Franklin. . . . Our men are sufficiently money-making. Let us keep our women and children from the contagion as long as possible. . . . True the book was prepared chiefly for those who are obliged to practice rigid economy in order to live and thrive. But could not some motive, besides merely the wish of accumulating wealth, have been urged as the stimulus to prudence and exertion?" (*Ladies Magazine* 3 [January 1830]: 42–43). On the other hand, it is not without significance that almost half of the authors in the core list of guidebooks for young men also wrote courtesy books for young

women, and that the topics and advice of the respective manuals are usually worlds apart.

6. Biographical and autobiographical profiles include the following: William Arthur, *The Successful Merchant; Sketches of the Life of Mr. Samuel Budgett* (1851?); John Frost, *Lives of American Merchants, Eminent for Integrity, Enterprise and Public Spirit* (1844); Freeman Hunt, *Lives of American Merchants*, 2 vols. (1856); idem, *Memoirs and Autobiography of Some of the Wealthy Citizens of Philadelphia . . . By a Merchant of Philadelphia* (1846); Charles Bailey Seymour, *Self-Made Men* (1858); William M. Thayer, *The Poor Boy and the Merchant Prince; or Elements of Success Drawn from the Life and Character of the Late Amos Lawrence. A Book for Youth* (1857); idem, *The Printer Boy; or, How Ben Franklin Made his Mark* (1860?). Brief profiles of the economically successful and powerful are often one of several significant components in the surveys of wealth and the wealthy, many of which focus on the wealthy as individuals and as a class in a particular community or region. One might cite examples such as William Armstrong, *The Aristocracy of New York; Who They Are, and What They Were* (1848); Moses Yale Beach, ed. *Wealth and Wealthy Citizens of New York City* (1842), subsequently retitled *Wealth and Pedigree of the Wealthy Citizens of New York* and *The Wealth and Biography of the Wealthy Citizens of New York*; Abner Forbes, *"Our First Men," or Catalogue of the Richest Men of Massachusetts . . . Credibly Reported to Be Worth One Hundred Thousand Dollars and Upwards* (1851); Abner Forbes and J. W. Greene, *The Rich Men of Massachusetts: Containing a Statement of the Reputed Wealth of About Fifteen Hundred Persons* (1851); Freeman Hunt, *Worth and Wealth* (1856), which also serves as an ethically infused primer on how to succeed economically; John Lomas and Alfred S. Peace, *The Wealthy Men and Women of Brooklyn and Williamsburgh* (1847); *Wealth and Biography of the Wealthy Citizens of Philadelphia . . . By a Member of the Philadelphia Bar* (1845); and Thomas L. V. Wilson, *The Aristocracy of Boston; Who They Are and What They Were* (1848), in which aristocracy and wealth are reciprocally dependent terms. As for studies lighting the way to wealth, some of the notable titles are: *A Calendar of Wealth, Fashion and Gentility* (1846); Edwin Troxell Freedley, ed., *A Practical Treatise on Business* (1852), earlier English editions of which are titled *Money: How to Get, Save, Spend, Give, Lend, and Bequeath It* and *Money: How to Get, How to Keep, and How to Use It*; idem, *Leading Pursuits and Leading Men. A Treatise on the Principal Trades and Manufactures of the United States, Showing the Progress, State and Prospects of Business* (1854), which was soon translated exactingly into German; idem, *The Legal Advisor; or, How to Diminish Losses, Avoid Lawsuits, and Save Time, Trouble, and Money, by Conducting Business According to Law, as Expounded by the Best and Latest Authorities* (1857); idem, *Philadelphia and Its Manufactures: A Hand-book Exhibiting the Development, Variety, and Statistics of the Manufacturing Industry of Philadelphia in 1857* (1858); idem, *Opportunities for Industry and the Safe Investment of*

Capital; or, a Thousand Chances to Make Money (1859); Charles Bailey Seymour, *Guide to Wealth; or, The Pathway to Health, Peace and Competence* (1856); George Sumner Weaver, *The Ways of Life* (1855), in part a discussion of success in business enterprise (Weaver was better known for his *Hopes and Helps for the Young of Both Sexes*, which in most of its topics and advice represents a conflation of the success manual for young men and the courtesy book for young women); and Robert Woodward, *Elements of Success* (1848).

7. John Todd, *The Young Man. Hints Addressed to the Young Men of the United States*, 7th ed. (Northhampton: Hopkins, Bridgman, 1856), p. 16; Timothy Shay Arthur, *Advice to Young Men on Their Duties and Conduct in Life* (Boston: Elias Howe, 1847), p. 51. In Arthur's view of manifest destiny, the advancement of man in the new world under the influence of Christianity and enterprise "must be permanent; for man now rises from the sensual into the scientific and rational, and finally becomes spiritual and celestial, and cannot again be deceived by appearances" (p. 16).

8. John Todd, *The Foundations of Success. An Oration Pronounced Before the Philomathaean and Phenakosmian Societies of Pennsylvania College* (Gettysburg: H. C. Neinstedt, 1844), p. 6.

9. William A. Alcott, *The Young Man's Guide* (Boston: Perkins and Marvin, 1839), p. 43.

10. Daniel Wise, *The Young Man's Counsellor: or, Sketches and Illustrations of the Duties and Dangers of Young Men* (New York: Phillips & Hunt, 1850), p. 107.

11. Charles Butler, *The American Gentleman* (Philadelphia: Hogan & Thompson, 1836), p. 31.

12. Bruce Barton, *The Man Nobody Knows: A Discovery of the Real Jesus* (Indianapolis: Bobbs-Merrill, 1925). This book was the best seller in 1925, topping even the English Bible in sales. The strong pact made with enterprise in these manuals is largely unrelated to whether the author is or is not a member of the clergy. Like the non-clerical authors, ministers are divided on the question of whether the new enterprise is cause for concern, religious examination, and at least modest warnings. The warnings, few and rarely directed against enterprise as such, raise a finger against excesses such as total obsession with moneymaking at the expense of other activities. As for the manuals written by ministers, evangelical authors John Abbott and Daniel Wise incorporate even less (and less superintending) Protestant dogma in their guidebooks than ministers like the Congregational Beecher, Presbyterian Todd, and Dutch Reform Van Doren, whose guidebooks are non-theological, and whose citations of passages and anecdotes from the Bible serve the subject at hand. Religious and moral duties are, in the main, compatible with enterprise and confirmed by it. By his works, the faith of the man of enterprise is known.

13. Van Doren is the only author to discuss at any length a new cultural problem specified by Emerson in his "Historic Notes of Life and Letters in New England": "In the law courts, crimes of fraud have taken the place of crimes of

force. The stockholder has stepped into the place of the warlike baron" (*Lectures and Biographical Sketches*, vol. 10 of *The Complete Works of Ralph Waldo Emerson*, ed. Edward W. Emerson [Boston and New York: Houghton Mifflin, 1903], p. 328).

14. Wise, *The Young Man's Counsellor*, pp. 29–30, 33.

15. Butler, *The American Gentleman*, especially pp. 13–45, for his lexicon of this order; Arthur, *Advice to Young Men*, pp. 8, 83.

16. Todd, *The Young Man*, pp. 16, 32–35.

17. Todd, *The Young Man*, pp. 46, 28–29.

18. Howe, *The Unitarian Conscience: Harvard Moral Philosophy, 1805–1861* (Cambridge, Mass.: Harvard University Press, 1970), p. 227.

19. Todd, *The Young Man*, pp. 139–40.

20. For Lyman Beecher's warning, see *The Autobiography of Lyman Beecher*, ed. Barbara M. Cross (Cambridge, Mass.: Harvard University Press, 1961), 1: 192. Henry Ward Beecher's dedication appears on an unnumbered leaf at the beginning of *Seven Lectures to Young Men, on Various Important Subjects* (Indianapolis: Thomas B. Cutler, 1844). Thoreau did not much care for the younger Beecher. "If Henry Ward Beecher knows so much more about God than another," Thoreau wrote in his *Journal*, "if he has made some discovery of truth in this direction, I would thank him to publish it in *Silliman's Journal*, with as few flourishes as possible" (1906 J 11:438).

21. Todd, *The Student's Manual; Designed, by Specific Directions, to Aid in Forming and Strengthening the Intellectual and Moral Character and Habits of the Student* (Northhampton: Bridgman and Childs, 1854), p. 14.

22. Todd, *The Young Man*, p. 15.

23. Wise, *The Young Man's Counsellor*, p. 13.

24. Henry Ward Beecher, "Preface" (unnumbered page), *Seven Lectures to Young Men, on Various Important Subjects* and (beginning with the 2nd ed. in 1845) *Lectures to Young Men, on Various Important Subjects*.

25. William Howard Van Doren, *Mercantile Morals; or Thoughts for Young Men Entering Mercantile Life* (New York: Charles Scribner, 1857), pp. 180, 181.

26. Wise, *The Young Man's Counsellor*, pp. 13–14.

27. Dorus Clarke, *Lectures to Young People in Manufacturing Villages* (Boston: Perkins & Marvin, 1836), p. v.

28. Alcott, *The Young Man's Guide*, pp. 25–26.

29. William T. Hamilton, *The Responsibilities of American Youth! An Address Delivered at Orville, Dallas County, Ala.* (Mobile: Strickland & Benjamin, 1851), p. 15.

30. Todd, *The Young Man*, p. 140.

6

Walden *as Parody*

Although participating in a cultural and literary discourse in which the conventions of the guidebook were honored, *Walden* had to fight to survive in the very culture that was its gynaeceum. In a time when Thoreau's culture appropriated many of the conventions represented in the guides to a young man's success and translated these conventions into rather specific means toward specific ends, his own translation through parody was allowed no more than a marginal presence, as the sales records of *Walden* confirm and as *Walden* itself projects through its witty parable of the Indian basket weaver and the speaker's decision to avoid the necessity of selling his product.[1] In part because it resisted contemporary vernacular even while using it, in part because it contested the popular understanding of enterprise in the name of what it regarded as a more desirable enterprise, in part because early critics were unsure about this unconventional work and its relation to familiar conventions, *Walden* could not expect the kind of market success enjoyed by contemporary success manuals for young men. Yet *Walden*, which features many experiments and several faces and voices, presents itself, among other things, as such a guide to success, on its terms, by transforming conventions of a genre and habits of mind in the contemporary culture into a narrative of cultural behavior and destiny centered on the enterprise of Thoreau's version of self-culture. "I would fain say something" concerning "you who read these pages," the speaker announces at the outset, you "who are

said to live in New England; something about your condition,
especially your outward condition or circumstances in this world, in
this town, what it is, whether it is necessary that it be as bad as it is,
whether it cannot be improved as well as not" (*Walden*, p. 4). In
short, *Walden* constitutes a serious parody of the guide to success
and a number of its conventions.

What I have in mind in characterizing *Walden* as a "serious
parody" of the guide for young men will be addressed by examining
the internalized reader of *Walden* (the recipient of the advice), the
relation of the recipient of advice to the advisor, the kinds of advice,
and the strategies employed by the advice-giver. Since the latter
point, the question of strategies, has the strongest bearing on identifying and demonstrating parody of young men's guides, sections II,
III, and IV of this chapter concentrate on what I see as the three
principal strategies of *Walden* as unconventional guide. These are,
respectively: lexical and semantic manipulation; reconstitution of
economy as lexical term and as concept touching on other terms;
and the unconventional rhetorical performance by the first-person
persona. At the outset, however, I offer a survey of recent theoretical appropriations and practical applications of the term *parody*
that bear on the question of *Walden*'s relation to the young man's
guide.

For several years now, Thoreau scholarship has exhibited some
interest in Thoreau as parodist and in *Walden* as parody. A passage
in Lawrence Buell's *Literary Transcendentalism* offers a useful
starting point for a brief survey of recent developments. On the
subject of the conventions of travel literature and *Walden* as travel
literature, Buell raises the possibility of serious parody without
describing Thoreau's achievement as such: "*Walden* is not in a class
by itself, but a variant or extension of a form which all share loosely
in common." Though we may differ with Buell's observation that
"actual travel is useless, in the Transcendentalist view of things," his
characterization of *Walden* as "an aesthetic mongrel" is appropriate, if somewhat unsatisfactory, when understood in terms of his
description of *Walden* as a "variant" and "extension" of a species of
literature with identifiable conventions. Buell's hints are, I suggest,
tantamount to attaching *Walden* to travel literature by the linkage
of parody.[2] In "Rural Architecture in Andrew Jackson Downing
and Henry David Thoreau: Pattern Book Parody in *Walden*,"

Richard and Jean Masteller discuss Thoreau's literary act of resistance, by means of parody, to architectural excesses as found in the popular house pattern books of the 1840s and 50s. More recent articles examine Thoreau's parodic use of the Westminster Catechism in his effort to bind improved means to improved ends and his parody of agricultural reformers and their programs.[3] And several general studies touching obliquely on the subject of parody in *Walden* have appeared. The earliest concerns itself with playful and ideologically poised operations in *Walden* and focuses on Thoreau's principal rhetorical means toward his end of reconstituting language and values: paradox, wordplay, and apothegm. The traditional notion of parody as burlesque presides over a study of Thoreau's comic sense, whereas the influence of more recent views of parody is clearly evident in a discussion of voices in *Walden*, a study that defines parody as a countervoice that questions the primary voice only to confirm its reliability, yet perhaps also supplementing it through its contestatory challenge.[4]

If one assumes, as I do, that literary parody involves appropriation and manipulation of particular conventions associated with a species of literature, then the argument for *Walden* as parody of the guidebook for young men assumes that Thoreau participated in the life of the guidebook genre through imitation, deviation, extension, outright rejection, and other means of appropriation. To posit that parody is an act of appropriation and transformation is not to define it, however. In fact, the generalization calls to mind a number of structuralist and poststructuralist views of parody. I think it fair to say that a tendency in recent theoretical discourse and criticism to implicate the term *parody* in a wide range of historiographical and metaliterary issues has had the salutary effect of enriching and elevating the term but at the cost of turning it into something approaching a suprataxonomical, all-inclusive signifier, indeed, a virtual synonym for the relation of a literary text to various aspects of itself, to other texts by the same author and by other authors, to a literary genre, to the very presence of so-called normative literary practice, to canons, to literary history, to Western tradition, to the discourse of an age, to criticism of the text, to criticism of a text that criticizes itself, and so on.[5] Thus some further explication of the term as I understand and use it seems advisable.

Let me begin my definition of *parody* by quoting Linda Hutcheon's admirably concise summary of the Russian formalist view of the term: "Parody develops out of the realization of the literary inadequacies of a certain convention. Not merely an unmasking of a non-functioning system, it is also a necessary and creative process by which new forms appear to revitalize the tradition and open up new possibilities to the artist." In this view, parodic art deviates "from the norm and includes that norm within itself." Consequently conventions "become energizing and freedom-inducing in the light of parody."[6] Such a view of parody raises any number of questions: When is a convention inadequate? For whom? In what respect? How does one realize its inadequacy? Why should the generative force or motivation behind parody depend on a recognition that a convention is inadequate or has failed? How can parody revitalize a tradition while contesting it? Is parody a creature of the very domain it resists? Are there essential, authoritative "norms" from which parodic art deviates? Does parody liberate current literary practice, literary art as a whole, the author, other authors, the reader, the critic?

Although crucial to the Russian formalist view of parody, the notion of inadequate conventions (*inadequate* is Hutcheon's term, but fairly represents the formalist position) is itself an inadequate one. Nonetheless, the idea of an author using conventions against themselves, against a tradition that valorizes them, against the author's own inclinations and frequent practice, or against the habits of the reader, so as to open up new possibilities as alternatives to the old ones, is a useful if somewhat fuzzy-edged notion. Hutcheon removes some of the fuzziness with her postulate that parodic art "parodies and imitates" the originary form "as a way to a new form which is just as serious and valid . . . as the form it dialectically attempts to surpass."[7] *Validity* is, of course, a loaded concept here, and her dialectical model tends to undercut the declared principle of parody as the resistance presented by one or more alternative forms rather than an antithesis that becomes the condition for a synthesis. As for the term *form*, it seems to me that *convention* is a more serviceable term since, on the one hand, *convention* is somewhat more receptive to the critic's need to place practical boundary markers on the term, on the other hand, *convention*, even more than *form*, accommodates aesthetic, linguistic, rhetorical, bibliographical, editorial, historical, cultural, and political considerations and implies that they impinge on one another.

In the case of the guides for young men and *Walden, convention* includes features such as general format, kinds of topics and subtopics, topical arrangement and relation, chapter titles, running titles, opening chapters, comparative emphasis (which topics and chapters tend to function as points of orientation?), rhetorical devices, and lexical and idiomatic patterns (habits of articulation). What Richard Poirier characterizes as a "fantasia of punning" in *Walden* "designed to subvert the comfortable idioms that unite the communities of finance capitalism,"[8] is, in effect, an authorial act of absorbing a particular environment but of appropriating certain of its conventions only to refashion them or to offer alternative versions alongside them. One might illustrate this from the Greek term *parodia* and its verb form *pareo*: one of the ways to open up this once narrowly defined term and to attribute to the term the capacity to offer another version alongside a familiar one is to impute to the stem *par* the meaning of *para* (as in "parallel," "parataxis," "paraphrase," "parallax," and "paradox"). This is *parody* as I use the term.

Let me take this idea of parody a step farther by suggesting that the parodic act (1) may expose to parody any, indeed all, conventions and the authoritative norms, dogmas, and habits they imply (Mikhail Bakhtin's view); (2) it may expose only a select number of conventions without contesting the idea or existence of conventions; (3) it may accept and rely on a number of conventions while manipulating only a few of them; (4) it may constitute a friendly or unfriendly takeover of conventions; (5) it may counter dogmatic norm with dogmatic norm and one fixed protocol of language with another (as the rebellious Prometheus does in his imitation of Jupiter prior to his unbinding in Shelley's "Prometheus Unbound"); (6) it may attempt to replace normative conventions with antinomianism; (7) it may seek to supplement a malnourished lexicon, rhetoric, or formal design; (8) it may attempt to revitalize a convention simply by locating it in a new context; or (9) it may parody itself in its very parodic maneuvers against conventions.[9] As I see it, a parodist may manipulate particular conventions as found in a work, group of loosely related works, or genre without creating a new genre and without limiting the newness of his new achievement to one kind of parodic treatment, or to parody, for that matter. The weight of my descriptions is borne by the term *convention*, not *genre*. *Walden* includes several kinds of parodic treatments; the parody of the young man's guide to success is one of these, and the various parodic activities, together with other experiments by Thoreau, resulted in what scholars with a formalist taxonomy of genre have regarded as a hybridized form.

Parody offers another version of particular literary and cultural conventions, and this maneuver suggests a form of co-optation. If one attaches to convention the concept of power (as I do), then parody as co-optation implies a resistance/accommodation that involves a simultaneous appropriation, manipulation, and a redistribution of power as convention and transformation of convention as power. The parodist's new version imitates the originary version and thus resembles it, yet contests it and thus differs from it. Difference can manifest itself, for example, in lexicon, in idiom, in rhetorical features, in topical arrangement. Both resemblance and difference suggest that in reading the parodic work there is much to be gained in understanding it comparatively and in determining in what kind of relation it stands to the parodied documents or corpus of documents. The likeness/difference relation will usually disclose how comic or serious the parody is, how narrowly selective it is, how dogmatic, how limited to the literary domain, how political, how moral, how deeply implicated in cultural discourse and values. As a parodist in a culture of enterprise, Thoreau conscripted parody as an instrument of co-optation. Like any artist, he faced the problem of power and its distribution.

I

Walden would fain say something to "you who read these pages . . . ; something about your condition, especially your outward condition or circumstances in this world, . . . whether it cannot be improved as well as not" (*Walden*, p. 4). Improving one's "circumstances in this world" is a thematic ligature between the voice of experience and the "you" addressed in an account the experienced speaker hopes will be "startling and informing" (p. 10), and is also *Walden*'s most obvious link to the young man's guide. As general as this "you" seems to be, this recipient has already been identified in terms of one conventional type of guidebook wisdom: "Perhaps these pages are more particularly addressed to poor students." The *poor* readers are not flattered by the pun. "As for the rest of my readers, they will accept such portions as apply to them. I trust that none will stretch the seams in putting on the coat, for it may do good service to him whom it fits" (p. 4). And whom does the coat fit? "I see young men, my townsmen, whose misfortune it is to have inherited farms, houses, barns, cattle, and farming tools; for these are more easily acquired than got rid of" (p. 5). The coat fits others. "I address myself now to those of my readers who have a living to get," the speaker declares in the midst of his inventory of income and outlay at Walden (p. 60), deftly using as fulcrum for his statement the ambiguous word "living." The speaker does not offer advice "to those who find their encouragement and inspiration in precisely the present condition of things, and cherish it with the fondness and enthusiasm of lovers," nor to "those who are well employed, in whatever circumstances." Rather, he will address the "discontented," those who are "idly complaining of the hardness of their lot or of the times, when they might improve them" (p. 16).

Important elements in his lexicon of direct address to the "you" and in his creation of a readership are the terms *advice* and *advise.* Yet his counsel suggests a relation to the reader and a purpose not associated with the conventional guidebook: "Will you be a reader, a student merely, or a seer?" (p. 111). That question, with its play on "seer" and its distinction between the traditional recipient of guidebook advice and *Walden*'s advisee, explicitly confirms what has become evident in the passages quoted in these paragraphs: that *Walden* presents itself as a guidebook for young men, that the speaker adopts the guise of the first-person guidebook counselor, that his readers may not be typical guidebook recipients, that his advice may be quite unconventional, and that traditional authority and popular wisdom may stretch the seams of *Walden.* "One young man of my acquaintance, who has inherited some acres," the speaker notes in a personal anecdote characteristic of guidebooks for young men, "told me that he thought he should live as I did, *if he had the means.*" What counts, of course, is the use to which the anecdote is put: "I would not have any one adopt *my* mode of living on any account. . . . I would have each one be very careful to find out and pursue *his own* way, and not his father's or his mother's or his neighbor's instead" (p. 71). This acknowledgment of the past, tradition, elders, and the accumulated experience of others, yet resistance to them, is already clearly signaled in the second paragraph of *Walden*, in which the speaker obtrudes his affairs on his audience because his affairs have been called "impertinent" by his townspeople.

In admitting the charge of impertinence into his discussion of his program while reassuring the reader that his program is "natural and pertinent," the speaker can use the double entendre of *impertinent* to his advantage and, prospectively, to the reader's "improvement." The "following pages" of *Walden*, although pertinent to the reader, will strike conventional readers, such as his "townsmen," as irrelevant to success and not pertaining to the matter of a success manual. Understood thus, the charge that *Walden* is "impertinent" dismisses its counsel as unsuitable, out of place, incongruous, trivial, trifling. Most of the mischief associated with the term *impertinent* belongs to the speaker; yet the mischief resides mainly in his response to the charge of impertinence. He states ever so politely and thoughtfully, "I will therefore ask those of my readers who feel no particular interest in me to pardon me if I undertake to answer some of these questions in this book" (p. 3). The polite dismissal of certain readers and expectations in a sense justifies the charge of "impertinence" with its other cluster of meanings: impropriety, rudeness, presumptuousness, forwardness, insolence to authority and to one's superiors, and unmannerliness. What is impertinent in one scheme of things, however, is pertinent in another. Only in the eyes of those who regard his counsel as pertinent will he be defended from being a trifler.

Thus we are not surprised by an even bolder reversal in the tenth paragraph of *Walden*, where the speaker not only turns the catechism on its head but also crowds out "echoes" of "what old people say" with his declaration that "Age is no better, hardly so well, qualified for an instructor as youth, for it has not profited so much as it has lost." With respect to practical counsel to young men, "the old have no very important advice to give the young, their own experience has been so partial" (pp. 8–9). The attributive "partial" loops back to the speaker's deliberately ambiguous citation of "the narrowness of my experience" in his paragraph on pertinence and impertinence and to his association of "prejudices" with elders immediately after referring to the catechism. "I have lived some thirty years on this planet," the speaker adds, "and I have yet to hear the first syllable of valuable or even earnest advice from my seniors. They have told me nothing, and probably cannot tell me any thing, to the purpose. . . . If I have any experience which I think valuable, I am sure to reflect that this my Mentors said nothing about" (p. 9). So much for the guidance of elders and traditional authority.

But something more important is going on here. Conventional roles have been reversed. The narrator-as-young-man is instructing and chiding his elders in a guidebook for young men and for the benefit of young men.[10] As for the ancients, although the parody-minded speaker now and then effectively drafts them into his program of resistance to tradition and conventional forms, more often than not they are relegated to the community of elders and a revered past that can offer only useless advice. To quote an example, "the learned societies and great men of Assyria,—where are they? What youthful philosophers and experimentalists we are! There is not one of my readers who has lived a whole human life. . . . Yet we esteem ourselves wise, and have an established order on the surface" (pp. 331–32). The conventionally profitable is chalked up in the loss column.

The complex reversals of roles and the shifting expectations produce, not surprisingly, another kind of impertinence, an unmannerly dismissal of codes of respectability as irrelevant to this unconventional guidebook. Contrary to most guides for young men, *Walden* does not include a treatise on manners as part of its advice. Nor does *Walden* assume that manners are next to morals or the other side of morals or that proper manners are a key to professional success. Rather, manners are identified with conventional values and behavior: "We have had to agree on a certain set of rules, called etiquette and politeness, to make this frequent meeting tolerable. . . . We meet at the post-office, and at the sociable, and about the fireside every night; we live thick and are in each other's way, and stumble over one another" (p. 136). When the socially successful invite the famous to their dinner table, the "interest and the conversation are about costume and manners chiefly; but a goose is a goose still, dress it as you will" (p. 329). By linking morals, manners, social standing, and professional success, respectable elders have become impertinent (irrelevant and trifling) in their rules and professional example. "Shall the respectable citizen thus gravely teach, by precept and example, the necessity of the young man's providing a certain number of superfluous glow-shoes, and umbrellas, and empty guest chambers for empty guests, before he dies?" (p. 36).

By dismissing manners from its pages, *Walden* banishes a large corpus of guidebook prescriptions to "the established order on the surface," the order regarded by the mannered as their reality and reified by the "earnest advice from my seniors." Yet *Walden* does not shy away from prescribing rules or invoking precepts. Its many aphorisms, for instance, are more often than not pointed advice and general precept dressed up as proverb. "I do not mean to prescribe rules to strong and valiant natures, who will mind their own affairs whether in heaven or hell" (p. 16), the speaker informs us, leaving an enormous latitude for precepts, but only for those who need the coat he has woven and will not tear its seams. And so *Walden* offers unconventional precepts for the "you," the readers internalized by the text. Advice giving in *Walden*, then, is remarkably like and unlike that in the young man's guide. While presuming the role and assuming the responsibilities of the guidebook for young men, *Walden* also warns its readers not to "seek so anxiously to be developed, to subject yourself to many influences to be played on; it is all dissipation" (p. 328). Aware of his advice-laden paragraphs and chapters, the speaker nonetheless informs the "you" early on that "I will only hint at some of the enterprises which I have cherished" (p. 16). Rather specific advice on early rising, reading, food, drink, apparel, dwelling, furniture, exercise, conversation, leisure, farming, chastity, and the like is offered as the means for the recipient "to find out and pursue *his own* way" (p. 71). That way leads in the direction of what the speaker memorably poeticizes as "*extra vagance*." Specific rules and counsel are viewed by *Walden* as part of the economy of means toward the end of "*extra vagance*," a condition that, with reference to institutionalized conventions and prevalent values, is "free and uncommitted" (p. 84).

Beyond merely acknowledging the presence of aphorisms in *Walden*, I wish to note that *Walden* is one of the most aphoristic literary documents associated with the so-called American literary renaissance. This feature of *Walden* reinforces rather than contradicts its use of conventions of language for unconventional ends. The compositional history of *Walden* reveals a noticeable transformation in the aphorisms from its first to its final version. Both versions are strongly aphoristic; the main difference lies in the relatively atomistic nature of aphorisms in the first version, in which the more aphoristic the prose, the more autonomous both sentences and paragraphs are of one another. This is most evident in the material eventually constituting the first two chapters. In the final version, aphoristic precepts are part of a more unified and complex weave, which is to say that as means to Thoreau's ends they have been integrated into the larger company of means in both the narrative and the exposition. The published version of *Walden* features a complex use of aphorisms. For example, the speaker uses and debunks slogans, practices an epigrammatic habit yet also contests the "wisdom" of epigrams, turns social truths on their side or head, and quotes the classics on husbandry yet violates local farmers' traditional advice. In all of this activity he uses commonplace sayings in order to challenge their confinement and subvert their authority or move beyond their traditional limits.

As a literary work that appropriates the conventions of the guidebook for its own purpose and in so doing attempts to offer a "natural and pertinent" book, *Walden* takes a calculated risk. The speaker's observation that "it is not all books that are as dull as their readers" (p. 107) suggests that he is aware of the risk. The opening paragraphs of *Walden* press the argument that the "account" of the "I" is not designed to win applause or assent without having engaged the reader confrontationally through its rhetorical means, especially its words of "a new aspect" and its unconventional "I." "What is called eloquence in the forum is commonly found to be rhetoric in the study," explains the "I" in "Reading," thereby linking the "I" with "rhetoric," and unmistakably distinguishing this "I" of *Walden* from the "orator" who "yields to the inspiration of a transient occasion" (p. 102), and who, we might add, is strongly featured in the majority of the success manuals of the 1830s to the 1850s.[11] Most books, including most guidebooks for young men, are dull, and so are their readers. Publications of this order are covered, no doubt, by the petulant and condescending asseveration in "Reading" that "this sort of gingerbread is baked daily and more sedulously than pure wheat or rye-and-Indian in almost every oven, and finds a surer market"(p. 105). One detects a note of special pleading in the assertion in the "Reading" chapter that the best books "have no cause of their own to plead, but while they enlighten and sustain the reader his common sense will not refuse them" (p. 103).

Books are defended from being common and trivial, the speaker argues in "Reading," if they "put a new aspect on the face of things for us." Or, to switch metaphors in the mode of *Walden*, books are uncommon if they encourage a new hearing and understanding. The test of a good book, including the *Walden* account, is offered in the same chapter: "There are probably words addressed to our condition exactly, which, if we could really hear and understand, would be more salutary than the morning or the spring to our lives" (p. 107). Good books are like good advice: by addressing words "to our condition exactly," they help the reader find his own way. *Walden* hopes to join the company of those books referred to honorifically in "Reading" because they dare the reader "to read well," an exercise which the speaker describes as "noble" and which "will task the reader more than any exercise which the customs of the day esteem" (pp. 100–101).

An appropriate subtitle for "Reading," with its pointed and loaded distinctions between "common" and "uncommon," would be the "advantage" (in the guidebook's profit/loss sense of that term) of uncommon schools, uncommon authors, uncommon books, uncommon readers, and uncommon understanding in a common, provincial, nineteenth-century American culture and its surface order. "We boast that we belong to the nineteenth century and are making the most rapid strides of any nation," the speaker taunts and pleads as though to separate uncommon readers from common ones. "If we live in the nineteenth century, why should we not enjoy the advantages which the nineteenth century offers?" Why, for instance, "should we leave it to Harper & Brothers and Redding & Co. to select our reading?" (pp. 108–9). Aside from the fact that Harper & Brothers had turned down Thoreau's *A Week* in 1847, this largest publishing house in the United States and, by the time *Walden* was published, the largest in the world, was probably associated in Thoreau's mind with its legion of volumes designed specifically for school libraries in New York State's school districts, its massive series of inexpensive novels by English authors (many of them pirated), and several other popular series such as the Harper's Boy's and Girl's Library, Harper's Family Library, and Harper's Fireside Library.[12]

The assumptions of the "Reading" chapter challenge both reader and writer, and place the instruction-minded "I" and the parody-minded author of *Walden* on the side of Socrates in his debate with the Sophists. Like Socrates, the speaker fears that writers and speakers who make concessions to particular audiences by appealing to the conventions and conventional responses of their audiences will persuade readers and listeners to pursue what is pleasurable to them, to be confirmed in their habits, and to avoid new understanding.

II

Lexical manipulation and semantic play are crucial means in *Walden* of appropriating received forms with the aim of violating narrow boundaries in pursuit of "a larger sense than common use permits." "We must laboriously seek the meaning of each world and line, conjecturing a larger sense than common use permits out of what wisdom and valor and generosity we have," the "I" lectures readers in the "Reading" chapter (p. 100). Conjecturing a larger sense is a demanding labor; reconstituting the lexicon shared by speaker and recipient is one of the most formidable kinds of cultivation in *Walden*. And the force of the "must" here goes a long way to explaining Thoreau's protracted and sometimes exasperating process of writing and rewriting *Walden*. By parodying the lexicon of the young man's guide, Thoreau aims to free words from their common use, from institutionalized narrowness, to enlarge their register, to increase their intellectual and moral resonance so that they will be "addressed to our condition exactly." Such labor will "possibly put a new aspect on the face of things" (p. 107).

A most obvious example of lexical manipulation because of its visible aspect is the enlargement/transformation of a lexeme. Both expansion within the lexeme (for example, "extravagance" to "*extra vagance*") and extension of a lexeme into a series of words (for example, "nobleman" to "noble villages of men" [p. 110]) are instances of transforming a key word by physically expanding it. An ironic version of such an enlargement (diminution through expansion) is the shift reported in "Economy" from "professor" to a mere profession of professing. *Poor economy* is the reminder in the latter case. That ironic transformation is typical of the speaker's penchant for trivializing and rejecting conventional signification by deliberately moving the signifier out of the security of its narrowness, a strategy heavily relied on, for instance, in his investigation of the "necessaries of life."

Thoreau's etymological maneuver with "extravagance" is, of course, much more than a mere physical expansion of a lexeme. By semantically opening up this lexeme, Thoreau makes it more adequate to the conception of *Walden* while betraying its adequacy in the narrowly yarded vernacular of his culture. The example of "extravagance," which will be examined more extensively later in this chapter, gets closer to the heart of *Walden*'s attempt at serious speech, a renegotiation of language that I have characterized as serious parody and that Stanley Cavell calls "heroic writing." In his view, such renegotiations "assume the conditions of language as such; re-experience, as it were, the fact that there is such a thing as language at all and assume responsibility for it—find a way to acknowledge it—until the nation is capable of serious speech again. . . . A written word, as it recurs page after page, changing its company and modifying its occasions, must show its integrity under these pressures. . . . If we learn how to entrust our meaning to a word, the weight it carries through all its computations will yet prove to be just the weight we will find we wish to give it."[13]

Yet the renegotiation as characterized by Cavell can itself keep several kinds of company. One can view Thoreau's "heroic writing" (especially in its lexical manipulations and semantic play) as an attempt at polysemous featurings of some essence. In this view, held by most of the Thoreau scholars who have written illuminatingly on Thoreau's language experiments, Thoreau explores the multi-meanings of key signifiers narrowly used by his culture. His various new/old deployments of terms and conventions are simply extensions of something stable and central. Such a reregistration of language revitalizes and greatly enriches the language without fundamentally reconstituting it, that is, without fundamentally contesting and displacing conventions. Clearly some of Thoreau's own comments on what he was up to support such a view of his work. Without denying the importance to Thoreau of just such a program, I agree with Cavell's suggestion that Thoreau's language program in *Walden* involves more than expanding and enriching the language of his culture. As the rest of this chapter underscores, his transformations of the terms *economy* and *extravagance* disclose no true center for these terms. They are constituted and reconstituted by history, by Thoreau's culture, and by Thoreau. As argued in this section, the same must be said for a large number of terms associated with the young man's guide. But in that process of reconstitution, in which Thoreau demands a role for himself and for literary art, the constitution and reconstitution of language approach or retreat from what Thoreau sees as the potentialities of the language rather than its essence. This kind of heroic writing is more radical and contestatory in its relation to convention. And this kind of parodic writing, I suggest, is the principal purpose behind Thoreau's strategies.

Clusters of words that *Walden* shares with guidebooks for young men need to be read with such a purpose in mind. One can cite as example the semantic cluster of the following terms: "mode," "example," "imitate," "past," "ancestors," "tradition," "elder," "authority." Perhaps an even more pertinent semantic cluster includes the terms "instruction," "teach(er)," "education," "tutor," "mentors," "students," "advice," "advise," "proposal," "rules," "precepts," "principles," "prescribe," and "guidance." Furthermore, Thoreau's transformation of the key guidebook term and concept of "improvement" involves the reconstitution of terms such as "advantage," "advance," "trade," "profession," "occupation," "vocation," "morals," "manners," and "gentleman." One can cite many additional terms and clusters involved in the strategy of parodic appropriation, deauthorization, and reauthorization of linguistic/ideological forms, as, for example, the vocabulary of *enterprise*, discussed earlier.

Thoreau's semantic expansion and reconstitution of what he regarded as the severely limited, culturally univocal term *enterprise* is evident in his manipulation of a lexicon related to *enterprise*, terms such as "business," "profit," "loss," "wealth," "luxury," "refinements," "clothing," "fashions," "mansions," "labor," "industry," and "idleness." For instance, in *Walden*'s tribute in the "The Bean-Field" chapter to productive cultivation, the speaker confides that "labor of the hands, even when pursued to the verge of drudgery, is perhaps never the worst form of idleness" (p. 157). And "Ponds" mnemonically celebrates "days when idleness was the most attractive and productive industry" (p. 191). Here, both the paradoxically idle activity and the act of remembering such "activity" and appropriating it in the literary account are cause for joy. Manipulations of this kind disclose a strong and persistent impulse "to absorb, then to refashion, then to displace the commonly accepted meanings of words and idioms,"[14] especially operative words and idioms of the young man's guide.

In refashioning words and displacing meanings, however, the morally motivated experimenter inhabited by the very culture he strongly criticizes is caught in an unavoidable dilemma. To refashion words like "enterprise," "improvement," "advancement," "advantage," and "profit," means to move boundaries or move beyond them. But to move boundary markers or to violate boundaries insisted on by common use does not imply the absence of any and all bounds for what the concluding chapter of *Walden* calls the language of "*extra vagance.*" To free words, idioms, and phrases from their narrow yards "depends on how [they] are yarded" and a capacity to acknowledge and understand that yarding (p. 324). In writing a parody of the guidebook, Thoreau sees to it that a large number of terms crucial to guidebook discourse break out of their narrow guidebook yards and, by the same token, out of their institutionalized service in his American culture. Yet to escape confinement is, at the same time, both a reification and redefinition of confinement.

Thoreau's treatment of higher law, a concept and terminology common to the four guidebooks on his shelves and to a number of the American success manuals of his day, is a particularly illuminating example of the inescapable tension in the parodist's striving for a "larger sense than common use permits." Even "Higher Laws" can become a narrow yard. Even this chapter of *Walden*, the speaker recognizes, is not exempt, any more than, for example, the lexicon of instruction or of enterprise in the young man's guide is exempt, from the judgment that the "volatile truth" of *extra vagance* "continually betray[s] the inadequacy of the residual statement" (p. 325). The humorous, unsettling, self-parodic colloquy between hermit and poet immediately following "Higher Laws" strongly suggests such a recognition. "Higher Laws" begins by establishing the seeming counter pulls of wildness and spirituality. The manipulation in "Higher Laws" of the language both of wildness and of spirituality places the "I" outside of the conventional bounds of the internalized readers. The speaker reconstitutes "higher law" so deliberately and profoundly that its unconventionality threatens even him. Is his "larger sense" too unconventional, we wonder, or is it *extra-vagant* in a way as to threaten the open-ended program of *extra vagance*? "In view of the future or possible," the speaker exhorts the reader, "we should live quite laxly and undefined in front" (p. 324). The collaborative, companionable "we" includes him and the *Walden* account with the recipients of the exhortation.

"Higher Laws," then, demonstrates the opportunity and dilemma of the parodist who uses parody for the purpose of what *Walden* calls *extra vagance*. *Extra vagance* gains its meaning in terms of confinement, and any new confinement, including the "liberal" new boundaries of the *extra-vagant* "I"; it does not gain its meaning in relation to the prospect of an infinite, boundary-free field. Such a free prospect is intimated by the speaker's declaration, "I desire to speak somewhere *without* bounds." The linkage, however, is to the term *desire*, not to the desired condition of freedom from any and all "bounds." No matter how trivial, conventional language is appropriated and transformed. Reconstituted forms establish a new sense of reference, apparent stability, and spiritual governance. Yet their influence in renewing the present and mastering the problem of "dullness" and "drowsiness" is countered from within by the tendency to master the future, to make it clearly defined in front. Thoreau's parody of conventions and conventional guidebooks welcomes but also resists such mastery, as we have seen in this section with examples of semantic expansion and reconstitution, and as we will see in the next section with Thoreau's extraordinary use of *economy*.

The speaker's reference to the labor of "conjecturing a larger sense than common use permits" is prefaced by the imperative "we must." *We* is a term of negotiation, here, as elsewhere in *Walden*, between the "you" and "I." The imperative *must* reports both desire and unquestioned urgency. Near the end of *Walden* the speaker summarizes his intention as speaking "*without*" (outside of) the "bounds" of his common speaking, "like a man in a waking moment, to men in their waking moments" (p. 324). The principle that supports his intention is offered in the form of a precept: that his reconstitution of language "should continually betray the inadequacy of the residual statement" (p. 325).

III

In the preceding chapter, I noted in passing John Frost's *The Young Merchant* as an instructive example of a thoroughly economical application of the term *economy* in a book that, nevertheless, still obligates the term to moral service and, in his case, probably moral pretension. Frost's chapter on the "Moral Qualifications" of the young merchant is subdivided into separate discussions of fourteen moral qualifications, the first seven of which are "Honesty," "Candour," "Firmness," "Prudence," "Truth," "Justice," and "Economy," and the final one of which is "Nil Desperandum." From the company that *economy* keeps in this chapter, we would expect a discussion that reclaims some of the classical and early modern history of *economy*. The opening sentence of the "Economy" subdivision seems intent on doing just that: "The present is peculiarly an age of extravagance." The second paragraph, moreover, opens with "There is no virtue so unduly appreciated as economy, nor is there one more truly worthy of estimation."[15] Yet Frost's treatise on "Economy" turns out to be a kind of unintended allegory on the fortunes of the term *economy*. The first two chapters seem intent on accommodating some of the rich history of the term and a range of significations; thereafter the discussion unmistakably narrows its focus and the term *economy* becomes a synonym for niggardliness (favorable connotation) and a sign for the kind of self-sacrifice praised in most of the success manuals—the steady, arduous, disciplined, and honorable building of a fortune. In the sweep of a few chapters we have an exemplification, probably an unwitting one, of what has happened to the term *economy* from the time of Fordyce to the time when Emerson and other Concordians purchased stock in the railroad about to be constructed from Boston to Fitchburg, the railroad completed in 1845 and made memorable in the *Walden* account.

Thoreau's chapter "Economy" is, among other things, a philological tour de force in which, under the obligations of the conventional guidebook motif of economy, all of these meanings of *econ-*

omy, and others, are appropriated for his purpose, which we eventually discover to be *extra vagance*. The aim, as I have suggested in regard to other key words in *Walden*, is to open and greatly extend the register of a term that was rapidly being narrowed but also to contest cultural habits linked to contemporary usage. Although not dismissing the understanding and use of the term *economy* in the young man's guide, *Walden*, by "conjecturing a larger sense than common use permits out of what wisdom and valor and generosity we have" (p. 100) and thus directly opposing the cultural inclination to narrow the term, reinterprets it in terms of new aims and in the name of power ignored (both dismissed and not yet discovered) by his culture.

The *extra-vagant* maneuver with *economy* consists largely of reclaiming the rich history of the term from classical roots to present usage. And one might say that Thoreau's renegotiation of *economy* forms the basis for his project in *Walden*. To restate this in Cavell's words, the language of the "Economy" chapter "establishes the underlying vocabulary of the book as a whole."[16] In examining the language of "Economy," one does well to begin with the term *economy*. Rigorously schooled in classical and hellenistic Greek, Thoreau was quite familiar with the Greek lexical and semantic source of the term *economy—oikonomia* (Latin *oeconomia*, a term that houses only a few of the Greek meanings). He also knew that the root of *oikonomia* is *oikos*, which has the principal meaning of "house" and secondary meanings of "meeting place" and "cage" (especially a cage for domesticated birds). The term *oikonomia* has a rich register; its principal significations are (1) the management of a house, household, family, or estate; (2) husbandry (the cultivation of the flora of a property, especially of fruits and vegetables); (3) thrift (in the sense of getting much out of little); (4) directives, rules, or precepts; (5) the arrangement and relationship of the parts of a whole; and (6) stewardship (putting to the best possible use that which one has received or that which one is expected to administer).

The importance of the root *oikos* to Thoreau's parodic purposes with *economy* is matched by the importance of house building in "Economy." The longest narrative unit in "Economy" concerns house building at Walden Pond (pp. 40–69). It is also the most extended and richly suggestive metaphor in *Walden*. By the end of

"Economy," the house-building account and metaphor have assumed remarkable power in establishing the vocabulary and transformative agendas of *Walden*. Although the materials for the rebuilder's foundation are standard items from his environment, he "must every where build on piles of [his] own driving" (p. 21). The house building itself features an even more obvious and memorable transformation of materials. The grimy and warped timbers and boards of a trackside shack the narrator purchased for four dollars and twenty-five cents from Irish laborer James Collins were bleached and warped straight again in the sun, then used by the narrator as his primary materials in building his "airy" house at the Pond. In a sense they were made to serve old purposes, timbers to frame the house and boards to cover the frame. Yet the house was unmistakably new in location, shape, general outer appearance, inhabitant, and purpose. The inside, as it appeared to the speaker when he moved in on Independence Day, is described in the pages immediately following the "Economy" chapter: "The upright white hewn studs and freshly planed door and window casings gave it a clean and airy look. . . . To my imagination it retained throughout the day more or less of this auroral character. . . . This was an airy and unplastered cabin, fit to entertain a travelling god." Like "Olympus," it was "but the outside of the earth" (pp. 84–85). The speaker's record of house building is his principal exemplification of *economy* in the chapter to which Thoreau eventually gave that term as its title.

The house building recounted differs sharply from other kinds of construction such as Concord barns "seventy-five feet by forty," their "'Augean stables never cleansed'" (p. 5), the building of "a workhouse . . . a museum, an almshouse, a prison, or a splendid mausoleum" (p. 28), or the building "for this world a family mansion, and for the next a family tomb" (p. 37). Constructions of these kinds follow the plans of honored conventions and signify conventional economy and respectability. What the "I" has to say about such building is invariably tainted with a strongly oppositional spirit and levity.

"Economy is a subject which admits of being treated with levity," a passage in "Economy" culled from Thoreau's 1852 Journal opines, "but it cannot so be disposed of" (*Walden*, p. 29). That opinion is more immediately pertinent and natural in *Walden*'s parodic purposes than in the Journal passage in which it first appeared as an independent aphorism. Of course *economy* can be disposed of with levity; any number of writers come to mind who had done so prior to Thoreau's experiment. Moreover, guidebooks and success manuals and their purposes with the term and theme of *economy* will be treated with some levity in *Walden*. But they will not be so disposed of. For instance, the narrator's construction of an "airy" cabin and *extra-vagant* account has made economy and *extra vagance* mutually dependent and inseparable. Thus, while treating with levity John Todd's warning against the baseless labor of building castles in the air—Todd undoubtedly invokes a cliché of the time—the narrator offers the reader the serious reminder that "If you have built castles in the air, your work need not be lost; that is where they should be. Now put the foundations under them (*Walden*, p. 324). The "I" of *Walden*, a textualized Thoreau, shares Thoreau's command of Greek and etymological expertise on the term *economy*. He also knows the recent history of the term and its roles as signifier in the guidebooks for young men.

By the time of Fordyce and West, the use of *oeconomy* to signify the art of building and managing a household or the manner of supervising the resources and expenditures of a household was largely obsolete. Other habitual associations and the term itself, however, were not obsolete. Certainly the fusion of the moral and economic in usages of *economy* was still habitual practice, as the guidebooks for young men make abundantly clear. In Fordyce the term *oeconomy* impinges on his discussion of charity, in West on her discussion of philanthropy. Thus one important meaning of *oeconomy* in their guidebooks is the administration of social priorities and the resources in a community. A more common meaning in Fordyce, West, Franklin, and Hawes is the morally sensitive and economically astute management of money, finances, and expenditures. The economical young man is he who sees to it that the incoming and outgoing are reciprocally adjusted in such a way as to give him an advantage. That advantage is characterized as both moral and economic improvement. The same moral/economic considerations are reflected in images of "economy" in the success manuals: to get as much as possible out of one's resources, to save time, labor, materials, money, and emotional energy.

In this context one should consider the tables of receipts and expenditures in "Economy" and "The Bean-Field." In his *Advice to Young Men* Timothy Shay Arthur repeats a commonplace in young men's guides in picturing in destructive terms the temptation of foolish spending and extravagance. "One means for the correction of this fault," he recommends, "may be found in a regular account of receipts and expenditures." Cultivating careful inventorial habits is traditional guidebook advice, and the direction and directedness of Arthur's recommendation typify the American success manuals of Thoreau's time. Regular and careful keeping of accounts will help the young man to accumulate money, and "money should be considered as a means by which man has power to act usefully in the world, and he ought to endeavor to obtain it with that end in view."[17] The majority of the readers addressed in "Economy" are identified through thoroughly familiar material signifiers. What appears to be the adoption of the language of material economy is a luring of the "you," but clearly not in the interest of accommodation or conciliation. The ledgerlike accounts of *Walden* are in keeping with its precept of economy and its advice on improving both the means and ends of economy. As such, however, they are not practical lessons on how to accumulate wealth but documentations of successes and failures in the experiments of *Walden*.

Pecuniary tables serve as inventories of *Walden*'s unconventional enterprises. On the cost of his house the speaker declares, "I give the details because very few are able to tell exactly what their houses cost," poignantly loading moral and psychological weight on the verb *cost*. His construction, he notes, pleases him more than any of the houses on Main Street and surpasses them (pp. 48–49). The interest of *Walden* in constructions that surpass conventional ones is one of the important meanings accommodated by the terminology of *extra vagance*. As for assisting the reader with judicious advice, the luring of the "you" is both an act of appropriating the conventions by which the "you" defines security and an attempt to draw readers out of their narrow security. Some of those readers will have recognized a special appropriation of *economy* in *Walden*'s inventories of cost effectiveness. Early nineteenth-century British and American sermonizing and theological writings attest to

the staying power of a theological management of the term *economy*, in theological vernacular a reference to spiritual or divine
government. In this context *economy* often referred to the inner
righteous kingdom or the personal republic of higher law. It could
also mean the judicious handling of precept.

Extra vagance through economy, but through an economy that
conjectures a much larger sense than common use permits—this
strategy is not at all contradictory to the speaker, although it
frequently contradicts the conventional reader. "We must learn to
reawaken and keep ourselves awake," declares a speaker who
"wished to live deliberately," who at Walden Pond was "tasked to
make his life, even in its details, worthy of the contemplation of his
most elevated and critical hour," and who is determined to publish
"in my next excursion" the meaning of whatever information he has
gotten (pp. 90–91). In these evocative passages we have a definition
of *economy*, yet the evocative language does not respect narrow
and precise definition. The definition is also more than that; it is a
kind of awakening of language, an economy that is itself a process
of learning to reawaken and that in this parody of the guidebook
serves as the improved means toward improved ends.

The significance of Thoreau's decision in 1852 or so to title the
first chapter of *Walden* "Economy" is more fully appreciated when
one recognizes the simultaneous expansion, over the course of
numerous revisions, of the themes of economy and *extra vagance*
and their inseparability. As the conception of *Walden* enlarged, the
theme of economy became more central and the language and
motifs of the first chapter not only impinged on every aspect of
Walden but also drew the other chapters beyond their earlier
bounds. What Thoreau sent to the publisher was "a true account
. . . in my next excursion" of the "paltry information" he and his
readers had gotten and continued to get. More importantly, it was
an account of how much can be done with this information (pp. 91,
90). One recalls the feat of transforming James Collins' shack into
the artist's house at the Pond and the centrality of the account of
this house rebuilding to the "Economy" chapter. The economical
house building is followed by a chapter on house management and
time management. This, in turn, is followed by chapters on economical reading; on a surprisingly advantageous economy of
sounds; on a thrifty and bountiful solitude; on a resourceful social

circle; on the most promising kind of cultivation; and, eventually, on the spiritual economy ritually cited in catechisms, sermons, and success manuals but through *Walden*'s parodic maneuvers pulled beyond the narrow limits of perfunctory acknowledgment.

In order to reclaim language, *Walden* practices a rigorous economy, an economy that recognizes "how you are yarded," creates the urgency to leap the fence, "kicks over the pail," and "leaps the cowyard fence." Only in conjunction with the *oikonomia* of *Walden* is its *extra vagance* proposed, clarified, and validated. Yet the principal meaning of the etymological root of *economy* is house, and a house can master its inhabitants by containing them too much, as suggested by a secondary meaning of the same root—cage. Narrowness, after all, has meaning only in terms of potentialities beyond its confines. And so the economist who begins the story of his enterprise by admitting that he is "confined . . . by the narrowness of my experience" (p. 3) concludes his account with the reminder that secures the credibility of *extra vagance* by pushing the term beyond the confines of *Walden*: "it seemed to me that I had several more lives to live. . . . It is remarkable how easily and insensibly we fall into a particular route" (pp. 324, 323).

IV

In the opening sentences of *Walden*, the speaker, concerned with the appearance of "impertinence," freely admits obtrusiveness. The effect is to test the term *impertinence* while supposedly testing his respect for convention and his sense of decorum. If anything, this "I" understates his obtrusiveness. He is much more obtrusive than the "I" in Fordyce, West, Franklin, Hawes, and the numerous success manuals that feature a first-person persona. Moreover, unlike the speakers in the majority of the young man's guides, the obtrusive persona of *Walden* refuses to ask for the reader's understanding and pardon for his strong, first-person presence. This "I," who resembles, yet differs markedly from, the first-person speakers so common to the guidebook, represents Thoreau's principal form of parody at the rhetorical level. A rhetorical "I" committed to a program of *extra vagance* by means of unconventional economy displaces the companionable and patronizing "I" that one would expect in a treatise on success. Hearing and understanding in readers have something to do with "rhetoric," we are told, and "rhetoric" is related to the nature of the speaker, who is not oratorical. To paraphrase parts of the second paragraph of *Walden*, the calculated omnipresence of a rhetorical "I" will be the most revealing feature of this account. The "I" will speak about a "you" but also about the "I," and will address "you" but, in so doing, will remind the "you" that the "I" is putting on the very coat he asks the "you" to try for fittedness. Thus the hearing and understanding of this economist's account have much to do with the use of the "I" addressing a "you."

Apparently, the petulantly condescending reviewer of *Graham's Magazine* was quite unaware of the rich irony in his ridicule of the presiding "I" of *Walden*, an irony made all the stronger by the acknowledgment in the review that Thoreau's decisions concerning his persona were ideological ones: "Mr. Thoreau, it is well known, belongs to the class of transcendentalists who lay the greatest stress on the 'I,' and knows no limitation on the exercise of the rights of that important pronoun."[18] The most obvious irony is the appropriateness of "no limitation." Equally ironic, however, is the indictment as a whole, to which the most appropriate rejoinders are the performance of the persona in *Walden* and the declaration of the speaker at the beginning of "Life without Principle," "I take it for granted, when I am invited to lecture anywhere . . . that there is a desire to hear what *I think* on some subject . . . and not that I should say pleasant things merely, or such as the audience will assent to; and I resolve, accordingly, that I will give them a strong dose of myself" (*Reform Papers*, p. 155). As *Walden* announces in its second paragraph, this account will feature not only a first-person persona but also a strong dose of that "I."

"In most books, the I, or first person, is omitted," the speaker declares in the second paragraph, where he deliberately and emphatically obtrudes himself "on the notice of my readers." "In respect to egotism," there may not be much of a "difference." "We commonly do not remember that it is, after all, always the first person that is speaking." Such a common forgetfulness, inattention, or unreflectiveness is encouraged to beat a hasty retreat in *Walden*; "I should not talk so much about myself if there were any body else whom I knew as well." The economist persona, whose account is confined only by his understanding of *extra vagance* and the conditions of that *extra vagance* in his treatise on uncommon success, will speak "much about myself" (p. 3). In paragraphs one and two, "I" occurs five times and fourteen times respectively, "my" two times and nine times, "myself" one time in each, and "me" four times in the second paragraph. These frequencies are not a momentary feature designed to make a point through repetition or exaggeration and then dropped. In all, the first-person pronoun occurs almost three thousand times in *Walden*: "I" 1,816 times, "my" 723 times, "me" 306 times, and "myself" 65 times.[19] This powerful presence of the "I" is implicated in the ringing declaration of the concluding chapter that "I am convinced that I cannot exaggerate enough even to lay the foundation of a true expression" (p. 324). Parody as rhetoric, rhetoric as appropriation and transformation, exaggeration, and "true expression" meet in the persona of *Walden*.

Whether the "I" speaks of himself or "about your condition," the speaker insistently and consistently addresses a "you who read these pages" (p. 4). "You" occurs 295 times, "you" in a pronoun-verb contraction 2 times, "your" 106 times, "yours" 2 times, and "yourself (singular and plural) 16 times. This "you" is not one but many. As evident in numerous passages from *Walden* quoted in the preceding paragraphs, the "you" frequently refers to real or imagined townsmen deliberately internalized as readers. A few of these readers are companionable as hearers and compatible with the "I" as interpreters. For instance, the confiding voice in "Solitude" and "Visitors," the saunterer with his field notes in "Baker Farm," and the combination of vigorous encouragements and benedictions in "Conclusion" assume a "you" who resembles the "I" or, at the very least, respects the discourse of these chapters. In most cases, however, the different kinds of townsmen inhabiting the "you" suffer from a poor "outward condition" (p. 4), one manifestation of which is "illiterateness." This functional illiteracy is not an inability to recognize written words, but the intellectual, moral, and imaginative illiteracy of readers of *Walden*. "I confess," the "I" explains with more than a hint of annoyance, that "I do not make any very broad distinction between the illiterateness of my townsmen who cannot read at all, and the illiterateness of him who has learned to read only what is for children and feeble intellects." Much more frequently than not, then, the "you who read these pages" are "underbred and low-lived and illiterate" (p. 107). Real and imagined townsmen appear in many guises, and the speaker addresses each in terms of that townsman's aspirations, values, and terminology. "I have never yet met a man who was quite awake," the "I" informs his readers (p. 90).

But the "you" of *Walden* accommodates more than real or imagined townsmen. As a key multiple constituent in this guide to success, the "you" constitutes the auditory of the guidebook with its proclivity for conventional values and ideas of success. Since the "you" is assumed to share these values and ideas, the I/you exchange in *Walden* is largely one-way ("I" to "you") and confrontational. I have not found a guidebook for young men that is as persistently confrontational as *Walden*. Rather than encourage the "you" with conventional language and social and professional signs of success, the "I" pointedly seeks to disabuse the "you" of conventional guidebook wisdom and to stand between the "you" and the kinds of traditional authority that supports and honors that wisdom. "I have tried trade," the speaker instructs those keen on succeeding in trade and commerce, "but I found that it would take ten years to get under way in that, and that then I should probably be on my own way to the devil. I was actually afraid that I might by that time be doing what is called a good business."[20] He has also tried "school-keeping," but "lost my time into the bargain. As I did not teach for the good of my fellow-men, but simply for a livelihood, this was a failure" (p. 69).

Reversals of success and failure (as these are conventionally defined) contribute to the confrontational address in *Walden* by adopting conventional categories in order to empty them of the meaning given by the "feeble intellect" of the "you." The reversals also fill the categories with meaning generously offered by the impertinent "I." The same reversal-as-confrontation maneuver with its strategy of displacement is evident in addressing the "you" in his numerous versions: student, teacher, tutor, farmer, woodchopper, would-be entrepreneur, traveler, young gentleman, and young artist, to specify some of them. The "you" thus constitutes the kind of readership the conventional guidebook assumes, internalizes, and honors.

"I desire to speak somewhere *without* bounds," the speaker declares, lodging himself outside of his readers' bounds but inside the *extra-vagant* circle of that "somewhere" (p. 324). Only because the responses of the readers are bound by narrow conventions, however, does his differentiation from the "you" and a speaking outside of his readers' narrow bounds have any meaning. But the "I" who differentiates himself from the "you" on the basis of *extra vagance* suggests a further differentiation—in this case among the "you"— on the same principle. Since *extra vagance* is not an essentially definable condition and the response of the "you" to confinement is neither uniform nor consistent, *extra vagance* may beckon the "you" in various ways and to varying degrees, or not at all. "I desire that there may be as many different persons in the world as possible; but I would have each one be very careful to find out and pursue *his own* way" (p. 71).[21] Yet, as in the strongly rhetorical poems of Whitman, although the "I" sometimes regards his voice as but one among a plenitude and sometimes as a plenitude within the "I," more often the "I" is determined to expose the fallacious forms of thought, speech, and behavior of the "you." In the latter case, the "I" is privileged by the authority of understanding and wisdom, and therefore both advice and censure offered by the "I" are reliable and directly pertinent to the "you."[22]

The bond yet the difference between speaker and reader is a feature not limited to their relationship; it is also a feature of the speaker in relation to himself. Notwithstanding the pertinence of the speaker's observation "I have never yet met a man who was quite awake" to our understanding of the I/you relationship in *Walden*, the very next sentence is a reflexive response: "How could I have looked him in the face?" (p. 90). The "you" is not simply the face of the other (who is like or unlike the "I") but also an aspect of the "I," a mirroring, and in this respect a reminder that *Walden* is an account of self-examination and of self-culture. This I/you doubleness (definition of the "I" through the "you" and vice versa) is explicitly noted in the "Solitude" chapter, an appropriate context for collapsing the "you" and "I" or, perhaps better said, for the projection of aspects of the "I" in terms of a "you." "I only know myself as a human entity; the scene, so to speak, of thoughts and affections; and am sensible of a certain doubleness by which I can stand as remote from myself as from another. However intense my experience, I am conscious of the presence and criticism of a part of me, which, as it were, is not a part of me . . . ; and that is no more I than it is you" (p. 135). The other side of confronting the "you" through rhetorical maneuvers is to "stand as remote from myself as from another" and, in criticizing "you," to criticize the "I."

"Criticism" and encouragement of the "you" is criticism and encouragement "of a part of me." To stand outside the bounds of the rhetorically created "you" and the "I" unfixes the "I" by transcending a particular codification of voice, a codification essential to the criticism of the "you" and characteristic of young men's guides. Such a transcendence permits the "I" to participate in and enact the very *extra vagance* that awakened readers will respect and desire. Appropriating the conventions of a confused society and a trivialized species of literature thus both criticizes those conventions and refashions them. Even the "I" must submit to such a remaking. As Sherman Paul noted several decades ago, *Walden* is, among other things, a fable of renewal.[23] That renewal includes a renewal of conventions and the placing of new boundary markers. Whether boundaries, including new boundaries, will continue to be sites of trespassing is the question that persistently accompanies the speaker's initiatives.

Regardless of whether the "I" or "you" is being addressed, the indubitably clear strategy is one of taking both guidebook conventions and the conventional thinking and language of a superficial yet energetic American culture out of their bounds and, to borrow an appropriately suggestive term from Bakhtin, carnivalizing them. As I understand it, Bakhtin's *carnival* is not an exact synonym for *parody* as employed in this study, but it does include the meaning of exposing to parody entrenched conventions without rejecting the idea of convention or the principle of the normative. To carnivalize is to contest the conventional and dogmatic with the potential for the new and different discerned in the very conventions and dogmatic norms being contested. Thoreau's parodic treatment of the young man's guide has little of the Rabelaisian mockery and travesty associated with *carnival*, but like the activity Bakhtin describes, Thoreau's parody has no external vantage point and resists all attempts at mastery and control, including its own. An instructive Bakhtinian treatment of *Walden* notes that Thoreau's desire to carnivalize is implicated in a crucial doubleness—one that will no doubt already have been inferred. I refer to the parodox of the rhetorically and ideologically controlling force of the "I" in its contesting of the "you" on the one hand and the expressed "desire to speak somewhere *without* bounds" on the other hand.[24]

That desire is memorably registered in the concluding pages of *Walden*:

> It is a ridiculous demand which England and America make, that you shall speak so that they can understand you. Neither men nor toad-stools grow so. As if that were important, and there were not enough to understand you without them. As if Nature could support but one order of understandings, could not sustain birds as well as quadrupeds, flying as well as creeping things, and *hush* and *who*, which Bright can under-stand, were the best English. As if there were safety in stupidity alone. I fear chiefly lest my expression may not be *extra- vagant* enough, may not wander far enough beyond the narrow limits of my daily experience, so as to be adequate to the truth of which I have been convinced. *Extra vagance!* it depends on how you are yarded. The migrating buffalo, which seeks new pastures in another latitude, is not extravagant like the cow which kicks over the pail, leaps the cow-yard fence, and runs after her calf, in milking time. I desire to speak somewhere *without* bounds; like a man in a waking moment, to men in their waking moments; for I am convinced that I cannot exaggerate enough even to lay the founda-tion of a true expression. Who that has heard a strain of music feared then lest he should speak extravagantly any more forever? In view of the future or possible, we should live quite laxly and undefined in front, our outlines dim and misty on that side; as our shadows reveal an insensible perspiration toward the sun. The volatile truth of our words should continually betray the inadequacy of the residual statement. Their truth is instantly *translated*; its literal monument alone remains. (*Walden*, pp. 324–25)

In *Walden*, argument, rejoinder, provocation, censure, ridicule, and exhortation encourage *extra vagance*, but such a codification of a superior voice also draws an authoritative new boundary inside of which that superior "I" articulates his desire to speak somewhere outside of bounds. Parody requires the destabilization of conven-tions. But the concept of stability and the action of destabilization have no pertinence in this context except in relation to each other. There is only a relative destabilization in *Walden*. Since the *extra-vagant* "I" is also a boundary-marking "I," *Walden*, in its parody of the young man's guide in the service of *extra vagance*, cannot and does not offer passports to absolute freedom (a condition that, in any case, can exist only as pure abstraction). *Extra vagance* as absolute freedom from culture, time, conventions, and received language is conceivable only as absolute formlessness, a condition or state that the economist of *Walden* would regard as the most pressing and most rudimentary occasion for the practice of economy. The *extra-vagant* economist establishes his distinctive enterprise within and outside the habits and expectations of the economic enterprise of Thoreau's America. As such, *Walden* belongs to the very world it seeks to displace.

As a parody of success books for young men, *Walden* reclaims language—for the "I" of *Walden*, for the renitent "you" of *Walden*, and, above all, for *Walden* as a "new system," a "world with full and fair proportions; in which, though the old cities and dynasties had passed away, fairer and more glorious ones had taken their places" (p. 327). Few in Thoreau's culture will understand or appreciate *Walden*'s language of *extra vagance*; nonetheless, his culture will support his order of understanding, his vocation will be justified by it, and the future will somehow bear him out.

Notes

1. Although *Walden* sold much more successfully than *A Week*, it took five years for the first printing of two thousand copies of *Walden* to sell out. *Walden* was not republished until after Thoreau's death. *A Week* sold only 219 copies in four years; in 1853 the publisher ordered Thoreau to take home the unsold copies.

2. Lawrence Buell, *Literary Transcendentalism: Style and Vision in the American Renaissance* (Ithaca: Cornell University Press, 1973), pp. 188–207. For the quoted passages see pp. 202, 197, 200. Certainly Buell's view adds much to our understanding of the oft-quoted declaration of the speaker of *Walden* that "I have travelled a good deal in Concord" (*Walden*, p. 4). It could be argued, in fact, that as a "variant" of the excursionary narrative of *A Week*, *Walden* represents a serious parody by Thoreau of his own earlier work, an interpretation that undoubtedly attaches itself to the parable in "Economy" of the Indian basket weaver and its declaration of a new purpose. In this context John Aldrich Christie's *Thoreau as World Traveler* (New York: Columbia University Press, 1965), especially pp. 245–71—an impressive inventory of Thoreau's travels, travel reading, citation of travel literature, and allusions to travel books and authors—might be seen as a study that misses an important oppor-

tunity in its last two chapters, where Christie discusses the travel book in terms of formal generic characteristics.

3. Richard N. and Jean Carwile Masteller, "Rural Architecture in Andrew Jackson Downing and Henry David Thoreau: Pattern Book Parody in *Walden,*" *New England Quarterly* 57 (Fall 1984): 483–510; Sargent Bush, Jr., "The Ends and Means in *Walden*: Thoreau's Use of the Catechism," *ESQ* 31 (1st Quarter 1985): 1–10; Robert A. Gross, "The Great Bean Field Hoax: Thoreau and the Agricultural Reformers," *The Virginia Quarterly Review* 61 (Summer 1985): 483–97.

4. Joseph Moldenhauer, "The Rhetoric of *Walden,*" (Ph.D. diss., Columbia University, 1964), pp. 99–250; Edward L. Galligan, "The Comedian at Walden Pond," *South Atlantic Quarterly* 69 (1970): 20–37; Henry Golemba, "The Voices of *Walden,*" *ESQ* 31 (4th Quarter 1985): 243–51.

5. While not interested in conducting an etymological, archeological, or literary-historical examination of *parodia* or in returning the term to any putative former masters, I am concerned that the broadening of the term to occupy the same ground as literary theory and the apotheosis of the term to the status of a natural law of literary history and theory may represent a lexical/semantic exchange and taxonomical maneuver that obscure in the interest of clarification and that displace without fundamentally changing anything. I readily admit, however, that recent commentaries on parody have been thoroughly instructive for me and that the influence of some of these commentaries is apparent in my use of the term *parody*.

6. Linda Hutcheon, *Narcissistic Narrative: The Metafictional Paradox* (Waterloo, Ontario: Wilfred Laurier University Press, 1980), p. 50. Other recently published English language discussions of parody that I have found instructive include: idem, "Parody Without Ridicule: Observations on Modern Literary Parody," *Canadian Review of Comparative Literature* 5 (Spring 1978): 201–11; idem, *A Theory of Parody: The Teachings of Twentieth-Century Art Forms* (New York: Methuen, 1985), especially pp. 30–83; Mikhail Bakhtin, "From the Prehistory of Novelistic Discourse," in *The Dialogic Imagination*, ed. Michael Holquist, trans. Caryl Emerson and Holquist (Austin: University of Texas Press, 1981), pp. 41–83; Wayne Booth, *A Rhetoric of Irony* (Chicago: University of Chicago Press, 1974), pp. 91–134; Henryk Markiewicz, "On the Definitions of Literary Parody,' in *To Honor Roman Jakobson* (The Hague: Mouton, 1967), II: 1264–72; Margaret A. Rose, *Parody//Meta-fiction* (London: Croom Helm, 1979); Howard D. Weinbrot, "Translation and Parody: Towards the Genealogy of the Augustan Imitation," *ELH* 33 (December 1966): 434–47.

7. Hutcheon, *Narcissistic Narrative*, p. 25. Henry Golemba espouses a similar dialectical view in his opinion that parody offsets "a thesis with amplitudinal antithesis" ("The Voices of *Walden,*" p. 244).

8. Richard Poirier, *A World Elsewhere: The Place of Style in American Literature* (New York: Oxford University Press, 1966), p. 85.

9. Joel Porte raised the possibility of self-parody in *Walden* by suggesting in passing that Thoreau learned authorial self-parody from Emerson. See his "Transcendental Antics" in *Veins of Humor*, ed. Harry Levin (Cambridge, Mass.: Harvard University Press, 1972), p. 182.

10. A similar strategy is employed in "Resistance to Civil Government," in which the speaker identifies the "American government" as a tradition without credibility: "what is it but a tradition, though a recent one, endeavoring to transmit itself unimpaired to posterity, but each instant losing some of its integrity?" (*Reform Papers*, p. 63).

11. "Eloquence" and "locution" had perhaps been tainted for Thoreau as early as his underclassman years at Harvard, where he had been instructed in elocution by Jonathan Barber, who taught freshmen from 1829 to 1835. Barber is remembered for his efforts to train students in a system of gestures, a training for which he constructed a spherical bamboo cage in which the student stood and "gestured through the appropriate open spaces between the slats according to a system which identified each space with a particular emotion." The cage was found one morning "hanging from a barber's pole opposite the college yard" (David H. Grover, "Elocution at Harvard: The Sage of Jonathan Barber," *Quarterly Journal of Speech* 51 (February 1965): 65.

12. Harper & Brothers of New York owed its mighty success in large part to its policies of calculated and aggressive piracy, strong lobbying against a copyright treaty with Britain, refusal to join publishers' associations created to reduce abuses in the book trade business, accounting procedures designed to increase the "on-record" cost of publication so as to minimize the author's profits, aggressive leadership in magazine publication, and its numerous popular series for the common reader. Redding & Company of Boston, a much smaller publisher, produced work by several New England writers, including Longfellow. Why Thoreau would mention these two firms as promoters of poor reading is open to conjecture. None of the sixteen success manuals discussed in section III was published by Harper or Redding. One of Harper's principal New York competitors, Scribner, published Van Doren's *Mercantile Morals*, and several of the other manuals were picked up by smaller New York publishers after these works had demonstrated profitability.

13. Stanley Cavell, *The Senses of "Walden"* (New York: Viking Press, 1974), pp. 33–34. Cavell's approach to Thoreau's linguistic aims and experiments appears to submit one of Nietzsche's celebrated propositions to a number of reasonable qualifications without trying to claim any more neutrality for itself or for Thoreau than is manifestly evident in Nietzsche's formulation. In his *Genealogy of Morals*, Nietzsche argues: "the cause of the origin of a thing and its eventual utility, its actual employment and place in a system of purposes, lie worlds apart; whatever exists, having somehow come into being, is again and again reinterpreted to new ends, taken over, transformed, and redirected by some power superior to it; all events in the organic world are . . . a *becoming*

master, . . . and becoming master involves a fresh interpretation, an adaptation through which any previous 'meaning' and 'purpose' are necessarily obscured or even obliterated" (Friedrich Nietzsche, *On the Genealogy of Morals and Ecco Homo*, trans. Walter Kaufmann [New York: Random House, 1967], p. 77). The word translated as "adaptation," *Zurechtmachen*, is a rich substantive that houses suggestions of "appropriation," "adjustment," "a making ready," "preparation for a purpose," "correction," and "redirection." Whereas a critic like Harold Bloom is very much in the orbit of the Nietzschean proposition just quoted and is receptive to the claim that appropriation may be radical enough to obliterate previous versions, Cavell rejects the either/or of the proposition, the cosmically devouring terminology of "whatever" and "all," and the principle of radical transfer of power (or displacement) as a result of the *Zurechtmachen*. Thus Cavell can admire Thoreau's ambitious undertaking without dismissing other powers at work in his culture and in our contemporary culture and without ignoring what the history of forms Thoreau appropriated and the history of Thoreau's reception have to say about Thoreau's redistribution of power.

14. Richard Poirier, *A World Elsewhere*, p. 85. For longer than two decades now Poirier's treatment of writers like Emerson and Thoreau reveals an insistent attempt to stake out a position apart from Arnoldian cultural priests, formalist-minded modernists, and post-modernists (including the new historicists). At times his insistence has been raised to a high state of vigilance against contamination by any of these large, diffuse groups. But more to the point, his position on literary artists is that they deserve critical attention (and get his attention) because of their struggle against pressures of reality—time, space, nature, culture. Uncustomary stylistic experiment, the writer's equivalent of sorts to the reader's illusion, is associated, in his mind, with momentary transcendence of these pressures. Thus Thoreau's struggles against conventions are his means to the end of limited and transient individual freedom and true (in contrast, presumably, to false) selfhood. Poirier's most recent book states his view succinctly. Wordsworth and his American counterparts Emerson and Thoreau (all of them Poirier heroes), believe that "salvation consists in our being allowed to experience the reality of being a 'Man' at least in the writing and for the duration of the reading." Writer, reader, and critic must, therefore, "work very hard to overcome their customary, indoctrinated expectations about language, and then work harder still so as to discover in other, stranger uses of language a hint of realities denied in and by the historical world" (*The Renewal of Literature* [New Haven: Yale University Press, 1988], p. 40). In short, reclaiming language is the agent of personal renewal. My basic position on the matter of Thoreau's attempt to reclaim language has been that such a refashioning and displacement is crucial to a larger parodic agenda, that the refashioning is usually not first and foremost an aesthetic concern with style (although Thoreau was an exacting stylist), that it has much wider ramifications than Poirier allows, and that Thoreau is not disinterested in social

languages (such a disinterest would mean, among other things, a disinterest in himself).

15. John Frost, *The Young Merchant* (Philadelphia: R. W. Pomeroy, 1839), p. 51.

16. Cavell, *The Senses of "Walden"*, p. 87.

17. Timothy Shay Arthur, *Advice to Young Men on Their Duties and Conduct in Life* (Philadelphia: Elias Howe, 1847), pp. 28, 27.

18. Review of *Walden*, *Graham's Magazine*, 45 (September 1854): 298.

19. For these statistics I have relied on J. Stephen Sherwin and Richard C. Reynolds, *A Word Index to "Walden"* (Charlottesville: University of Virginia Press, 1960).

20. According to Horace Hosmer, the Thoreau family pencil business could have been developed into a large and thriving enterprise, but Mr. Thoreau was secretive about his process of producing New England's finest graphite, showing no inclination to expand his business. The Thoreaus finally had their graphite trade stolen from them. As for Henry Thoreau, he was the realization of the family's hope that he become a writer and did not seek to advance the family business. See George Hendrick, ed., *Remembrances of Concord and the Thoreaus* (Urbana: University of Illinois Press, 1977), especially pp. 17, 32, 35, 84.

21. A passage in Thoreau's Journal recounting his meeting with loggers in the woods near Concord turns on a metaphor that summarizes, it seems to me, the likeness/difference between the "I" and the "you." Each abides by his own mill privilege, to use the terminology of the logger and sawmill. No doubt "our employment is more alike than we suspect. . . . I have my work in the woods where I meet them, though my logs do not go to the same mill. I make a different use of skids" (NNPM MA 1302:15).

22. Thoreau's language of "desire" and his use of the first-person voice to suggest a plenitude within the "I" invite psychoanalytic speculation. I think especially of Jacques Lacan's rewriting of Freudianism to combine psychoanalysis with a study of society, specific cultural conditions, and language theory.

23. Sherman Paul, *The Shores of America* (Urbana: University of Illinois Press, 1958), pp. 323–53.

24. See Malini Johar Schueller, "Carnival Rhetoric and Extra-Vagance in Thoreau's *Walden*," *American Literature* 58 (March 1986): 33–45. Schueller explicates this doubleness in terms of a Bakhtinian monologic/dialogic tension.

Afterword

My approach to Thoreau has presented me with a number of choices, several of which have been identified in the Preface and body of the book and two of which I note here. First, my study began as a tripartite project designed to examine Thoreau's participation in three forms of discourse in his culture—republican, moral/aesthetic, and economic. The original plan of the work obviously represents a more comprehensive treatment than the completed version. Yet my enterprise developed its own economy, which could not be disposed of as easily as typescript pages on republicanism and moral/aestheticism. The deferred issues represent a subsequent enterprise. Second, my original purpose was to concentrate on how Thoreau was "yarded," to use his metaphor. My decision to abandon the subjects of republicanism and moral/aestheticism was influenced principally by a growing recognition of the need for an altered, bipartite project, the first part of which would focus on Thoreau's containment by his culture ("how you are yarded") and the second of which, while fully acknowledging the confinement just noted, would try to sound out Thoreau's metaphor of *extra vagance*, which he linked directly to his confinement, on the one hand, and his economy as a writer, on the other.

When Thoreau added to his concluding pages of *Walden* that the "universe is wider than our views of it" (p. 320), he was acknowledging the power of the "restless, nervous, bustling, trivial Nine-

teenth Century" to master, or at least to create the impression that
in practice it mastered, New Englanders' perceptions (p. 329). Thoreau's *our views* probably refer to views besetting the citizens of his
region, but Tocqueville had noted a similar problem in the culture
at large: the spectacle of a libertarian and incomparably public
national society intolerant of diverse opinions. Safe in his status as
aristocratic foreigner, he wrote that "one must give up one's rights
as a citizen and almost abjure one's qualities as a man if one intends
to stray from the track which [the majority] prescribes."[1] Thoreau
made essentially the same observation when he complained of his
fellow citizens that "you cannot interest them except as you are like
them and sympathize with them" (1906 J 7:79). Yet he also noted in
his Journal that "the slope from the last generation to this seems
steeper than any part of history" (1906 J 3:317). Unprecedented
change had, in his view, produced an extraordinary sameness—
characterized by one of our premier contemporary literary historians as "the utilitarian, moralistic cast of mainstream culture."[2]
Thoreau's assessment of his culture offered an unconventional version of the French proverb "plus ça change, plus c'est la même
chose."

In Thoreau's challenge to what he saw as the prevailing understanding and practice of "enterprise," he was not satisfied with
enlarging the concept; such enrichment would not necessarily address the problem of conformity. Nor was his end displacement of
categories or change of behavior, although displacement figured
significantly in his means. To displace particular linguistic or behavioral expressions of his culture would not inevitably address the
fundamental orientation of the culture, the unquestioned habits
behind its responses. It is *Walden*'s principle of *extra vagance* by
means of economy that takes us to the heart of Thoreau's vocational agenda. In this respect, the preamble to his memorable
paragraph on *extra vagance* warrants attention. By means of a
favorite metaphor, he registered what he perceived to be the perennial problem of the individual within the cultural milieu, a problem
that presented itself in a particular version in his America—the
habitual problem of turning *milieu* into a synonym for *matrix*. Or
as the speaker of *Walden* puts it: "The surface of the earth is soft
and impressible by the feet of men; and so with the paths which the
mind travels. How worn and dusty, then, must be the highways of

the world, how deep the ruts of tradition and conformity!" (p. 323). To Thoreau's way of thinking, his enterprise of self-culture and the economy that it entailed did not escape cultural conditions or remove him from those conditions. His economy aimed to enfranchise and support a response different from the dominant response in the culture to conditions affecting his vocation. Surely "enterprise," "economy," and "vocation" admitted of more than a conventional, uniform interpretation, just as *Walden* should and just as any *extra-vagant* literature does.

It is all too easy, the advocate of *extra vagance* reminds his readers, to slip into the deep ruts of one's culture and non-reflectively to proceed in that path. Like Thoreau, scholars who write on him are editors inhabited by their culture and Thoreau's culture even as they seek to contain the latter. My attempt to address the subject of Thoreau and enterprise has been a continual lesson in that fact of life. One reminder of the highways "which the mind travels" has been the prolific traffic of Thoreau scholarship of the last several decades, much of which actually bodies forth an unmistakable sameness. Another reminder was my initial readiness to accept key items in Thoreau's lexicon as private yet determinate, a language that does not contest itself or its linguistic matrix.

During the writing of the book, a particularly instructive reminder of a common path of travel has been Kurt Heinzelman's erudite and sophisticated *The Economics of the Imagination*, much of the first chapter of which is devoted to Thoreau. The book got my full attention with its promissory note that by "analyzing the economic forms of poetic discourse and the poetics of economic discourse simultaneously, as equally significant and instructive exertions of the imagination, we may see how the development of the political economy changes the idea of the imagination and how, through the further labor of the imagination—through its expression in poetry—economic discourse is forced to speak in more responsive ways." Speaking of Thoreau, yet also of his own agenda, Heinzelman argues that "'to know how you stand' you must become aware of all the economies of space and time by which we all are yarded." That postulate can point to several different agendas, but in Heinzelman's case the examination of a "fictive economic discourse," a "body of systematized knowledge,"[3] produces, in the final analysis, the specie for a structuralist's transactions with supra-cultural language, grammar of the imagination, and codes of imaginative literature. Expecting a study whose "responsiveness" would include the obligation to historicize its subject, I responded to his study with admiration and disappointment.

A mentor as important as Heinzelman in testing the nature of my responsiveness has been Michael Gilmore, author of *American Literature and the Marketplace* (1985). Unlike Heinzelman, Gilmore raises unambiguous expectations and conforms to them. His Marxist analysis features a vigorous anticapitalist conscience. At times his discussion borders on a jeremiad against both the false consciousness represented by the marketplace in which American romantics conducted their transactions and the confused consciousness of literary artists as they sought for a share of power in that market. True to the emplotment of much current Marxist literary criticism and leftist historical analysis in America, Gilmore paradoxically tells his story in the tragic mode. In so doing, he persistently and illuminatingly historicizes, but he also subjects his historicized moments and conditions to judgments grounded in doctrines of reality and truth which expose the dilemmas and delusions inherent in the conditions examined.

In addressing the topic of Thoreau's participation in the economic vernacular of his time and place and in the cultural conventions associated with that vernacular, I have accepted as crucial to my responsiveness an interest in cultural criticism; by the same token, I regard as relatively unimportant as well as profoundly problematical the convention of assuming a better cultural period in the past in order to chart the culture's decline. Just as problematical is the Marxist obligation to expose and logically or rhetorically to eliminate history's false truths. To restate this last point with the help of an allusion to Francis Bacon's *New Organon* (*conventions* is substituted for Bacon's *idols*), the critic may participate in a program to expose and drive from the temple of Thoreau's culture or from the minds of today's readers conventions which inhabit either or both; on the other hand, to the best of his or her ability the critic may sound out the meaning and resonance of those conventions and the record of Thoreau's responsiveness without unnecessarily simplifying the scholarly subject because of impatience with the uncertainties of "sounding out."

The desire to sound out conventions of Thoreau's culture and Thoreau's inimitable responses to those conventions has encouraged me to combine several kinds of history (economic, social, and intellectual) with several kinds of literary criticism (archeological, linguistic, rhetorical, genetic, and dialogic[4]). My purpose has not been to divine his culture or any putative law of cultural discourse. Rather, my aim has been to tease out some of the storages of meaning, shifts in meaning, and multiple meanings in the economic discourse in which Thoreau participated through his writings and to regard storages, shifts, and multiplicity of meanings as the conditions for Thoreau's literary program of *extra vagance*—a program that he identified with his vocation of self-culture.

Throughout my writing, a passage from Thoreau's *Journal* has resonated as a reminder that places all other reminders in perspective. I readily admit about my work what Thoreau admitted about his: that we "hear and apprehend only what we already half know. If there is something which does not concern me, which is out of my line, which . . . my attention is not drawn to, however novel and remarkable it may be, . . . it does not detain us. Every man thus *tracks himself* through life, in all his hearing and reading and observation and travelling" (1906 J 13:77). This kind of tracking was included in Thoreau's metaphor when he wrote that he had travelled a good deal in Concord.

Notes

1. Alexis de Tocqueville, *Democracy in America*, (1835; reprint, ed. Phillips Bradley, New York: Alfred A. Knopf, 1945), 1:267.

2. Lawrence Buell, *New England Literary Culture from Revolution Through Renaissance* (New York: Cambridge University Press, 1986), p. 56.

3. Kurt Heinzelman, *The Economics of the Imagination* (Amherst: The University of Massachusetts Press, 1980), pp. 11, 31.

4. By *dialogic* I refer principally to Bakhtin, and to a particular application of his understanding of *voices* in literature. "I hear voices in everything and dialogic relationships between them," is his most succinct pronouncement on the subject. See Mikhail Bakhtin, *Bakhtin School Papers*, trans. Anne Shukman, in *Russian Poetics in Translation*, no. 10 (RPT Publications and the University of Essex, 1983), p. 4. His understanding of *voices* draws criticism

and, for that matter, literary history into the realm of discourse (ongoing cultural transaction at the level of language). And *dialogic* signifies any so-called theatre and performances in which culture and literature, and the many voices within the self and within the culture, intersect. Dialogy, in fact, is the intersection, or transaction, of voices within the self, within the culture, and between the two. That transaction, marked by varying degrees of conflict but not by uniformity or consensus, cannot be reduced to dialectic and cannot be analyzed dialectically.

Appendix

The guidebook for young men has not as yet received scholarly scrutiny, nor, strange to say, has it been identified as one of the species of conduct books in seventeenth- and eighteenth-century Britain. Resemblances between the guidebook and widely disseminated forms of literature in years spanning the latter part of the eighteenth and the early decades of the nineteenth centuries, the literary aims of many guidebook authors, the middle-class readership targeted by the guidebook, and genetic ties of the nineteenth-century American success manual and British self-help manual to the guidebook for young men strongly recommend scholarly attention to the guidebook.[1]

The guidebook had its counterparts of sorts in popular middle-class fiction, most notably so in the latter part of eighteenth-century Britain. The sentimental tale, in particular, was being used and touted by a number of contemporary authors to profess and presumably achieve the same ends as the conduct book. Despite the frequent censures in young men's guidebooks of the sentimental tale, opposition to the sentimental tale reveals something less than opposites; indeed, it suggests a fear of and resistance to co-optation. Thus it is not surprising that an author like West and several nineteenth-century American authors of successful guidebooks also produced sentimental romances and that brief didactic tales to illustrate the author's point are a common feature of the guidebook in America during Thoreau's time. The Franklin-Stuber *Life* represents another crossing of boundaries and a significant addition to guidebook writing in that Franklin explores the possibilities of autobiographical narrative as an effective mode of instructing youth in virtue, useful order, and success. Moreover, the Franklin text, like West's guidebook, had a literary aim, one that can be discerned in a number of guidebooks and American success manuals: to transform the conduct book into an acceptable, indeed pleasing, work when measured by the literary standards of their time, place, and principal readership. This aesthetic aim was, in Franklin's case, inseparable from his republicanism and prediction of a republican new world literature.[2] As for West's three-volume guidebook, its phenomenal success in Britain and America and its presence in Thoreau's personal library have something to do with her ability to create for her readers the appearance of a contemporary literary work.

By Fordyce's and West's own admission, the primer on manners, a type of conduct book, was on their mind as much as any fashionable new kind of literary production related or unrelated to the conduct book. In their view, one of the unfortunate signs of the changing times was the increasing preoccupation of conduct books with manners and the increasing number of conduct books devoted exclusively to manners and designed as guides for the young would-be gentleman. If popular fiction represented a threat from without, the book of manners represented a source of corruption from within. Rather than reject the conduct book as an unredeemable tradition, however, they sought, by contributing to it their kind of guidebook, to recover what they regarded as its honorable purpose. Consequently, they could claim a legacy of respectable antecedents, acknowledge duplication in a crowded field, and promote their guidebooks as a new and timely species of literature. According to them, the new species of guidebooks for young men addressed the current conditions of the British middle class and its young men.

The conditions of middle-class young men addressed by the guidebook are assumed to represent historic change. When West refers to "the revolution that has taken place in the habits of traders of eminence, and professional men," she has at least two things in mind: the flight of young men to urban centers to enter professions and the lack of supervision of these youths (West, 1:xxxvii–xxxviii). The guidebook conventionally portrays the city as a dangerous environment that tests the best resources of young men seeking careers there. "Where do temptations most strongly stand in the way and where does vice most strongly proliferate," asks Fordyce. His Scottish audience could have answered for him: "in rich and populous cities, and most of all in the metropolis [of London]" (Fordyce, p. 16). Hawes' opinion on the matter suggests both the city-as-Sodom convention and a telling social development in America: "Every season, great numbers of youth come from the country, to our larger towns and cities, to engage in the various departments of business and trade. . . . They have not firmness to resist the enticements of depraved companions. The consequence is, they fall in with the mass of corruption around them, and go to swell the monstrous tide of depravity and dissipation, which is rolling, as a mighty dessolation [*sic*], over the cities of our land" (pp. 40–41). (In "My Kinsman, Major Molineaux," completed four years after Hawes' guidebook appeared, Hawthorne manipulated the convention of the city as Sodom and effectively used the American cultural problem associated with its reiteration in a tale that resists resolution.)

One might offer West's self-conscious and morally aggressive defence of her *Letters Addressed to a Young Man*, first published in 1801 and in its sixth edition by 1818, as an illuminating perspective on the history of the conduct book and the perceived need for a new version of the young man's guide. This prolific contributor to *Gentleman's Magazine* argued that the "change in the *condition* of the middle and inferior classes of people, which has taken place within these three hundred years, is astonishing; and the changes of *manners* have at least corresponded. . . . Most unquestionably [the times] have altered, from bare sufficiency to luxurious indulgence; from general ignorance to universal information; from an almost *slavish* dread to an almost *boundless* freedom. . . . In no instance is this difference more visible than in the manners of young people to their seniors" (West, 3:366–67). According to the largely self-educated, antirepublican, antidemocratic, antideistic, antiatheistic, anti–Roman Catholic, anti–labor reform, antiromantic, antigothic, anti–modern literature Mrs. West, her *Letters Addressed to a Young Man* were addressed to her son in particular and British middle-class youths in general,[3] all of them threatened by dangerously persuasive propaganda. The evil propagandists "no longer audaciously demand to be heard at the bar of manly reason; they know that tribunal is unfavourable. It is to *juvenile* readers that they now apply; and in those amphibious ephemeral productions which escape criticism, and elude the attention of the learned, they contrive to wage an alarming war against the cause of order and morals" (West, 1:xxiii–xxiv).

West's "they" refers principally to pamphleteers and essayists who have garnered popularity by disseminating what she regards as perverse treatises on subjects such as morality, religion, nature, education, art, manners, social acceptance, and professional success. "I know not whether it be in consequence of a settled design, or be purely accidental," she adds, introducing the possibility of a sinister conspiracy at large, "but since the time that the enemies of Christianity have been most active, an unusual number of books on the formation of the manners of youth have issued from the press. The attention of the public has been evidently excited by these productions. . . . Were this extraordinary attention paid to the rising generation from good motives, were it conducted on sound principles, and directed to beneficial ends, we might hope that it would produce the most salutary effects. But . . . I am afraid we shall soon wish to return to the days of the horn-book and the primer" (3:348–49). Indeed, the "*scarcity* of popular productions, undertaken on sound principles, conducted with ability, and adapted to local circumstances and general utility" is cited as the main justification of her work (1:xxviii–xxix).

This lack of respectable guidebooks is also West's strongest argument in defence of her polemical voice. Morals and manners have not kept pace with "the revolution that has taken place in the habits of traders of eminence, and professional men" (1:xxxvii–xxxviii). In an age of phenomenal commercial and industrial expansion, urbanization, and increasing professionalism, she will vigorously champion "that industrious simplicity which once distinguished professional and commercial men, the tradesmen, the manufacturers, and the yeomanry of this kingdom" (1:xiii). On the one hand, then, West points with moral concern to the influx of young men into towns and cities to enter trades and professions, the absence of "restrictive power" over these youths (1:xxxviii), the almost total lack of family-like guidance and support by employers or others, "the rapid increase of luxury and refinement, and the fascination of fashion" (1:lii); on the other hand, she cites more hopefully the increase in literacy and the demand for publications (including novels, popular romances, serials, guidebooks, and treatises on various subjects), in short, an appetite for knowledge and reading. It "becomes expedient, therefore, to satisfy [the] cravings" of the present age "by an increased store of wholesome nutriment" for its youth (1:xxvi).

West's remarks reveal how much she is struck by what she perceives as the uniqueness of her opportunity and the uniqueness of her three-volume guidebook. "It occurred to the writer," she opines, "that her instructions (being adapted to the peculiar circumstances of the times, and the station of youth to whom they were addressed) differed essentially from any work of the kind which had fallen under her notice. This may be owing to her limited information" (1:x). Undoubtedly she pressed the argument of the uniqueness of her project with Bishop Percy, whom she approached for assistance in promoting her works.[4] Undoubtedly Percy, the bishop of Dromore, acknowledged both Britain's moral need and West's financial exigencies in complying with her request.

But the popularity of West's guidebook is no more related to the public-relations efforts of a supportive and influential Anglican bishop than the popularity of Franklin's *Life* as a young man's guide is related to the encouragements of Abel James or Benjamin Vaughan. More to the point is West's reference to "the peculiar circumstances of the times, and the station of youth to whom [the guidebook's instructions] were addressed." Franklin's reception offers a particularly rich site for examining evidence of popularity and genealogical influence. In 1748, he published an American edition of George Fisher's *The Instructor; or, Young Man's Best Companion*, an English guidebook and handbook for would-be young tradesmen. In preparing his edition, Franklin changed spellings, deleted and added a number of items, and expanded other items, in effect altering (although not really displacing) the voice presiding in Fisher's book. This initiative on Franklin's part (to my knowledge, the first example of an Americanized version of a British guidebook) coincided with his retirement, at age forty-two, from his highly profitable printing business. His accumulated wealth and the prospect of ongoing future income from his business confirmed his status as a living exemplar of extraordinary success in colonial Pennsylvania. Twenty-three years later he wrote the first installment of his *Autobiography*, a project that would preoccupy him intermittently in the last two decades of his life. The first two installments of this work, its most familiar parts, were conceived largely as a guidebook for enterprising young men in an even younger, yet rising, nation. As such, these two installments represent a new and more Americanized version of Franklin's undertaking in his decision to edit and publish Fisher's *The Instructor*.

Thoreau's respect for and appropriation of Franklin represents a further development in this genealogy, but not the only one or, for that matter, the only kind. The following anonymous title of a nineteenth-century publication suggests a different appropriation: *The Universe's Rules of Life, Or, The Way to Wealth and Happiness. Selected from the Works of Dr. B. Franklin, and Other Eminent Authors*. A similar appropriation of Franklin was the aim of James Turnbull, one of the many profit-minded authors in America in the 1830s and 40s to make it his business to write about business success. In 1835, he published a guidebook consisting entirely of materials compiled from popular guidebooks. This book, titled *Advice to Young Tradesmen, on the Formation of Business Habits Calculated to Insure Respectability and Success in Life*, draws heavily on Franklin and John S. C. Abbott. Turnbull was not the first and certainly not the last to feature Franklin in a book charting respectable paths to success. For example, in 1858 Charles Bailey Seymour published his popular *Self-Made Men*, which includes a substantial chapter on Franklin that subsequently was also published separately in several editions. One or two years later William Makepeace Thayer published an equally popular work titled *The Printer Boy; or, How Ben Franklin Made his Mark*. The guidebook was susceptible of a range of appropriations, then, which were not limited to a particular genre or literary status, and which did not share a uniform principle of success, as *Walden* reminds us with its parables on the Indian basket weaver and the artist of Kouroo.

Notes

1. Studies at least tangentially touching the topic of conduct books include: Terry Belanger, "Publishers and Writers in Eighteenth-Century England," *Books and Their Readers in Eighteenth-Century England*, ed. Isabel Rivers (New York: St. Martin's Press, 1982), pp. 5–25; Jane Bingham and Grayce

Schalt, *Fifteen Centuries of Children's Literature: An Annotated Chronology of British and American Works in Historical Context* (Westport, Conn.: Greenwood Press, 1981), pp. 75–130; John E. Mason, *Gentlefolk in the Making: Studies in the History of English Courtesy in Literature* (Philadelphia: University of Pennsylvania Press, 1935; reprint New York: Octagon Books, 1971), especially pp. 253–90; Neil McKendrick, John Brewer, and J. H. Plumb, *The Birth of a Consumer Society: The Commercialization of Eighteenth-Century England* (Bloomington: Indiana University Press, 1982), pp. 286–315, 329–34; Henry Knight Miller, *Essays on Fielding's "Miscellanies": A Commentary on Volume One* (Princeton: Princeton University Press, 1961), pp. 164–228; Patricia M. Spacks, *The Adolescent Idea* (New York: Basic Books, 1981), pp. 19–190 passim; idem, "'Always at Variance': Politics of Eighteenth-Century Adolescence," in Spacks and W. B. Carnochan, *A Distant Prospect: Eighteenth-Century Views of Childhood* (Los Angeles: William Andrews Clark Memorial Library, University of California, Los Angeles, 1982), pp. 1–24; Leland E. Warren, "Of the Conversation of Women: *The Female Quixote* and the Dream of Perfection," in *Studies in Eighteenth-Century Culture*, ed. Harry C. Payne (Madison: University of Wisconsin Press, 1982), 11:367–80; idem, "Turning Reality Round Together: Guides to Conversation in Eighteenth-Century England," *Eighteenth-Century Life* 8 (May 1983): 65–87.

2. Franklin's achievement with the guidebook anticipates the kind of appropriations and transformations of conventions that we tend to take for granted in nineteenth-century American literature: for example, Poe with the gothic tale; Poe, Thoreau, and Melville with popular excursionary literature; Hawthorne with the sentimental romance, sketch, and historical novel; or Howells with the popular courtesy books of postbellum America. Many other examples can be cited. Ideologically speaking, each such achievement was in its way a modern instance of relatively modest challenges to beliefs and practices in American culture; yet their work also represented more radical proposals in their attempt to build a durable and imposing American house of art on an egalitarian, mass-culture plane. They used for their purposes forms important to the mass culture and gave these forms new possibilities. The evidence suggests something other than an enshrinement of "pure" art. That many of these artists expressed alienation from their culture does not alter the fact that they lived in that culture, were inhabited by it, drew on it, and considered possibilities of transforming it.

3. West characterizes her intended readership as the modestly educated, enterprising class that gives "energy to our exertions, and stability to our constitution" (1:xi). A book on "the more exquisite refinements of manners," although hardly evil in itself, would present "some danger of perverting that decency of character which is appropriate to their station in life" (1:xi–xii).

4. A year before *Letters Addressed to a Young Man* appeared, Mrs. West confessed in a letter to Bishop Percy that the "catalogue of my compositions previous to my attaining twenty would be formidable. Thousands of lines

flowed in very easy measure. I scorned correction, and never blotted" (*The Dictionary of National Biography* [London: Oxford University Press, 1950], 20:1242. Today West's use of the preterit has its ironic side in that her critique of her juvenalia will strike many readers as appropriate, in more than one respect, for her guidebook.

Index